MYSTERIOUS
CHINA

READER'S DIGEST

Travels & Adventures

MYSTERIOUS CHINA

Published by The Reader's Digest Association Limited
LONDON • NEW YORK • SYDNEY • CAPE TOWN • MONTREAL

◆ COVER:

Main picture: **A lone fisherman guides his bamboo raft across a wide, but placid river in the Guilin area, here suffused by the warm glow of early-morning light.**

Smaller pictures, from top to bottom: **Robin Hanbury-Tenison (right) and his wife Louella on their first pair of mounts, Tang and Ming. An adolescent giant panda enjoying itself in the wild. Peasant-farmers carrying their wares to market in traditional double baskets. Only a few of the lifesize terracotta warriors that were unearthed near the tomb of Emperor Qin Shi Huangdi (d. 210 BC). A paper parasol protects this woman from the fierce sun of southern China.**

Spine: **The living embodiment of an archetypal figure: the inscrutable Oriental sage.**

◆ FRONTISPIECE:

A Chinese Buddhist monk listens to the music of the river flowing past the Pavilion of Pure Sound, near Mount Emei—a holy mountain in Sichuan province.

◆ TITLE PAGE:

A lotus blossom, sacred symbol of the Buddha.

◆ OPPOSITE:

One of China's many magnificent butterflies—a yellow swallowtail, here sipping nectar from a hibiscus flower.

◆ CONTENTS PAGES:

Left: **The dilapidated gateway to the tomb of a Ming emperor—one of 13 comprising the Ming necropolis north of Beijing.**

Right: **Robin Hanbury-Tenison (right) and his wife Louella on their first pair of mounts, Tang and Ming.**

◆ PAGES 8–9:

Built from local white marble, the Three Pagodas of Saintly Worship at Dali, in Yunnan province, are all that remain of an ancient temple complex.

◆ PAGES 42–43:

Even after the passage of many centuries, the Great Wall of China shows that it was built to last.

MYSTERIOUS CHINA was edited and designed
by The Reader's Digest Association Limited, London.

The Reader's Digest Association Limited
11 Westferry Circus, Canary Wharf, London E14 4HE

A Ride Along the Great Wall: Original full-length version
by Robin Hanbury-Tenison
published by Century, an imprint of Random House UK Ltd.
© 1987 by Robin Hanbury-Tenison
British condensed version © The Reader's Digest Association Limited, 1995

Contributors

Consultant Editor: Donald Payne
Special Adviser: Dr Richard Louis Edmonds

Editor: David Scott-Macnab
Assistant Editor: Charlotte Rundall
Associate Editors: David Blomfield, David Compton
Copy Editors: Caroline Arthur, Jacqueline Krendel
Researcher: Julia Bruce
Designer: Louise Dick
Assistant Designer: Stephen Strong
Picture Researcher: Caroline Hensman
Assistant Picture Researcher: James Robinson
Additional material by: Caroline Blunden,
Dr Richard Louis Edmonds, John Ellison Kahn,
Tim Locke, Tobias Newman
Watercolour illustrations: Mark Entwisle
Calligraphy: Mali Edmonds
Cartography: Malcolm Porter
Index: Brian Amos

◆ The publishers and project team would like to express their gratitude to the Royal Geographical Society for its ongoing help and advice. They would also like to thank Robin Hanbury-Tenison and the many individuals who have contributed to the preparation of this volume.

Contents

A RIDE ALONG THE GREAT WALL

Condensed from A RIDE ALONG THE GREAT WALL by Robin Hanbury-Tenison

— page 44 —

♦ *with special features*:

Index and Acknowledgments

PART 1 AN EVOCATION

THE MIDDLE KINGDOM

The Middle Kingdom

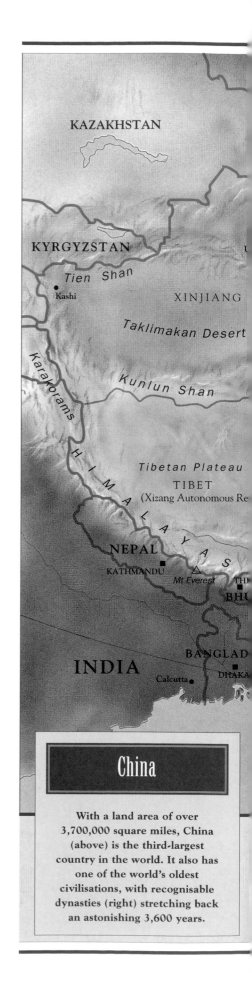

CHINA IS AN UNDISPUTED COLOSSUS of the East, and in many ways of the whole world. Covering over 3,700,000 square miles, including the disputed territory of Tibet, China is the third-largest country in the world today, after the Russian Federation and Canada. And with over one billion inhabitants, it is easily the most populous country on Earth: of every five people alive today, one is Chinese. Theirs is one of the world's oldest civilisations—for thousands of years, technologically and culturally far in advance of any other. Little wonder that as far back as the 6th century BC the Chinese considered themselves an elite people living at the centre of the universe, in a territory they called *Zhongguo*—'The Middle Kingdom'.

In the Beginning

According to Chinese mythology, *Zhongguo*, the world and the universe all owe their existence to a giant named Pan Gu, who once lived in an enormous egg. This he sliced in half to create Heaven and Earth, and then stood, like Atlas, between the two halves, holding them apart. After countless millennia, Pan Gu died; his left eye became the sun and his right eye the moon, while his body turned into mountain ranges and his blood into flowing rivers. His perspiration became rain, his hair became vegetation, and his bones were metamorphosed into minerals and rocks. Somewhat unflatteringly, the myth goes on to tell us that the human race arose from the lice on Pan Gu's body.

For modern scientists, a somewhat different cataclysm gave rise to much of the topography and climate of China as we know it today.

The story, as they tell it, is that about 40 million years ago the subcontinent of India, which had been slowly moving north on one of the vast plates that make up the surface of the globe, collided with the continent of Asia. This was one of the most

China

With a land area of over 3,700,000 square miles, China (above) is the third-largest country in the world. It also has one of the world's oldest civilisations, with recognisable dynasties (right) stretching back an astonishing 3,600 years.

RUSSIAN FEDERATION

RUSSIAN FEDERATION

ULAANBAATAR

MONGOLIA

HEILONGJIANG

Harbin

'ai Shan

Gobi Desert

INNER MONGOLIA

(MANCHURIA)

JILIN

Vladivostok

GANSU

Shangdu

LIAONING

SEA OF
JAPAN

Jiayuguan

Hohhot

Yellow River

Great Wall

Shanhaiguan

BEIJING

NORTH
KOREA

PYONGYANG

Yinchuan

Tianjin

Bo Hai

SEOUL

Taiyuan

HEBEI

SHANXI

SHANDONG

SOUTH
KOREA

QINGHAI

NINGXIA

Lanzhou

Yellow River (Huang He)

YELLOW
SEA

SHAANXI

Wei

Xi'an

HENAN

JIANGSU

JAPAN

Nanjing

Chengdu

HUBEI

Wuhan

ANHUI

Shanghai

EAST CHINA
SEA

SICHUAN

Yangtze (Chang)

Leshan

ZHEJIANG

HUNAN

JIANGXI

GUIZHOU

FUJIAN

TAIPEI

Dali

Kunming

Guilin

Tropic of Cancer

YUNNAN

GUANGXI

GUANGDONG

TAIWAN

Mandalay

Canton (Guangzhou)

Hong Kong

URMA
ANMAR)

HANOI

Macau

VIETNAM

SOUTH CHINA SEA

PHILIPPINES

LAOS

HAINAN

Pre-Imperial China				BC AD		Imperial China			
			221	The Early Empire	316	The Middle Empire	1279	The Late Empire	1911
1600	1027		256		581	618	907 960	1368	1644
eolithic Period	Shang	Zhou	475	206	The Three Kingdoms	Sui	Tang	Song	Yuan (Mongol)	Ming	Qing (Manchu)
			Warring States Period	Qin			Five Dynasties		
				206 BC	Han	AD 220 265 589	Northern and Southern Dynasties		
					Western Jin				

dramatic events in the geological history of our planet, and the consequences were spectacular: large areas of China and southern Asia that had previously lain below the ocean waves were levered up to become dry land, and thousands of square miles of rock were buckled and squeezed by the force of the collision to form the major mountain ranges of central Asia—the Himalayas, the Pamirs, the Karakorams and the Tien Shan.

The emerging mountains not only changed the appearance of the continent, they also came to have a serious impact on its climate and vegetation. For at the time of the collision, central Asia was a lush region, a land covered by huge forests and swamps. But as the Himalayan massif rose, it progressively blocked the monsoon rains driven in from the sea, and thereby slowly killed off the ancient forests over a large area. As a result, in place of these forests—in the 'rain shadow' of the mountains— now lie the parched Tibetan Plateau and two of the Earth's most fearsome deserts: the Taklimakan and the Gobi.

These arid tracts cover more than a quarter of China, but are only one aspect of the country's overall appearance, which is as varied as it is spectacular.

A Landscape that Takes One's Breath Away

Whatever image one has of a Chinese landscape, it can be only a stereotype of one particular region, so diverse is the country's terrain. In the north and northwest—in Inner Mongolia and Xinjiang, for example—stretch gently undulating plains that are bitterly cold in winter and stiflingly hot in summer. At best, they consist of sparse grasslands; at worst, of stony desert with vast saltpans devoid of vegetation and looking distinctly like the surface of the moon.

The southwest is hardly more hospitable. Here, across Tibet and Qinghai, lies the great Tibetan Plateau—sometimes called the roof of the world—at an average altitude of 14,000 feet above sea level. This is one of the highest inhabited regions on Earth: a harsh, desiccated world, largely unsuitable for settled agriculture, and capable of supporting only relatively small numbers of nomadic herders. Hardly surprisingly, less than two per cent of China's population lives here. And visitors who come to view the region's dramatic scenery often find themselves breathless—usually with awe, but also as a result of the scarcity of oxygen at this daunting altitude.

Farther east, however, the Earth is much more bountiful, especially on the Loess Plateau of north-central China (in Ningxia, Gansu and Shaanxi). This is a distinctive area of flat plains cut by deep ravines; of terraced hillsides that look as dry

▲ A classic Chinese landscape of steep, conical hills rising from a flat, fertile plain near Guilin in Guangxi province.

▲ Contrary to appearances, this dusty hillside is composed of some of the most fertile soil in China—loess—which is why it has been laboriously terraced.

▲ The bizarre 'trees' of the Stone Forest near Kunming have been sculpted by rain over millions of years.

Stone Forests and Animal Mountains

CHINA CAN BOAST within her borders the highest mountain in the world (Mount Everest) and the second-lowest depression (the Turfan Depression), representing a range in altitude of over four-and-a-half miles. Moreover, with her southern lands in the tropics and her northernmost province on the same latitude as Hudson Bay, China experiences a wide range of climates, and these help create an astonishing variety of landscapes. Often described as a series of steps, from the high Tibetan Plateau in the west to the fertile plains of the east and south, China's landscape includes some of the most breathtaking vistas in the world.

The dreamlike, steep-sided mountains of traditional Chinese painting may seem like impossible exaggerations, but they do actually exist—in the area around Guilin, in southern China. These rugged, cone-shaped hills, rising improbably from the surrounding plain, were created over millions of years as rivers eroded the softer limestone rocks that once filled the gullies between them. For centuries, if not millennia, the fantastic shapes of these hills have inspired artists, poets and storytellers, many of whom are responsible for the bizarre names—for example, Elephant Trunk Hill—that are typical of the area.

Erosion is also responsible for the aptly named Stone Forest near Kunming in Yunnan province.

Here, corrosive rainwater, slowly eating its way through cracks in the limestone rock, has created a strange yet uniquely Chinese landscape of closely packed pillars, some up to 100 feet high.

Even these beautiful and unusual formations cannot, however, compare in majesty to the mountains of the west, where the Himalayas, Tien Shan and Karakoram ranges virtually encircle the far-flung territories of Tibet and Xinjiang. In fact, fully two thirds of China is mountainous, which has led to another characteristic feature of the Chinese landscape: terracing, in order to maximise agricultural production and so feed the largest population on Earth.

▲ Glittering in the middle distance, the clear, blue waters of Lake Karakuli lie serenely below one of the dramatic peaks of the Karakoram range of mountains—one of the mighty barricades of China's far west.

A Wildlife Extravaganza

CHINA IS SO VAST and encompasses so many types of habitat—from bleak desert to towering mountains, to lush tropical rain forest—that it is home to a fascinating variety of wildlife. Some of the world's most gorgeous birds—such as Temminck's tragopan and the mandarin duck—are found here, together with many animals uniquely adapted to their own particular environments.

One of the best-known, yet rarest, of Chinese animals is the giant panda, which may have existed for over 20 million years, making it one of the oldest mammals on Earth. This endearing, playful creature lives in the high, cold bamboo forests of Sichuan and Gansu, at altitudes of 10,000 feet or more. Healthy adult pandas have no natural enemies other than humans, who have recently driven the species to the edge of extinction through hunting and commercial exploitation of the bamboo forests that are the pandas' only home.

Destruction of the bamboo forests also threatens the diminutive red panda, also known as the cat bear. Little bigger than a small fox, the red panda looks more like a raccoon than anything else, and experts disagree about whether it is indeed a raccoon, or in fact the only known relative of the giant panda.

Perhaps most striking of all the animals living in China is the Siberian tiger, the largest of all tigers, weighing in at some 600–700 pounds. Tragically, there are only a few hundred Siberian tigers alive in the wild today, leading many conservationists to doubt whether the species will survive much into the next century.

◀ Giant pandas are shy, solitary creatures which spend most of their time eating; a fully grown adult will consume about 45 pounds of bamboo every day.

▲ A mandarin drake—renowned for its fidelity as well as its colours. It mates for life, which is why wedding presents in China traditionally often include a pair of mandarin ducks.

One of the last remaining Siberian tigers reclines majestically in the snow of Heilongjiang province. ▶

▲ After foraging for food all night, this red panda has found a nice sunny nook in which to spend a restful day.

▲ China is home to many beautiful birds, including several spectacular species of pheasant—among them, Temminck's tragopan (seen here).

as dust, but bear crops because they are ingeniously irrigated by a complex system of canals and channels. Known locally as 'the land of yellow earth', the Loess Plateau derives its name from its fine, yellow soil (known to geologists as loess), which was deposited here in vast quantities during the last ice age by harsh winds sweeping southwards over the Mongolian desert. Fertile and easy to work, loess sustained China's earliest prehistoric farmers as well as its first major cities—such as Chang'an, near modern Xi'an—which is why the plateau and its surrounding river valleys are often called the cradle of Chinese civilisation.

Yet to the southeast the land is even more fertile. Studded with lakes and crisscrossed by an intricate network of rivers and canals, this is the China of most Westerners' imagination: a world of paddy fields, terraced hillsides, placid water buffalo, and farmers in broad-brimmed hats tending their crops. A happy combination of soil and climate allows three, and sometimes even four, harvests a year—of rice, sugar cane, vegetables and citrus fruits—making this one of the most intensively farmed and densely populated areas on Earth.

And the landscape here is often fantastically beautiful. Along the Li River in Guangxi province, for instance, little conical hills have been eroded into exotic shapes, as their names plainly declare: for example, Climbing Tortoise Hill, and Hill of Five Tigers Chasing a Goat. Similarly, in neighbouring Yunnan province, limestone deposits have been sculpted by rainwater into strange, treelike pinnacles known collectively as the Stone Forest, and with fascinating individual names—among them, Layered Waterfall, and Phoenix Preening its Feathers.

Varied but Endangered Wildlife

Of course, the phoenix does not occur in China—or anywhere else for that matter—except in myth. And in the more heavily populated areas of the country, many wild animals have long since joined the phoenix as creatures of storybooks rather than inhabitants of the landscape. This would be tragic under any circumstances, but the scale on which it is happening in China is particularly lamentable, not least because of the variety of the country's indigenous animal life: no fewer than 14 per cent of the world's bird species live here, and 20 per cent of its reptiles.

The rich diversity of China's fauna is directly related to the diversity of its landscape and associated plant-life. For instance, about 13 per cent of the country is covered by forests—comprising conifers (firs, pines and larches), deciduous trees (maple, birch and oak), and even, in the extreme south, tropical evergreens. These woodlands are home to a wide assortment of wildlife, including magnificent Siberian tigers, diminutive muntjac deer, numerous species of monkeys, and even elephants. The forested mountains of central China also harbour the country's best-known, and perhaps best-loved, animal—the giant panda, which is not, as is commonly supposed, a true vegetarian, but rather a carnivore that has adapted relatively recently to eating the plant that dominates its habitat: bamboo.

This beautiful creature, with its clownlike face, consumes huge quantities of bamboo—as much as 45 pounds of it a day. Unfortunately, the panda's digestive system is still better suited to processing meat, which means that it derives only just enough energy from its meals to stay alive—in fact, pandas expend almost as much energy chewing and digesting bamboo as they gain from it. As a result, they are extremely ponderous and slow moving—and consequently unable to catch prey that would be a valuable source of protein. Instead, they have to rely on insects and the occasional rotting carcass to supplement their otherwise monotonous diet.

Elsewhere, in the arid deserts and high plateaux of this vast country, a surprising number of animals eke out a living in very different circumstances. The climate here is extremely harsh and the vegetation often consists of little more than sparse grasses and small shrubs; yet wolves, foxes, lynxes, mountain goats, hares, eagles and pheasants, as well as herds of wild asses, camels and yaks, defy the odds and pursue a somewhat precarious existence in what can be an intimidatingly grim environment.

China's Human Face

Being so vast in area and so diverse in its landscapes, China was bound to have great diversity among its people too. Yet for many Westerners, long accustomed to thinking and speaking simply of 'the Chinese', it can come as something of a surprise to learn just how varied the population actually is—in ethnic and religious background, in culture and language, and even in appearance. Despite fervent attempts by the Communist authorities to forge a unified and uniform Chinese nation, the country remains stubbornly unhomogenised. North still differs from south, and east from west; for a great many people persist in clinging to their traditions and their own cultural identity.

Certainly, there is a dominant or mainstream group—the ethnic Chinese, or Han people, as they are known, who make up over nine-tenths of the population. Their name derives from the Han dynasty (206 BC–AD 220)—the first to rule for any significant period over a unified country. Yet even among those who call themselves Han, there are noteworthy differences. Many of

▲ Mongol nomads, many of them wearing blue—the colour of good fortune—enjoy a musical get-together.

These proud Kirghiz horsemen, living on the edge of the Taklimakan Desert, are Muslims of Turkic descent. ▼

A Kaleidoscope of Peoples

CHINA IS A LAND OF MANY FACES. The country has 55 officially recognised minority groups comprising perhaps 80 or 90 million people—a large number by most standards, yet in reality only a very small fraction of China's total population of 1.2 billion. The rest consider themselves part of the majority Han community, and have traditionally tended to look down on their minority compatriots.

Not that the Han themselves are anything like uniform in appearance and culture. Their languages, for instance, though related, differ from region to region. And thanks to intermarriage over the centuries with indigenous peoples into whose homelands they spread, southern Han tend to be shorter and darker than their northern counterparts.

It is among the minorities, however, that differences in appearance and culture are most marked. The Mongols along the northern border cling to their traditional way of life as nomadic herders, forever moving to new pastures with their ancient version of the mobile home, a large circular tent called a yurt. In the northwest, other hardy peoples such as the Kirghiz and the Uigurs, whose ancestors were of Turkic stock, are still usually set apart by their more European-looking facial features, and

by continuing to identify themselves as Muslims. In the south, by contrast, the minorities generally resemble groups in the neighbouring countries of southeast Asia: the Miao, or Hmong, for example, belong to the same people as the Meo of Vietnam and Laos. Among the traditions for which the Miao are renowned are their elaborate silverwork and the ornate embroidery with which they decorate their clothes.

▲ Enjoying a stroll in the sunny grounds of Beijing's Forbidden City, this father, mother, grandmother and baby in a bamboo pram are all members of China's vast majority group—the Han.

Traditional costumes are not reserved for festivals or tourists' photographs— they are often part of daily life, as is shown by this woman from Yunnan. ▼

▲ Fine embroidery, heavy silver jewellery and a distinctive costume identify this cheerful girl as a Miao—one of the five million who live in southern China.

the Han people living in southern China are actually descendants of the peoples who originally resisted the southward spread of Han armies and settlers. These southern Han are in many ways much closer to the people of Vietnam and Thailand: they are shorter and darker, for example, than the northern Han, who are, in turn, more akin to Mongols, Manchus and Koreans in their appearance.

In cultural matters too, the Han display considerable diversity. Though they all use chopsticks as their main eating utensils, their eating habits and cuisines vary widely from region to region. And although all their languages are similar in grammar and structure, there are at least seven of them that are distinct enough to be mutually incomprehensible.

As well as the Han, China also contains within her borders no fewer than 55 minority groups, many of whom are fiercely independent and proud of their ancestral customs and way of life. This is especially apparent in the far north and west of the country—regions that are sometimes called 'Outer China'.

The Rugged Herders

For centuries, if not millennia, the sprawling hinterland of the north—the region beyond the Great Wall—has been the source of some of China's greatest political and military turbulence. The begetters of these problems were herders—fiery, nomadic peoples who scorned both settled agriculture and settled communities, preferring to roam the wide open spaces of the Asian steppe with their herds of horses, sheep and camels. For most of their history, they had no overall leaders, but they had a fearsome reputation for inflicting lightning raids on their neighbours. In time, their very names—Hun, Mongol, Tartar—would strike terror into the hearts of the men and women who lived within range of their swift, and apparently inexhaustible, horses. And the Chinese authorities took them very seriously—so much so that they built the Great Wall to keep them at bay.

In the 13th century, however, the Mongols did more than merely harry the farming folk and soldiers of the frontier: they overran the Great Wall and conquered the whole of China. As a result, when the Chinese managed to drive the invaders out some 150 years later, they took every possible measure to ensure the nomads would not come back—eventually even annexing the Mongols' territories themselves.

Nowadays, the Mongols are much more subdued. Their lands have been divided into two distinct regions: the independent Mongolian Republic (generally known as Mongolia), and Inner Mongolia, a province of China. What is more, over the last 45

▲ This herder's thick sheepskin hat bears testimony to the intense cold that can descend on the plains of Xinjiang.

Tibetan nomads plod towards fresh pasture, their livestock—a small herd of yaks—acting as pack animals. ▶

Heavy blankets of felt laid over a light wooden frame are the essential materials of the ubiquitous Asian yurt. ▼

China's Wild West

THE INHABITANTS of China's vast northwestern province of Xinjiang describe their land as having three 'too manys' and three 'too littles': 'too many winds and too little rain, too much sand and too little grass, too many stones and too little soil'. Much the same could be said of the Tibetan Plateau to the south of Xinjiang: lying at an average elevation of 14,000 feet, the plateau experiences one of the most severe climates in the world—one of intense sunshine, bitter cold and little rain. Conditions such as these mean that, over vast areas of western China, settled farming is all but impossible—except in a few fertile river valleys.

But rather than abandon their apparently inhospitable homeland, many of the people that live in these areas—including Uigurs, Kazakhs, Kirghiz and Tibetans—have adapted themselves to the only way of life possible: nomadic herding. Whenever pasture becomes too thin for grazing, people simply pack up their belongings, round up their livestock, and move on. Everything they own, therefore, needs to be portable—right down to the house. This might be a simple felt tent, or the more elaborate yurt—a round, domed dwelling also made from

▲ **Wearing their best clothes—in the woman's case, an embroidered chuba, or gown—these Tibetan nomads are on a religious pilgrimage.**

felt, but in this case wrapped around a frame of willow wands. This ingenious structure takes less than two hours to erect and is more weatherproof than a tent in winter because extra layers of felt can easily be draped over it.

Naturally, the more you own, the more you have to carry, so nomads are people of few possessions. Unlike settled people, they don't tend to produce bulky artistic objects such as ceramics or sculptures. Instead, they channel their creativity into things they can always take with them—such as jewellery and clothing, which is often richly colourful and decorated with intricate embroidery.

years the Chinese authorities have done all they can to force the Mongols away from their ancient herding ways and onto settled communal farms. Even so, Mongol culture is far from dead. They have retained their distinctive folklore, cuisine and traditional sports, such as archery, horse racing and wrestling. And on the great open plains one can still see the round felt yurts of nomads—independent families who have steadfastly clung to the freedom of a time-honoured way of life.

Other nomadic herders have been fortunate in being left more in peace by the authorities—particularly in the western-most province of Xinjiang. This is an extraordinary region of the most dramatic contrasts, especially between fertile oases fed by meltwater from the Tien Shan, Altai Shan and Kunlun Shan mountains, and burning deserts that are among the hottest places on Earth. Between these extremes there are also plains that are roamed by nomadic Kirghiz and Kazaks—Muslims of Turkic origin, whose culture is in many ways more akin to that of Afghanistan, Kyrgyzstan and other central Asian countries than China proper. Like the Mongols, they too live in yurts and are renowned for their horsemanship.

Equally independent are the nomads of Tibet and Qinghai—regions where, apart from a few fertile river valleys, the land is too unproductive, rainfall too light and the cold too severe for tilling the earth. In consequence, hardy pastoralists wander the plains with their woolly yaks and portable felt tents, perpetuating customs and a way of life that have endured for millennia.

The Cultivators of the South

In marked contrast with the harsh outer reaches of China, the southern and eastern lands teem with life. The south, especially, is nurtured by year-round tropical warmth and fed by monsoon rains—ideal conditions for the proliferation of farming and settled communities, not to mention human cultures.

Apart from the ubiquitous Han, more than two dozen minority groups reside in China's southern provinces, many of them clinging tenaciously to their distinctive traditions, and so keeping alive the variety that has always characterised these regions. Some groups are associated specifically with the hills, while others farm the bounteous lowlands—a world of rice fields, tame water buffalo and wide, life-sustaining rivers.

◄ **With the distinctive hills of the Guilin area towering behind them, farmers feed harvested rice plants into an old-fashioned threshing machine, while a youth leads a water buffalo—the customary beast of burden in this area—to new pastures.**

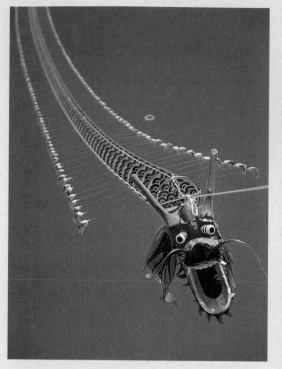

▲ This magnificent flying dragon exemplifies the skill and artistry of Chinese kite-making.

Motherland of Inventions

IMAGINE BONFIRE NIGHT without fireworks, or navigation without a compass, or even windy autumn days without any kites to fly. These familiar objects, and many other everyday items we take for granted in the West, owe their origins to the ingenuity of the Chinese in ages past.

Papermaking, for instance, was unknown in Europe before the 11th or 12th century AD, but can be traced back in China to the 3rd century BC. It is hardly surprising, then, that the Chinese developed a variety of interesting uses for paper—among them the construction of kites, often in fantastic shapes of birds, insects and dragons. Kites were flown by hobbyists for recreation, by Taoist monks as a meditative exercise, and even by some intrepid enthusiasts for experiments in manned flight.

The 4th century BC saw the Chinese using the world's first magnetic compasses in the form of lodestones—pieces of naturally magnetic iron ore—and in about AD 132 they had developed another sensitive directional instrument: a seismograph, able to detect earth tremors hundreds of miles away. It was not until the year 1703 that the first working European seismograph was invented.

Possibly the most momentous of China's discoveries, however, was gunpowder. It was first created in the 9th century AD, apparently by alchemists who were seeking—ironically enough—the elixir of life! In due course, it came to be used for fireworks, which then probably inspired the invention of military rocket-launchers. Guns and cannons followed—to be enthusiastically adopted by the powers of Europe as soon as they heard about such weapons in the late 12th century.

Gunpowder was quickly seized upon for military inventions, such as this 'bee's nest' rocket-arrow launcher. ▲

◀ A working model of the earliest-known lodestone compass, which was used for quasi-magical, rather than nautical, purposes.

▲ Fireworks, an early by-product of the Chinese invention of gunpowder, explode over Beijing's Tiananmen Square as part of May Day celebrations.

A reconstruction of the world's first bronze seismograph. In response to an earthquake, a ball would drop from one of eight spouts into the mouth of a waiting toad, thereby indicating the direction of the epicentre. ▼

Among the hill-dwellers are people such as the Yi, who are eminent in their knowledge of Chinese herbal medicines; and the Hmong, or Miao, who make elaborate silver jewellery and finely detailed embroidery, the intricate patterns varying in many subtle details from one region to the next.

The lowlands are home to China's largest minority, the Zhuang, who number over 15 million. Their houses are often built on stilts, with their livestock sleeping below, and in remote regions, even today, they have a reputation for practising magic and ancient shamanistic rites. Like many other southern people, the Zhuang are closely related to the people of neighbouring countries, such as Thailand, Burma, Vietnam and Laos.

For centuries, as far as the Han Chinese were concerned, all foreigners, including the minority peoples they ruled, were mere 'barbarians'. And they expressed their disdain in the very structure of their writing, by basing the symbols, or characters, for the names of various minorities on the character for 'dog'. Only in recent years have more sensitive characters been promoted, with the 'dog' element replaced by the symbol for 'man'.

Yet the Han have themselves, unquestionably, been enriched by their contact with the diverse cultures of the minorities, absorbing ideas, customs and skills without consciously knowing it. And in this process of absorption and assimilation, the Han, an already capable people, became even more creative.

A Land of Discoveries and Inventions

One of the most noteworthy features of Chinese culture is that it has, through the ages, encouraged both a spirit of curiosity and a practical-mindedness in its people. The result has been an extraordinary creativity, leading to inventions that Europeans acquired only much later, either through borrowing or through independent rediscovery.

China pre-dated Europe, for instance, in developing the arts of papermaking and book production; in the pleasures of setting off fireworks and flying kites; in using the compass and various astronomical and seismographical instruments; in printing paper currency and using the decimal system; in firing guns and building suspension bridges; in wearing sunglasses and satin fabrics; in eating off fine porcelain, and even in drinking whisky.

Possibly the most momentous of all these inventions was gunpowder, discovered by Taoist alchemists in the 9th century AD. Ironically, it was while searching for the elixir of life that they came up with what turned out to be such a powerful agent of destruction. But if the alchemists were disappointed, other inventors were delighted; they quickly exploited the powder's explosive properties to produce flamethrowers, rockets, bombs, and eventually guns and cannon. For a very short time China had a stupendous military advantage over the rest of the world—only the technology could not be kept secret. The recipe spread like wildfire, reaching Europe during the 13th century, when China was still a semi-mythical place which no Westerner had ever yet visited.

Yet gunpowder was a relatively late invention in Chinese terms. One of their greatest breakthroughs dates back at least 4,000 years, to the very boundaries of recorded history. No one knows exactly when silk production—or sericulture—began, but according to ancient tradition the wife of the semi-legendary Emperor Huang Di (the Yellow Emperor) gave royal support to the industry as early as 2700 BC. What is certain is that, for thousands of years, China enjoyed a monopoly that it guarded with utmost care: the threat of death hung over anyone who might think of betraying the secret of farming silkworms, unravelling their cocoons and weaving the threads into a luxurious fabric that was admired and envied throughout the world. Even after the secret did get out, in about 140 BC, Chinese silk remained pre-eminent in quality, ensuring that China retained its supremacy in the silk market until the early 20th century.

A Mosaic of Languages

It is from the most distant past that China also derives two of its most intriguing cultural creations: its family of languages and its system of writing.

Owing to the great size of China, and the many minority peoples living within its boundaries, a great number of completely unrelated languages are spoken there—Uzbek, Mongol, Tibetan, Miao and Manchu, to name a few. However, the great majority of Chinese people—about 90 per cent of the population—speak one of about seven related languages (experts disagree on exact numbers), of which the dominant and best known are Mandarin, or *Putonghua*, and Cantonese. These seven languages all belong to the same general family, but are as mutually unintelligible as French and Portuguese. All the more confusing, therefore, that they are often all referred to simply as 'Chinese'.

No one language fully deserves that title, but if any has a stronger claim than the others it is surely Mandarin, which is spoken by fully three-quarters of the Chinese population (some 900 million people) and has been established, in its Beijing dialect, as the official language of the People's Republic. As a mother tongue, Mandarin has more speakers than any other language in the world, including English.

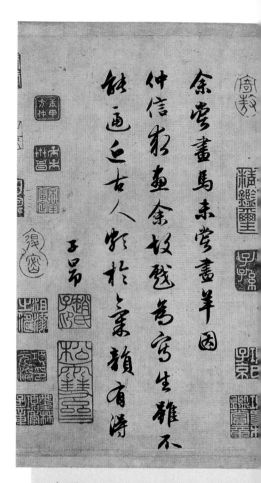

▲ Chinese characters, many of which derive from simple pictures, are often considered an art form in themselves.

▲ There is no easy way to learn Chinese characters, but an early start and lots of practice do help.

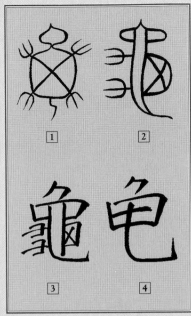

▲ The evolution of the Chinese character for 'tortoise', from the earliest pictographs (1–2), to the classical Chinese character (3), and its simplified modern form (4).

A Universal Language

THINK HOW CONVENIENT it would be if English, French and Portuguese, while remaining quite distinct in the way they sound, were identical when written down. People unable to speak intelligibly to each other could nevertheless converse happily by exchanging notes. Difficult to imagine, perhaps, but a comparable situation exists in China, where there are at least seven distinct spoken languages (not simply dialects, as they are sometimes called) that are all written down in much the same way.

The trick lies in the writing system used in China. Instead of an alphabet, which employs letters to indicate sounds, Chinese writing consists of 'characters', which indicate objects, actions and ideas, and which can be read out loud in quite different ways, according to the language of the reader.

The earliest characters, over 3,000 years old, were simple pictographs—such as a crescent to represent the moon; many then developed into more complex ideographs that indicated abstract concepts. Most characters have now evolved so far that their origins can be difficult to recognise,

▲ Newspapers and political pamphlets clutter a wall in Beijing. Their readers may all speak different Chinese languages, but they will all understand the written script.

yet the principles governing them remain largely unchanged—for example, in the way that two characters are combined to produce an independent word: the idea 'good', for instance, is represented by the characters for 'woman' and 'child', and the character for 'forest' consists of the

character 'tree' drawn twice over. A very intricate character might consist of as many as 33 separate strokes; little wonder, then, that many of the most commonly used characters were simplified in the 1950s as part of a literacy campaign inaugurated by Mao Ze-dong.

Sages and Spirits

CHINA HAS AN ANCIENT and illustrious tradition of scholarship and learning—one that affords special reverence to wise men and philosophers such as Confucius, who was concerned with the right ordering of society, and Lao Zi (Lao-Tzu), the founder of Taoism, who sought a path of personal development. The country, by and large, has never been much moved by mystics or religious visionaries with a mission to convert others. Perhaps for this reason China also has a unique record of religious toleration. No Chinese army has ever been to war on religious grounds, and even under Communism, freedom of worship is guaranteed by the constitution—although, in practice, the authorities have not always been so broad-minded.

But China also has another tradition, stretching back thousands of years, perhaps even to the myths of Bronze Age hunting communities—a tradition of ancestor-worship, magic, alchemy, shamanism, ghosts and spirits. This tradition never had a name; nor, until it came into contact with the teachings of Confucianism, Taoism and eventually Buddhism, did it develop any systematic or orthodox form.

Gradually, however, these traditions—some high and scholarly, others simple and superstitious—began to influence and even merge with one another. Hybrid practices developed, reflecting a

▲ **Taoist monks recite prayers in the presence of sacred texts at the White Cloud Temple, Beijing.**

uniquely Chinese mixture of Taoist philosophy, Confucian ethics, folk belief and Buddhist ritual—the various elements emphasised in different proportions by different people. Alongside the old, austere Taoist school, for example, there developed a Taoist religion with prayers, rituals and deities completely alien to the philosophical tradition. Yet, for the tolerant Chinese, such contradictions are not a problem; for many, the greatest truth is encapsulated in the ancient saying: 'The three [Taoism, Confucianism, Buddhism] are one'.

▲ Confucius' birthday is still observed by many Chinese; here, it is celebrated with decorous pomp in Taipei.

▲ An ivory Buddha, with Chinese features, seated in a turquoise alcove.

◄ Stone animals form a 'spirit way' in the Forest of Confucius, the cemetery of the sage and his descendants, near Qufu.

Like Cantonese and its other five relations, Mandarin is distinctive in being a 'tone language'; that is, the meaning of any word or syllable is determined not just by its vowel-sounds and consonants, but also by its pitch or lilt—by the *way* it is spoken. Modern Mandarin has four ways of sounding a word—four 'tones', as they are called: a high, level tone; a rising tone; a falling tone; and a tone that drops and then rises again. The word *ma*, for example, can therefore mean any of four quite different things, according to the tone in which it is spoken: 'mother', 'hemp', 'horse' or 'to scold'. So, the sequence *Ma ma ma*, spoken with the correct tones, will mean 'Mother scolds the horse'.

Written in Chinese characters, this statement loses all its appearance of gobbledegook, for the simple reason that Chinese writing is not based on an alphabet; its characters are symbolic representations of objects or ideas, so the characters for 'mother' and 'horse', for instance, are quite distinct.

The great virtue of this system of writing is that, because its characters are essentially visual symbols, they are used and understood by speakers of all the core Chinese languages, and several others besides. This has always had a strongly unifying effect on China, allowing an official from Shanghai, say, to communicate in writing with a counterpart in Canton, even if they could not actually understand each other in conversation. Similarly, rulers could issue edicts or propaganda in written form, knowing they would be comprehended by any literate Chinese.

Ancient Ways of Thought

Rulers, officials and politicians were not, however, the only beneficiaries of China's ingenious script: it also made possible the early and widespread dissemination of the thoughts and writings of the country's foremost thinkers—men such as Confucius and Lao Zi (Lao-Tzu), who both rose to prominence during the later years of the Zhou dynasty (1027–256 BC).

Confucius (*c.* 551–479 BC), or Kongfuzi as he is known in China, was a scholar and civil servant. He was also a great teacher, whose aim was to establish a code of morals and apply it to government and society. Confucius wrote no books himself, but his teachings were collected after his death and preserved in *The Analects*, one of the world's most celebrated ethical texts.

At the heart of this work lies Confucius' assumption that all human beings are naturally equipped to distinguish between good and evil. One word occurs time and again: *ren*—literally, 'the kernel', meaning the innermost nature of human beings, which enables them to recognise and act in accordance with what is right. And virtue—or rather virtuous action—was for

▲ In traditional Chinese medicine, both plants and animal parts are believed to have curative powers. This stall's display includes a dried monkey's paw.

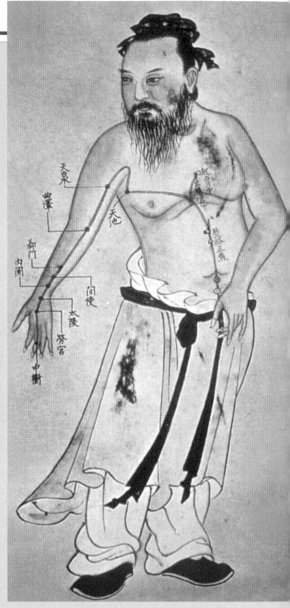

▲ An 18th-century drawing shows the acupuncture points for treating diseases of the heart and sexual organs. Modern practitioners use up to 2,000 points.

Health through Harmony

IT IS OFTEN SAID that while Western medicine is very good at classifying, identifying and treating illness, it lacks a unified theory of health. Chinese medicine, by contrast, is founded on just such a theory—one that views health as a state of balance or harmony between different energies in the body. Illness occurs when the balance is upset, or when the flow of *qi* (pronounced 'chi'), or life energy, becomes blocked.

In traditional Chinese theory, *qi* flows in paths, called meridians, that run throughout the body. Certain points along the meridians are considered particularly important and are used in treatments such as acupuncture and acupressure, aimed at unblocking or harmonising the flow of *qi*. Some *qi* is considered yin, or feminine, while some is yang, or masculine. Everyone needs a balance of the two, though the proportions differ between men and women, and even between individuals of the same sex.

The task of the traditional practitioner is to identify any energy imbalances, preferably before they become serious enough to cause symptoms (or disease), and to correct them by means of diet, exercise or traditional treatments such as herbal infusions and cupping. Although Western science follows a very different philosophy from that on which Chinese medicine is based, it does accept that some Chinese methods can be highly effective. While there is still no Western scientific explanation for acupuncture, for example, and while no anatomical features have ever been discovered to correspond to the meridians, the practical results achieved by traditional Chinese physicians are not in doubt.

It may look alarming, but acupuncture is said to be virtually painless, and this patient seems quite untroubled. A variant called moxibustion uses burning herbs instead of needles. ▶

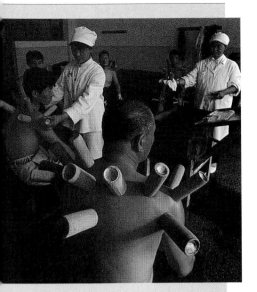

▲ This modern hospital still uses cupping: the heated bamboo tubes are supposed to suck poisons from the body.

▲ Interlocking teardrop symbols represent the balance of yin and yang—here on a protective lacquered amulet.

Confucius the necessary basis for both a just ruler and a just society, which he suggested should be governed like a family, with the ruler acting like a caring father.

Confucius' philosophy soon became popular, especially with the ruling classes, who appreciated its conservatism and support for traditional social hierarchies. As a result, Confucianism came to dominate official Chinese thinking for centuries—and many claim still does, even under Communism. Even so, there arose another, subtler philosophy, which would also prove highly influential. This was Taoism, whose founder, Lao Zi, supposedly lived in the 6th century BC, though some scholars claim that he may have been a purely legendary figure. At any rate, the central Taoist text that is ascribed to him, the *Tao Te Ching* ('The Way of Power'), dates from about 300 years later.

Unlike Confucianism, Taoism was not concerned with ethical codes; rather, it emphasised individual freedom and spontaneity, suggesting that these be achieved by following the *tao*, or 'way'—a natural course of action that cannot be defined but has to be instinctively recognised. In consequence, Taoism never developed into a social system; on the contrary, it became associated with mysticism and superstitious folk beliefs that in many ways ran counter to its original philosophical principles. Even so, over the centuries, Taoism has proved a valuable foil to the rigidity of Confucianism, and has strengthened the more aesthetic and individualistic aspects of Chinese society.

An even earlier school of thought attempted to explain nature in terms of two complementary principles: yin and yang. Yin is the female, nourishing force associated with the moon, water, cold and dark; while yang is the male, creative force associated with the sun, fire, heat and light. In time, elaborate systems of astrology, numerology and geomancy developed, based on these ideas and a belief in the need to achieve balance and harmony between the forces of yin and yang. From the earliest days, they were also vital concepts in Chinese medicine.

In Sickness and in Health

For Westerners who like to experiment with acupuncture and Chinese herbalism, but who would never dream of doing without antibiotics or even a dental anaesthetic, it can come as something of a shock to learn how important a role traditional medicine still plays in the Chinese health-care system. According to recent figures, thousands of operations—including critical brain surgery—are carried out annually with no form of pain relief other than acupuncture. Only in the cities is anything more than the most rudimentary of Western medicine usually available. For the rest of the population, traditional healers and simple remedies must generally suffice for all but the gravest illnesses—and often they serve very well indeed.

Yet Chinese medicine can seem very strange to Westerners, if only because its basic principles are entirely different from those underlying Western medicine. For a start, the Chinese system is holistic; that is, it considers the patient as a whole, including his (or her) mental outlook and emotional state, as well as any physical symptoms. Furthermore, its core ideas are based not on anatomy, but on traditional philosophy, and include notions such as balancing yin and yang energies, and strengthening the flow of *qi* (pronounced 'chi')—the vital force or life energy of every organism, believed to flow through the body in channels called 'meridians'. Every case is treated as unique, so two patients with the same physical symptoms may receive entirely different treatments.

A patient who goes to a traditional practitioner complaining of, say, poor concentration, fatigue and irritability, will find his skin colour, the appearance of his tongue and the tone of his voice being closely scrutinised. His pulse will be taken at numerous different points, and the doctor will ask about his way of life and perhaps how different seasons or times of day affect him. Eventually diagnosis and treatment will be pronounced— in this case, possibly a deficiency of yang energy in the 'kidney meridian', which needs to be corrected by a change of diet and some herbal medicines. The patient is likely to comply since, in traditional theory, the condition could lead to impotence and insanity if left untreated.

The Rise of Chinese Civilisation

Where, then, did this highly evolved culture with so many original ideas come from; and when and how did it bloom? The answers lie in the valleys of the Wei and Yellow rivers in north-central China.

It was here, in a region that has become known as 'the cradle of Chinese civilisation', that the first Neolithic settlements were established. And it was here too that the first major dynasty, known as the Shang (1600–1027 BC), held sway. From archaeological evidence that has come down to us, we know the Shang had a rich and accomplished culture; but it was also barbaric, practising mass human sacrifice and ceremonial beheadings.

The Zhou (1027–256 BC), who succeeded them, preferred a more orderly form of rule, and they also expanded their power base, establishing a feudal system of vassal states bound together by family ties.

▲ The Zhou dynasty (1027–256 BC) is renowned for its intricate bronzes, such as this four-legged pot and brazier.

▲ Having mastered the art of making ceramics and glazes very early in their history, the Chinese went on to develop these crafts to an astonishing degree.

The Flowering of Civilisation

CIVILISATION CAME EARLY TO CHINA. Archaeologists have found evidence of settled agricultural communities in the fertile valleys of the Wei and Yellow rivers 6,000 years before the birth of Christ. And while Stonehenge was being built in Britain (c. 2100 BC), the early Chinese were developing sophisticated techniques for weaving silk, and for making elaborate bronze artefacts and wafer-thin ceramics.

It was not until the 3rd century BC, however, that any true nationhood came to China. Up to this point, the area was divided between numerous states: some small, some large, and all at war with one or more of their neighbours. Then, in 221 BC, the state of Qin emerged as the dominant power, subduing all the others. With that, the king of Qin became the first emperor of all China, or Qin Shi Huangdi—'First Qin Emperor'—as he called himself.

The new emperor immediately drafted labourers in their hundreds of thousands to help construct the newly unified country's main defensive structure, the Great Wall. He also set about standardising the written language, weights and measures, and economic practices, all the while fiercely quashing any opposition to his reforms: to pre-empt dissent, Qin Shi Huangdi even ordered the burning of a great many books of learning, and then murdered all the

▲ **These magnificently expressive figurines were discovered in a royal Tang tomb.**

scholars and intellectuals who objected.

Only four years after Qin Shi Huangdi's death in 210 BC, the Han dynasty came to power, and over the next 200 years the crafts of papermaking, lacquerwork, silkmaking and bronzeworking reached new heights. The splendour of the first Han capital, Chang'an (near modern Xi'an), was unrivalled in scale and magnificence anywhere in Asia. Yet these achievements were only a prelude to the artistic and cultural triumphs of the magnificent Tang dynasty (AD 618–907), the undisputed high point of ancient Chinese civilisation.

▲ **Emperor Qin Shi Huangdi shows the darker side of his character in this depiction of two of his greatest atrocities: the burning of learned books and the mass execution of scholars and intellectuals who protested.**

◄ **A more impressive memorial to Emperor Qin Shi Huangdi is the Great Wall, which he was the first to conceive as a single, unified barrier for protecting China's northern frontier.**

But blood is not always thicker than water, and in about 475 BC rivalry between the various states had so intensified that the system collapsed, plunging China into 250 years of chaos, known as the Warring States period.

Eventually, out of all the turbulence and conflict, there arose one leader strong enough to subdue all others: Zheng, the king of Qin, who wasted no time in securing his position. He proclaimed himself First Emperor of China—or Qin Shi Huangdi ('First Qin Emperor') as he became known—and established strong central government of a sort never seen before.

Although his reign lasted little over a decade (from 221 to 210 BC), Emperor Qin Shi Huangdi revolutionised every aspect of Chinese life. He had a passion for standardisation, which he extended to laws, fines, weights and measures, even the written language; and he had a passion for grand projects. It was he who first had the idea of linking the defensive walls of China's various states into a single Great Wall along the kingdom's northern frontier; and he had the power to see it done.

Emperor Qin Shi Huangdi's other grandiose scheme was to have a life-size and lifelike model army of some 8,000 warriors and horses modelled in terracotta to stand guard in perpetuity in front of his tomb. These were discovered in 1974 and continue to inspire amazement and awe in all who see them.

As well as having immense energy and imagination, Qin Shi Huangdi also had another, darker side: he could not tolerate opposition, and he was utterly ruthless in dealing with it. Books that he disliked he ordered to be burnt; and when some 460 of China's greatest scholars objected, he summoned them to the palace, cut off their right hands and buried them alive.

Cycles of History

The grandiose Qin empire survived Qin Shi Huangdi by just four years. Exhausted by the effort of building the Great Wall and feeding the vast imperial army, the country ran short of food and supplies. Eventually rebellion broke out; then, in 206 BC, there arose from the ashes of the old regime a new imperial dynasty—the Han, one of the greatest China was ever to see.

The first Han emperor, Liu Bang, was a man of humble origins. An uneducated but shrewd peasant-farmer from the Wei valley, he followed Confucian teachings and ruled more

◀ **The round Hall of Prayer for Good Harvests, in Beijing's Temple of Heaven, is built in the traditional Chinese manner— from wood, without a single nail. Its three-tiered roof is covered with 50,000 blue-glazed tiles, symbolising the vault of heaven.**

At the Court of Kublai Khan

A STONISHING AS IT MAY SOUND, China had been unified for nearly 1,500 years before the first eye-witness accounts of this extraordinary eastern land reached Europe. These came from the brothers Nicolo and Maffeo Polo, Venetian merchants who travelled across the great Tien Shan mountains and then overland to China in the early 1260s. After a nine-year round trip, they returned to Europe with fantastic tales of their adventures, most notably, their cordial reception at the court of China's first Mongol ruler, the emperor Kublai Khan.

In 1271, the Polo brothers set out again, this time with Nicolo's 17-year-old son, Marco. Four years later, they reached Kublai Khan's summer palace at Shangdu. The young Marco, now 21, impressed the Great Khan and over the next 17 years he was charged with many missions on the emperor's behalf, travelling throughout the land as his personal ambassador. The stories he recounted on his eventual return to Europe seemed so far-fetched that he was accused of falsehood; yet the reality of what he saw was probably even more fantastic. When urged on his deathbed to take back some of his incredible tales, Marco is reported to have whispered, 'I did not tell half of what I saw, for I knew I would not be believed.'

Marco's caution was well founded, for what he had discovered was a country that was technologically far in advance of Europe in the production of steel, ceramics and explosives; that used paper money; and that had a sophisticated system of government over an area larger than all the squabbling nations of Europe put together. Little wonder that some people were never able to believe him.

▲ Wild flowers brighten the timeless Tien Shan mountains—crossed by Nicolo and Maffeo Polo on their first trip to China in the 1260s.

◀ Marco Polo, Kublai Khan's personal ambassador for 17 years, is here immortalised in a gilded Chinese statue of the 16th century.

• •

This mediaeval Spanish map shows Nicolo, Maffeo and Marco Polo passing through Asia Minor on their way to China. ▼

▲ A modern-day Mongol dressed in light armour, such as Kublai Khan's fearsome cavalrymen might have worn.

◀ Kublai Khan, the first Mongol emperor of all China, depicted here in a coat of white ermine and taking part in a hunt; note the cheetah seated behind the mounted courtier in the foreground!

humanely than his predecessors. He required laws to be justified as 'right' for the common people, and for the first time those in power were expected to live up to high moral standards.

Following in Liu Bang's footsteps, a succession of able and warlike emperors extended the Han empire swiftly to the south and west. Alongside military expansion, the Han took Chinese civilisation to new heights, especially in agricultural and technological developments—the invention of the compass and paper, for example. The strength and vigour of Han culture was such that it eventually became synonymous with the Chinese people, who even today refer to themselves as Han.

After little more than 400 years, however, the Han empire ultimately weakened and broke up into smaller states—one more turn of the cycle of order and disorder that seems to repeat itself throughout Chinese history.

China's next great age came under the Tang emperors, who from 618 to 907 presided over a state more developed and enlightened than any in Dark Ages Europe. Under Tang rule, China experienced a flowering of education, science, literature and other branches of learning. Diplomatic contacts were established as far afield as Persia and Byzantium, and the Tang capital Chang'an (near modern Xi'an) became the most cosmopolitan city in the world, tolerant of all faiths and traditions, and a meeting place for traders and travellers from all over Asia.

During the 8th century, China's great golden age began to dim. A series of disastrous military defeats, rebellions and massive peasant uprisings weakened the Tang empire to the point where it could no longer hold together, leading to a period of short-lived military dictatorships known as the Five Dynasties (907–960). These were eventually replaced by the Song emperors (960–1279), who themselves increasingly came under attack from the Mongols of the north—free-spirited nomads whom the imperial forces had never subdued. Several groups even set up their own empires in northern China, but the real *coup de grâce* came in 1276, when the Mongols overran the whole country.

The Mongols Assert their Might

At first glance, the Mongols might seem unlikely imperialists. Unsettled nomads without much use for lands or possessions, their loyalties were predominantly clannish and tribal, with internecine warfare a permanent way of life. In the 13th century, however, a leader emerged who set the wild horsemen of the steppes on the road to establishing the largest empire the world has ever known. His name was Temujin, but he came to call himself Genghis Khan—'Almighty Ruler'.

Not only was Genghis Khan the first man ever to unite the anarchic Mongol tribes, he was also a brilliant military strategist. In 1208, more than 100,000 Mongols swept down from the north, breached the Great Wall and invaded China. One by one cities fell, were looted and then razed to the ground. In 1215, Beijing (then called Chungtu) surrendered. With that, Genghis turned his attention abroad—to the Islamic states of central Asia, and thence to India, Georgia and southern Russia.

In 1227 Genghis Khan died; and in 1229 the succession passed to one of his four sons—Ogodai, who enthusiastically continued his father's programme of expansion. The armies of Russia and Europe crumbled before the Mongol hordes, who by 1241 had crossed the Danube and were threatening Vienna; then Ogodai died. Instantly, and to the bewilderment of the Viennese, the Mongols abandoned their campaign and raced for home to begin the lengthy process of choosing a new overlord.

Eventually a grandson of Genghis Khan emerged supreme—Kublai Khan, in time the emperor of all China, as well as of Korea, Tibet and parts of Indochina. Unlike his father and grandfather, Kublai was a nation-builder, not just a conqueror. His rule was enlightened and tolerant, dedicated to trade and the free passage of men and goods across a vast empire. Unlike the Chinese, he was outward-looking and actively sought contact with the West—the young Italian traveller Marco Polo was only one of many foreigners employed in his service.

At first the Mongols brought new vitality to an old culture. After a while, however, they became absorbed into a way of life very different from that of their native steppes, and one for which they were not by nature suited. After Kublai Khan's death in 1294, their empire declined, and in 1368 they were finally expelled by the Chinese. From start to finish, Mongol dominion over China had lasted less than 160 years, yet it over-turned centuries of isolation and extended China's reputation and influence into the very heart of Europe.

Traders from the Sea

With the expulsion of the Mongols, China entered its period of Ming rule (1368–1644); it also reverted to its old, closed ways, especially towards the West. But behind the cloak of mistrust, China was not sleeping. During the 15th century, seven major Chinese expeditions set sail, organised on a scale undreamed of in the West, with dozens of ships and thousands of men, including scholars, linguists, doctors and China's finest craftsmen. They kept detailed records of everything they saw and exacted tribute from lands as remote as Mozambique and Somalia.

▲ Portuguese seafarer Jorge Alvares, the first European to sail to China, landed in Guangdong in 1513.

Chinese porcelain, known in the West simply as 'china', is here being carefully packed for export to Europe. ▶

Trading with China

ONCE THE MONGOLS had been overthrown in 1368, China wilfully isolated herself from her neighbours and, with even more determination, from the West. As far as the self-sufficient Chinese were concerned, the 'barbarians' from beyond their borders had nothing to offer them. By contrast, the jostling European powers of the 16th century, hungry for both empire and trade, saw China as a massive source of untapped wealth, especially in silks and porcelain.

In 1498–9, the Portuguese explorer Vasco da Gama opened a sea route to India via South Africa, and in so doing unlocked the whole of the Far East to trade and exploitation on a scale never possible before. First, however, Europeans had to ingratiate themselves with the Chinese.

The Portuguese themselves landed in Guangdong in 1513, but failed to establish any trade agreement with the emperor. The Chinese, in fact, were so hostile that in 1522 they banned all European ships from their coastal waters. In 1557, however, local officials relented, allowing the Portuguese to establish a small trading base on the Macau peninsula.

In spite of the heavy rent, customs and harbour duties imposed by the Chinese authorities, Macau flourished on its exports of Chinese tea, silks and porcelain, Japanese silver, and spices from the East Indies. By 1574 its population had reached 10,000, prompting the ever-wary Chinese to erect a heavily guarded wall between the settlement and the mainland. Despite a variety of other problems, Macau remained the hub of European trade with both China and Japan until well into the 19th century.

Meanwhile, the Spanish and Dutch were also eager to gain a toehold in China and for 37 years they tussled over control of Taiwan, until in 1661 all Europeans were evicted from the island.

▲ A street scene in Macau by George Chinnery (1748–1847), showing the influence of Portuguese architecture.

The Portuguese colony of Macau grew rich on the export of tea, silk and porcelain tableware, such as this Ming jug with its classic blue pattern. ▶

▲ Portuguese sailors and their ships, as depicted on a Chinese lacquer screen of the 17th century.

Despite its early promise, China's age of exploration was short-lived. In 1433, the Ming, fearing the destabilising effects of foreign contacts, wound down their navy and ordered a total ban on coastal shipping. But China had to fight hard to maintain her isolation. In the late 15th century, a new age of seafaring dawned in Europe, with explorers and traders setting out across uncharted waters. When a route to the East was found, China, with its legendary wealth, became a prize too rich to be ignored.

The first Europeans to reach China by sea were the Portuguese, who landed on the coast of Guangdong in 1513 with offers of mutually beneficial trade. But, the emperor was uninterested: the European 'barbarians' could offer him tribute if they wished, and he would sell them some goods for civilising effect; in essence, however, China wanted nothing from Europe.

By 1557, however, the Portuguese had obtained a base at Macau, which thrived on exports and was soon the envy of Europe. Not to be outdone, the Spanish set up trading posts in the Philippines, and the Dutch established bases in Indochina and Japan, while both nations battled for control of Taiwan. All the while, mainland China remained aloof and largely sealed off.

During the 17th century, China experienced yet another dramatic change with the overthrow of its Ming rulers by the Manchus—founders of the country's last imperial dynasty, the Qing (1644–1911). But the Manchus brought no new attitude towards foreigners, and as late as 1793 the British ambassador, Lord Macartney, was expected to prostrate himself, or kowtow, at the feet of the emperor to petition humbly for his country's right to sell goods to the Celestial Empire. In the event, he refused, probably in the knowledge that, whatever he did, the emperor would steadfastly refuse to open Chinese markets to British goods. Such intransigence was to prove fateful for China.

British Traders Go Underground

The 19th century commenced with the Western powers deeply frustrated with China. Exports of tea, silk and porcelain stood at record levels, but almost nothing was allowed into the country. For large institutions, such as the British East India Company, the situation was intolerable, so they set out to remedy it.

Since they were prevented from pursuing unfettered trade through legitimate channels, British traders turned instead to a less salubrious business—the black market in opium, a drug that the ruling Manchus had banned as early as 1729 because of its obvious corrupting effects on the population.

But smuggling on a grand scale continued, and even increased with the tacit support of the British authorities. Eventually, in

▲ By the middle of the 19th century, the waterfront at Canton was a hive of foreign activity, as this painting shows. Each flag identifies the *hong*, or trading house, of a different Western nation.

After the First Opium War between Britain and China, the Treaty of Nanjing (1842), seen being signed here, gave Britain control of Hong Kong and access to five other major ports. ▶

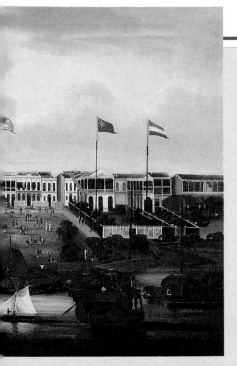

▲ A Chinese opium smoker lights his pipe in an opium den in the late 19th century.

Opium and Boxers

AFTER WAITING IN THE SIDELINES for many years, Britain finally gained a stake in China when she was allowed to open her first trading post at Canton in 1699. In reality, however, commerce was still severely restricted. A handful of government-appointed Chinese merchants controlled all trade from Canton and Europeans were not even allowed within the city walls. The Chinese were uninterested in anything that Britain had to offer and rejected all diplomatic advances. The British had to find something that China wanted—and this turned out to be opium.

The Chinese had known about opium for centuries, but when they started smoking it in the 17th century they became addicted in great numbers—so much so that in 1729 the emperor issued an edict banning the drug. But a huge black market continued to thrive on opium, which was imported from India in

staggering quantities by enthusiastic British traders. Chinese efforts to eradicate the trade culminated in the virtual imprisonment of Canton's entire foreign community, which in turn sparked off the First Opium War (1839–42) between Britain and China.

Britain, far better armed than her opponent, won a major military victory, and achieved an even greater triumph in the subsequent Treaty of Nanjing, by which she gained control of Hong Kong island and access to five other major ports. Two further wars and their treaties further humiliated the Chinese, especially when they were forced to reimburse Britain for opium lost during the hostilities.

Anti-European feelings gradually intensified and finally erupted in 1900, when the Boxers—members of a quasi-religious secret society—started murdering Christians, both Chinese and European. The Boxers also laid siege to foreign embassies in Beijing, prompting an invasion by a multinational relief force. The rebellion was soon quashed, and in its aftermath punitive peace terms were again imposed on China.

◀ Members of the secret society called the Righteous and Harmonious Fists—better known in the West as Boxers—do battle with Western troops in 1900.

The Turbulent 20th Century

As IT ENTERED THE 20TH CENTURY, Imperial China was already in terminal decline. The Manchu dynasty, after nearly 260 years in power, was hidebound by outdated tradition and self-imposed isolation. And under the corrupt, iron-willed and arch-conservative Empress Dowager Cixi (Tz'u-hsi), all attempts to reform and modernise the country were speedily suppressed.

Within three years of her death in 1908, however, a republican movement under Sun Yat-sen had won support throughout China, and in February 1912 the six-year-old emperor, Puyi, was forced to abdicate. Yet, even as he did so, the republicans were in turmoil: Sun Yat-sen, lacking the personal authority to keep up the momentum of his bold undertaking, handed the reins of power to Yuan Shikai, a regional military leader, in the hope of preventing civil war.

What followed was a turbulent period of internal strife—the warlord era—from which two major opposing factions emerged: the Nationalists, under Chiang Kai-shek, and the Communists, eventually led by the charismatic Mao Ze-dong. They proved to be bitter enemies, and as they fought one another by every means available a third great adversary appeared on the scene: Japan, which in 1931 took advantage of China's weakened position

▲ Chinese troops man the Great Wall in the 1940s in order to stem a Japanese advance.

and began occupying large areas of land, from Manchuria to Shanghai.

At first, the Chinese virtually ignored this invasion, largely because the Nationalists refused to be deflected from their efforts to destroy the Communists: Nationalist hatred of the Communists went so deep that they even made treaties with the Japanese in order to concentrate their efforts on only one foe. In contrast, the Communists began waging a determined guerrilla-style war against the invader, and in so doing won themselves

a large, enthusiastic following both in urban areas and in the countryside.

With Japan's surrender in 1945, China had four more years of civil war to endure, culminating in the retreat of the defeated Nationalists to the island of Taiwan. On the mainland, on October 1, 1949, a jubilant Mao proclaimed the founding of the People's Republic of China—a republic in which he would soon acquire a cult status that would, paradoxically, have been familiar to the emperors of old.

▲ Watched over by the ubiquitous Chairman Mao, young Red Guards—the agents of China's Cultural Revolution—put on a show of revolutionary zeal.

◀ The imposing memorial to Chiang Kai-shek in Taipei, Taiwan, where Chiang was president until his death in 1975.

▲ Puyi, the last emperor of China, as he appeared in 1934, after the Japanese had installed him as a puppet ruler of their state of Manchukuo (Manchuria).

Long after the death of Mao Ze-dong in 1976, his portrait still hangs over the Tiananmen Gate—the Gate of Heavenly Peace—in central Beijing. ▼

1839, after a direct plea to Britain to cease its destructive trade, the Chinese took action. Foreign traders in Canton were held and forced to surrender 20,000 chests of opium, which were publicly burned. The British response was to send in gunboats to bombard and seize Chinese ports—the beginning of the so-called Opium Wars which were to cost China dearly, both in terms of land—the Treaty of Nanjing that ended the first war ceded Hong Kong to Britain—and money: China was forced to reimburse Britain handsomely for the destroyed opium.

Not surprisingly, anti-Western feeling began to grow in China. The ruling dynasty, too, came under attack at home for presiding over China's humiliation. As the century progressed, its position became increasingly precarious. One blow followed another: first, a disastrous war with Japan, then a succession of failed harvests and a devastating increase in unemployment. In the hope of redeeming the national spirit, many Chinese turned to semi-mystical secret societies, such as the 'Righteous and Harmonious Fists', or Boxers as they became known—so called because of a type of shadow-boxing martial art they practised.

Initially predominantly anti-Manchu in attitude, the Boxers were cleverly diverted by the court against foreigners and Christians, who were blamed for all China's misfortunes. In 1900, open hostility broke out. The Boxers burnt churches and massacred missionaries and Chinese Christians. When they besieged foreign embassies in Beijing, the West could no longer stand by. An expeditionary force from six European nations, the United States and Japan was sent into action, culminating in the looting of the Imperial Palace. Afterwards, the West imposed crippling reparations, which drained the government and sealed the fate of the enfeebled Qings.

The Making of a Modern State

China entered the 20th century in crisis. Its effective ruler was the ultra-conservative Empress Dowager Cixi (Tz'u-hsi), who had reigned since 1862 in the name of two successive puppet emperors. When she died in 1908—by extraordinary coincidence, one day after the Emperor Guangxu—she had already arranged for the succession to go to Puyi, a boy of two-and-a-half.

A little over three years later, in February 1912, Puyi was forced to abdicate, because in November the previous year a republic had been proclaimed with Sun Yat-sen, a Western-trained doctor, as its president. But Sun Yat-sen did not last long either; under pressure from China's endlessly feuding warlords, he resigned after only a few weeks in the the hope of avoiding civil war—only to see the country slide inexorably into chaos.

Pandas and People in the 21st Century

▲ Young, orphaned cranes being taught to fly at Zhalong Nature Reserve.

This strange texturing of a desert dune represents a bold attempt to stop the desert from encroaching onto arable land. ▶

CHINA HAS A PROBLEM that would daunt any government: how to feed, house and provide basic services for her 1.2 billion inhabitants. And with 14 million new mouths to feed every year—the equivalent of one-quarter of the entire British population—it is not surprising that China has put issues like conservation some way down her list of priorities. And yet there is a growing awareness in the country of the importance of issues concerning the environment.

There are several practical reasons for this change in attitude: national parks attract tourists, who bring with them much-needed foreign revenue; and a conservation programme imparts international prestige and moral credit. Perhaps most tellingly of all, it is now clear that an overexploited environment eventually exacts a high price in human terms—through erosion, encroaching desert and loss of fertile land. It is a price that China can ill afford to pay.

While China's conservation projects are still mainly in their infancy, some are already showing results. Most of the 1,000 giant pandas left in the wild are now in 13 nature reserves, where they are studied, protected and assisted by means of scientific breeding programmes. There are also plans to set aside a further 14 zones in the near future for the benefit of the pandas and their dwindling habitat, the bamboo forest.

In Heilongjiang province a project is underway to protect China's cranes—revered since antiquity as symbols of longevity and, because of their elegant motion in flight, as companions of celestial beings. Thanks to the establishment of the Zhalong Nature Reserve, they now have a vast area of wetland, rich in frogs and other sources of food, in which to breed and rear their young away from the perils of the modern world.

And in Ningxia, to the west, an ingenious land-protection scheme is showing promising results in halting, and possibly even reversing, the effects of desertification. For China, with its vast tracts of overgrazed, overpopulated land, a positive outcome could make the difference between success and failure in feeding itself in the next century and beyond.

••••••••••••••••••••••••••••••••••••••

Not a teddy-bears' picnic exactly, but similar—part of a serious attempt to protect and study the giant panda. ▶

Eventually, after decades of upheaval, two dominant forces led by two gigantic personalities emerged: the Nationalist Party, or Kuomintang government, controlled by Chiang Kai-shek; and the Communist Party, dominated by Mao Ze-dong. The clashes and manoeuvres of these titanic antagonists have become the stuff of legend, especially the so-called Long March of the Communists, when 80,000 troops and 20,000 supporters set out on a year-long slog of over 7,500 miles to escape their enemies; fewer than 10,000 battered individuals survived the ordeal.

Yet the Communists were able to regroup, marshal their forces and in 1949 drive the Nationalists onto the island of Taiwan, while proclaiming a People's Republic on the mainland.

Under Communism, China has slowly modernised herself and there have been impressive achievements in fields such as health care and literacy. There have also been some staggering failures. Mao turned himself into a cult figure, whose whims determined the lives of hundreds of millions of people. And his misjudgements, when they did occur, brought disaster on a grand scale: for example, the notorious Great Leap Forward economic drive of 1958, which caused a famine in which some 30 million perished; and the terrors of the Cultural Revolution—a brutal ten-year purge (1966–76) of artists, intellectuals and professionals at the hands of young militants known as the Red Guards.

Since Mao's death in 1976, his successors have pursued a more pragmatic course. Peasants are once again allowed to own land and traders to make profits. Gradually, a more prosperous and open society has developed, characterised by a new-found awareness of China's huge economic power. On the other hand, human rights are still weak, and images of the Tiananmen Square massacre of 1989 uncomfortably fresh. Those who love China hope for a more peaceful and prosperous future, but recognise that the path ahead is unlikely to be entirely smooth.

Introducing *A Ride Along the Great Wall*

When Robin Hanbury-Tenison first jokingly suggested to his wife Louella that they might ride along the Great Wall of China, they both realised that it was an ambitious scheme. They could not take their horses to China, they spoke no Chinese and no one had ever done anything of the sort before. But they were not the sort of people to be put off by such trifles, and set to work in the firm belief that you will never know if something can be done if you don't even try to do it. And they did do it, with good humour and a strong spirit of adventure.

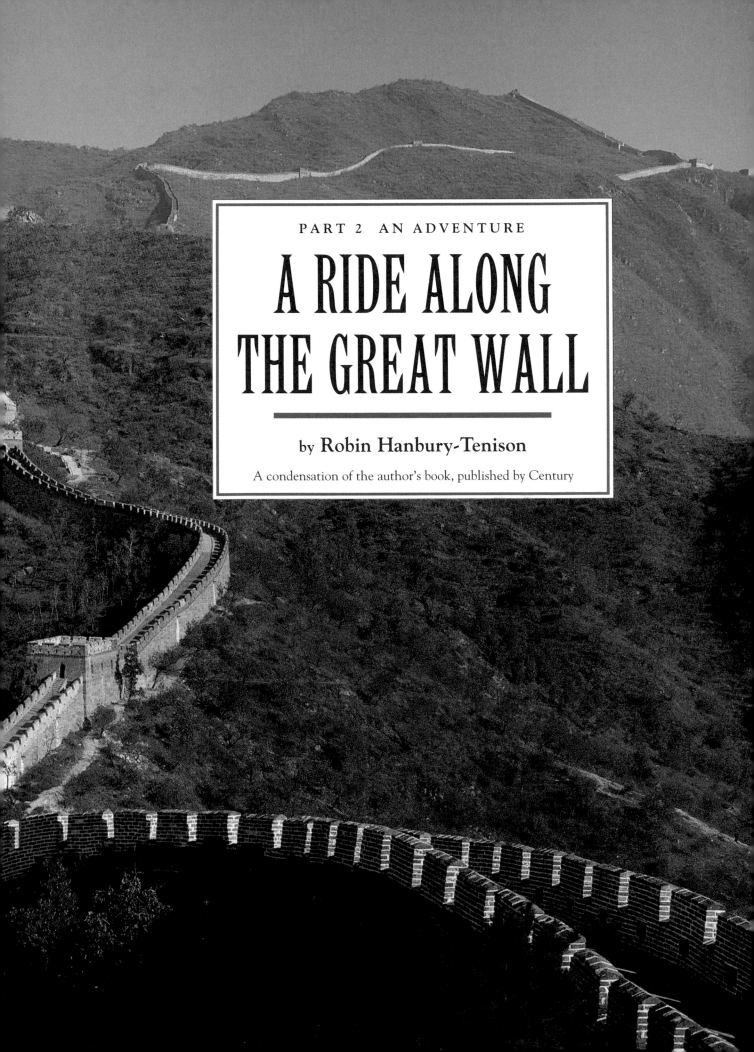

PART 2 AN ADVENTURE

A RIDE ALONG THE GREAT WALL

by Robin Hanbury-Tenison

A condensation of the author's book, published by Century

CHAPTER 1

Preparation

On completing a long journey, there is one question that springs irresistibly to the lips of almost all a traveller's friends and relations. 'Where are you off to next?' they ask. It is in the need to answer this question positively that most journeys are conceived.

So it was with China.

In 1984, my wife Louella and I bought two white Camargue horses on the Mediterranean coast and rode them back across France to our farm in Cornwall. This ride, which was originally undertaken simply as a romantic and pleasant way of bringing the horses home, seemed to touch a chord with all sorts of people. The BBC made a film for television about it, and at the very end, after the credits and when we assumed most viewers would have switched off, we slipped in a private joke.

As the camera pulled away from the two of us on our horses on a Cornish hilltop, Louella turned to me and asked, 'Where shall we go next?' I replied, 'How about along the Great Wall of China?' and she answered, 'Now, that really would be something!'

So, instead of asking 'Where next?' our friends asked us *when* we were off to China or, even more maddeningly, whether we had already done it. It seemed we would have to go.

The first thing we found out was that it was impossible. While the door to China is opening wider than ever before, and innumerable people from all over the world have 'viewed' the Great Wall—mostly the short restored section at Badaling near Beijing—there are still large parts of the country that are closed to foreigners and these include most of the regions through which the Great Wall runs.

Much as we would have liked to have done so, therefore, we simply did not dare just go to China and travel along our proposed route on horses. We would have been arrested at once and deported. We would have to do it legally and officially; very special permission indeed was going to be needed.

We went to see Robbie Lyle, a childhood friend of Louella's, who worked in the City and whose sphere of interest was China. When we told him of our plans he greeted them with enthusiasm. I have since learned that Robbie is an incurable optimist, the most valuable trait for anyone wrestling with Chinese bureaucracy. Several times over the next year of planning and negotiation, when I was cast down by what sounded like a final rejection of our proposals or a flat refusal of some specific idea, I would ring him up in despair to tell him the bad news. His reaction was always the same, and it was immensely cheering. 'Ah, good!' he would say. 'If they are that positive about it then they are about to give in.' And to our amazement he was nearly always right.

There are always excellent reasons for not doing things. There were, for instance, a great many things happening in our lives which made the idea of being away for three months seem at times far fetched. We did not want to leave our three children, who now included a baby boy, born nine months after our French ride. The farm, too, was undergoing a major upheaval. My sheep-farming partner had great plans for diversifying into red deer and Angora goats. Louella, however, decided that at this age the children would miss us far less than we would miss them, while I convinced myself that things would run better on the farm when I was not there. Of course, to try and make a long independent journey through closed regions of China was going to open a Pandora's box of problems. There was no precedent for it or anything like it in the last fifty years.

Yet the more we read about China the more excited we became at the prospect of going there, whatever the difficulties. Furthermore, we looked forward to the possibility of another long, happy ride together. As we summed it up at the time, there were really only three problems to be resolved: the permission, the money and the horses. We began to work on it, and Robbie suggested that I should fly out on a recce to present our idea to the authorities in November 1985 while he was in Beijing himself.

▲ The author and his wife Louella on the magnificent Camargue horses they rode all the way from southern France to Cornwall.

I decided to go via Hong Kong, as an idea was beginning to take shape which might resolve the second of our problems, that of money. Why not make this a sponsored ride and raise lots of funds for charity? For twenty-five years I had been making ambitious and arduous expeditions to tropical rain forests and across deserts. My themes were the misuse of our planet by thoughtless progress, and the destruction of the rain forests and of the people who live there; these I believe affect mankind's welfare and indeed our very survival. We made no pretence that our proposed ride had any such scientific merit, but we should let some good come from it. Hong Kong was a rich place and a lot of people seemed delighted at the prospect of helping us. I just needed to persuade them that we would succeed. Then I had to convince the powers that be in China itself that they should let us go. Finally I had to track down a couple of suitable horses.

It all seemed so easy when put like that.

In Search of Sponsors

'We are just about to cross the border into China,' said the plane's captain.

The Cathay Pacific flight to Hong Kong had been passing over Burma, one of the wildest and least accessible regions left on earth. Where five nations' borders almost meet on the Tropic of Cancer, hill tribes and warlords defy the authority of government, and local conflicts flare up continually. The landscape is so broken, the forested hillsides so steep and the rivers so fast flowing that there are few roads and travel overland is painfully slow.

Now, however, the character of the landscape below suddenly changed. A whole mountain top had been cleared of vegetation, and even from 30,000 feet I could see terracing on some of the slopes, dirt roads snaking along and clusters of tin-roofed houses glinting in the valleys. We were now over the most populous nation on earth. I had not expected their presence to be so instantly apparent from the air. This was my first sight of China and it was an exciting moment.

First, however, I was to address the Fundraising Committee of the Hong Kong branch of the World Wildlife Fund. I talked so much that I missed out on the delicious food provided. After telling them about my past track record of expeditions and books, I explained that much of my life had been devoted to conservation of one sort or another and I had worked with the WWF on several occasions. They were welcome to any money they could raise through our journey, and we did not mind being used in advertisements if necessary.

I packed several other meetings into my one day in Hong Kong. It is a place where a great deal can be achieved in a very short time. One of the vets at the Jockey Club most kindly gave me a lot of useful advice about buying horses.

'Look for straight tendons,' he said. 'Watch out for enlargements of the fetlock joints. Make sure there are no lumps or bumps around the joints and that you can bend them all the way. Trot them hard and test for lameness—if there's any trace of that don't touch them! Don't worry too much about "splints".'

▲ An aerial view of the stunning red-and-green patchwork landscape of Yunnan province, which borders on Burma. Here, every available patch of land seems to be utilised for growing crops.

Although I have ridden all my life, I make no pretence of being a 'horsey' person, and I have always had a problem remembering which bits of the horse are which. I tried to look intelligent and took lots of notes. I also wondered how much choice we would have when it came to the crunch. He told me that most of the horses he had seen on a recent trip, even up on the Mongolian grassland plains, had been for pulling carts. They had been in good condition, with very hardened hooves, so that we should be able to go unshod if there were no blacksmiths.

Greatly reassured to have met someone who knew what he was talking about and did not regard our plan as wholly mad, I hurried to a meeting with Owen Price, Managing Director of Dairy Farm. This huge company controlled all sorts of retail and manufacturing businesses, including a large chain of supermarkets. I had an introduction to Owen and planned to do my best to persuade him to supply us with rations for our ride. I prepared to launch into a long explanation about our plans and hopes to justify my request for help from his company. 'You see,' I said, 'we're planning to ride for charity along the Great Wall of China and we hoped you might give us some food.' Such requests always sound most

◀ A junk sailing across Hong Kong harbour against a backdrop of ultra-modern skyscrapers. Despite being one of the world's leading financial centres, Hong Kong retains many features of traditional Chinese life.

unlikely at the moment of making them. In the first place, my smart tropical suit disappears and I feel myself to be in rags with a begging bowl; in the second place, why on earth should he help us?

'Certainly,' said Owen. 'How much do you need?'

A City within a City

The next day I boarded the flight to Beijing. As I queued in the aisle, waiting for elderly Chinese gentlemen to stow their copious Hong Kong purchases in the overhead lockers, I caught the eye of the man who was sitting in my seat. He wore a faded leather jacket over an open check shirt and he looked like a film director. We sorted out the seats and I discovered that he was, indeed, a director.

He was Mickey Grant, and he had recently made the film of a run across China, called the Great Friendship Run, that had been accomplished by an

American called Stan Cottrell, who had started on the Great Wall just north of Beijing and finished at Canton (or Guangzhou as it is called in China) just north of Hong Kong. Mickey was planning further films in China and by the end of the flight we'd made plans for him to film our ride as well.

'How odd that we should be sitting next to each other!' Mickey said.

'Worse than that,' I said. 'You were in *my* seat. It's a perfect case of serendipity.'

Mickey introduced me to China. A youngish Texan, he was a most unlikely Mandarin speaker, but he had studied the language for three years and had a natural ability to communicate. We took a taxi to the Friendship Store, a large department store stocked with the produce of China and supposed to be used only by foreigners. In theory, it accepted only Foreign Exchange Certificates, but the two-currency system was beginning to break down and there were lots of Chinese people there.

At the fur section, for which the store is famous, I was momentarily subdued by the sight of leopard-skin jackets among the fox, wolf, mink and ermine coats. Although China is a signatory of the Convention on International Trade in Endangered Species (CITES), conservation is still a very new concept there.

'The best bit's downstairs,' said Mickey, who was into acupuncture and herbal medicines. It was an impressive display. There were 'dragon bones' (in reality, fossils of prehistoric animals) to be ground up, extracts of toads and lizards, as well as ginseng of all sorts. The instructions recommended cures for boils, hot palms, hot temper, biliousness and grinding teeth.

Two faces of Beijing: in the background, high-rise buildings of the modern city; in the foreground, a watchtower and moat of the Forbidden City, the residence of China's emperors for 500 years. ▼

Mickey bought a do-it-yourself battery-operated electric acupuncture kit and I almost bought a superb scale model of a painted rubber horse, showing the acupuncture points on one side and its insides exposed on the other. Feeling slightly hysterical, we sampled various sorts of Tiger balm and sniffed at strangely coloured miniature bottles of essences which the giggly sales girls told us were for every imaginable ailment from impotence to backache.

Back at the Great Wall Hotel we had a sandwich in the totally incongruous lobby. Two rather shabby old men in white tie and tails were making wonderful music on a piano and violin, while the glass external lifts shot up seven storeys past the plants and fountains above our heads. We sat up late talking and making ever wilder plans about filming our ride.

Robbie was not due to arrive for another day and so I had a chance to do some sightseeing. Happily a great friend, Nigel Sitwell, was also in town and we were able to share the pleasures of the day. We walked about the streets in crisp, sunny weather. Then we entered the Forbidden City and were confronted by the breath-taking succession of Heavenly Gates. I was astounded by the decorated roof tiles: dragons, birds, lions and horses in procession along the graceful curves of roofs. It is a magical place and feels strangely undisturbed, though it has been much restored. A visitor is made to feel alone with all the beauty. Only a few man-made structures are able to do this, to produce such an overwhelmingly sat-

▲ An ornate pavilion set among shady trees in a tranquil corner of Beijing's Forbidden City.

isfying effect that neither the build-up of excessive expectations, nor the crowds of other tourists, nor the factory chimneys and skyscrapers in the background can make one feel disappointed: the Acropolis, the Taj Mahal, St Peter's, and now the Forbidden City, too.

There is an endearing feeling of abandonment, and some grass grows in the courtyards and on unrestored roofs. Apart from all the great temples, museums and treasure houses, there are also intimate corners. Among the trees, giving freshness and a sense of country, there were rockeries with flights of steps and hidden bamboo gardens. It was easy to escape from the regimented hordes obediently reading the instructions and following the signs. We even found a small stall selling tiny, red, toffee crab apples on sticks. The toffee and the pips were tooth-cracking hard, but there was a refreshing and delicious explosion of apple taste in the middle.

The Great Wall of Bureaucracy

During the following week I suffered my first ordeal by Chinese bureaucracy of delays, frustrations and prevarications. Robbie arrived, full of energy and good humour. I am not used to being unable to fight my own battles, but I was by now aware that China was not a place where bluster, bribery or bending of the rules

▲ One of Beijing's many surprises: peasant farmers harvesting their crops in the time-honoured fashion barely a stone's throw from a modern university building.

would work; I would get nowhere without a lot of influence and luck. Robbie was my guide; blundering in on my own would do no good and so I had to contain myself impatiently.

In between exquisite, expensive meals with charming, influential Chinese friends of his, I tried to take some exercise as a form of therapy. Robbie liked to go jogging early in the morning, so I went with him.

In our track suits, with scarves over our faces and our breath white on the frozen air, we were as anonymous as the shapeless padded figures passing on bicycles; but we still drew the astonished stares to which all foreigners in China, as in much of the Third World, soon become accustomed. I have found that a good way to combat it is to decide to be mildly eccentric so that the stares can be rationalised as a natural response rather than the manifest doubting of one's very humanity, which these mass inspections often seem to be. The Chinese, due to a combination of long isolation and powerful independence, suffer to a greater degree than most from cultural and racial arrogance. Foreigners have always been regarded as uncivilised hairy barbarians, barely-human foreign devils. This attitude was reinforced for many years after the Communist victory in 1949 by Party propaganda which emphasised the evils of capitalism while at the same time criticising the 'revisionist' path of other Communist countries, notably Russia.

I suggested we run along one of the nearby canals instead of down the crowded main boulevards, where there was a real danger of being hit by the already dense early-morning bicycle traffic. The moment we turned onto the towpath we seemed to be in the rural China I had read so much about. There was a grove of pollarded willow trees, thin ice on the water's surface, a lock gate and then a narrow path twisting between old houses built round courtyards. We glimpsed tiny patches of garden where chickens and pigs scratched and rooted, old women bent over smoking stoves, neat sticks of firewood and husks of corn. Beyond lay some paddy fields, this close to the very heart of the city. Much of the countryside beyond the old city walls was still completely rural, but I had not expected to find it still there between the high-rise buildings.

As we trotted happily along, chatting about the day's programme of meetings, our nostrils were suddenly assailed by the most pungent odour imaginable. We passed a night-soil storage pit, holding our breath as long as possible. Later we agreed that it was good to see that even here in the capital the famous Chinese thrift, which extends as far as the use of all human waste, was still being practised. Nevertheless, we chose a slightly different route on subsequent mornings.

I also hired a bicycle and began to explore Beijing on that, finding it far the most sensible form of transport. Pedalling along in a crowd of purposeful Chinese was fun. Much of Beijing still consists of narrow lanes, where whole communities live behind protecting walls, virtually isolated from the big city around them. While it is impossible to enter these areas in a vehicle, it is easy on a bicycle and there I began to experience the taste and feel of China. From the squalor of inconceivably crowded hovels, where smoky charcoal briquettes are used for cooking, where refuse is hurled into the lanes as it used to be in medieval Europe and where glimpses into occasional eating houses reveal interiors reminiscent of Hogarthian gin taverns, emerge people whose clothes are neat and clean and who are clearly setting off to work in an office. Closer inspection shows that the whole set-up is, perforce, extremely efficient.

The keeping of cats and dogs in cities was made illegal some years ago, because they ate too much food and were thought to constitute a disease risk. As a result there are no messes to avoid and no scavengers. Refuse is collected, as is night soil; water is laid on, albeit usually cold, and life is clearly tolerable. The thing that surprised me most was the almost palpable cheerfulness. The horrors of the Cultural Revolution had been halted and reversed in the last few years and the cautious release of steam seemed to be increasing daily. I began to see the Chinese as a naturally ebullient and jolly people, rather than the dour ideologues they have seemed since Liberation. Their raucous cries, shrieks of laughter, heated arguments and loud conversations reminded me far more of a Mediterranean fishing village than an Iron Curtain country. Watching these cheerful people, I began to hope that if we could break through the screen that seems to surround foreigners in Chinese eyes, then we might have an entertaining time among them. Perhaps being mounted on horses would do the trick.

▲ All the hustle and bustle of a typical outdoor eating house.

Meanwhile there remained the problem of breaking through the real barrier of official resistance to our plans. Robbie had been working on this and had come up with an idea: 'You need a patron,' he said.

Patronage in Beijing

Robbie's own most influential friend was Mr Rong Yiren, one of the most powerful men in China, with whom and through whom he had already done a lot of useful business. Widely regarded as the man who has done most to bring about China's economic recovery since the Cultural Revolution, Mr Rong was Chairman of the China International Trust & Investment Corporation (CITIC—a company set up to draw in foreign investment) and many other bodies. It was decided therefore that Robbie and I would together host a banquet for Mr Rong. The quality and opulence of a banquet is directly related to the difficulty and significance of the matter on which the host seeks his guest's help. Since everyone knew that what I was asking was impossible, nothing but the best would do.

On the western edge of Beijing lies a beautiful garden of lakes and ponds, through which a river runs. There in the twelfth century the Emperor Zhang Zong had a fishing lodge erected, which has since become the central feature of what is now the Daioyutai State Guesthouse. Robbie had received permission for us to hold our banquet in the fishing lodge. This was a great honour, for which we would pay an equally great bill.

We arrived in one of the Red Flag limousines used by senior Party officials. These huge black cars, only 200 of which are made in China each year in a style unchanged since the 1950s, have plush seats, darkened windows and, for added

The author sought assistance from Mr Rong Yiren, one of the most influential figures in the Chinese business world, seen here enjoying a brief moment of relaxation. ▶

anonymity, lace curtains. We drove along tree-lined avenues, over marble bridges and past large dark mansions until we reached the fishing lodge. Here coloured lanterns greeted us, discreetly helped by floodlights, which lit our way over a little white bridge and into an ancient courtyard. Gnarled old trees grew from the paving stones; *cloisonné* urns decorated a terrace between red lacquer pillars and a venerable bronze bell. Inside, our banqueting table was decorated with priceless treasures—fine china, silver and glass—rescued from the ravages of this century's successive revolutions.

First we went to the parlour to greet our guests. However grand, these reception rooms all adhere to the same pattern throughout China. Armchairs and sofas embellished with lace antimacassars are arranged squarely around the walls. The host and chief guest sit at one side and everyone listens to their conversation. It makes for rather stilted chitchat, but fortunately Rob is masterful at this sort of thing. Mr Rong was a most impressive figure. Formidable at first, he mellowed in response to Rob's wit and by the time we went in to dinner everyone was laughing.

When my turn came to speak, I explained why I believed our journey would contribute to the goodwill between our two countries and finished by presenting Mr Rong with a copy of *White Horses*, my book on our ride through France. The general feeling was that the evening had been a complete success and a sound investment. From now on things should get easier. However, nothing tangible had been achieved, and since it was now clear that actual permission to make the ride was going to be a cliffhanger until the last minute, the one thing I might be able to do was to find the horses we would use.

It was impossible to find out anything on the subject of horses in Beijing and so I went to the place where the Wall begins, Shanhaiguan, 200 miles away, trusting that something would turn up. Mr Hou, a charming young lawyer from Mr Rong's company, CITIC, agreed to come with me and act as interpreter. But before we could go we had to buy our train tickets, since this had to be done the day before departure.

We made our way to the fine central railway station, one of the best examples of monumental architecture in Beijing. Built in the 1950s, it has two big clock towers (which show the right time) and a huge reception hall with escalators. It looks as though it could cope efficiently with any number of people, but fails to do so for two reasons. One is the staggering number of people who use the station. At all hours of the day and night it is crowded to overflowing. All over the pavements and car parks outside, groups of travellers from the far corners of China huddle by their piled-up belongings, as they wait for something to happen. The other ingredient of the chaos is the appalling ingrained bureaucracy of China,

▲ An exquisitely decorated lacquer plaque dating from the Ming dynasty (1368–1644). Many such treasures were lost during the Cultural Revolution, when China's rulers decreed that works of art should express only Communist ideals.

which causes even the most simple operation, such as the purchase of a ticket, to be surrounded by almost insuperable rules and regulations.

Foreigners have a special, elegant, echoing booking hall where life should run smoothly. One had only to enter to see that it did not. Timetables were unobtainable, and the large wall chart of the principal trains each day showed only the trains' ultimate destinations; so it was necessary to consult a map of China in order to work out if a certain train might stop at the station of one's choice. We worked it out and queued at the only tiny pigeonhole being manned. When our turn came we could see a cross-looking girl sitting sideways and ignoring us.

'Excuse me,' said Mr Hou. 'Could we have two tickets, soft class, to Shanhaiguan on the 8.40am train tomorrow?'

With a toss of her head and without looking up, she replied, '*Mei you!*' This literally means 'not have' and is the instinctive initial response, it seems, to all questions addressed to officials and shop assistants in China by foreigners and Chinese people alike.

'How about hard class?' I made Mr Hou ask. She shook her head as though he had asked for a special coach. 'The early train?' I suggested, since we were both quite ready to make a 5am start. Again a firm no, and so it went on as we tried trains and classes throughout the day. The queue behind us became restless and she shuffled tickets and money busily and did her best to pretend we were not there. As we were patiently working through the afternoon trains, she suddenly lost interest in the game and thrust two tickets and other vital bits of paper through the slot. They were soft-class tickets for the train we had originally requested and cost about £3 each for the 200-mile journey across the Hebei plain.

Hunting for Horses

Next morning we fought our way through the throng to our train. Our own sleeping compartment was a delight. There were four comfortable bunk beds draped with white sheets embroidered with blue flowers, a table with a lace tablecloth, lamp and pretty pink lampshade, a real begonia in a decorated pot and a television mounted on the wall. Grey velvet curtains with muslin netting behind screened the window and there were hooks to hang our coats from, as well as a vacuum flask of hot water for making tea. There was a thermometer on the wall, and the heating was full on. Less desirable were two Greek sailors, who lay in the top bunks smoking when awake and snoring resonantly when asleep, and a loudspeaker through which for the first twenty minutes a strident girl's voice instructed the passengers on what they were not allowed to have on board, such as explosives.

But I had my Walkman and a stock of Mozart tapes, which I always take on trains to cut out distractions, and at last I was travelling through the Chinese countryside. It seemed good riding country, with lots of dirt roads and cart tracks leading off to the horizon between rows of poplars. I played a childhood game of pretending I was on a horse cantering beside the train, leaping over obstructions as they loomed up.

One of the great pleasures of train travel in China is the large number of fine great steam engines to be seen. Although our own train was pulled by diesel, I saw them in every station and siding, puffing clouds of black smoke while white steam escaped between their great wheels. The drivers waved cheerfully when they saw me peering out at them, as did the jolly, red-faced girls in brightly coloured padded jackets working on the track. A shepherd grazed his flock of sheep on the embankment, and we passed a herd of very pink pigs which stopped their rooting and rushed off at the sound of the train.

It was very exciting to see the countryside and the regularly spaced villages, still partly screened by willows and poplars losing the last of their autumn leaves. As I gazed I tried to imagine what life was like for the people I could see riding on their carts behind mules, horses and donkeys, or trudging along under heavy loads. The villages consisted of row after row of identical bungalows, looking a bit like railway carriages with the wheels removed, and I missed the relief and focal point of a church, mosque or temple. The only imposing buildings, ancient or modern, I saw on the long journey were great factories, with rows of tall chimneys. They are the temples of modern China.

On our arrival in Shanhaiguan, a cheerful, round-faced policeman at the station offered to find us the only taxi and then decided to come with us. Mr Hou explained what we were there for and a general discussion followed, with an enthusiastic willingness to help us in our quest but much shaking of heads over the prospect of finding riding horses. I had to admit that I had not seen a single person riding a horse on the whole seven-hour journey.

We drove to see the Great Wall. The old town lies up against the Wall and most of its own walls are intact, with narrow gateways leading to the crowded streets beyond. The magnificent east gate of the great fort has been restored and bears the inscription 'The First Pass Under Heaven' in huge characters on the double-roofed tower. Beyond lies the province of Liaoning, part of old Manchuria, which for 2,000 years was peopled by barbarians who constantly threatened China's peace.

Several walls were built to divide this area's warring states and to define borderlines as early as the fifth century BC, but it was not until China was unified by Emperor Qin Shi Huangdi in 221 BC that they were first linked up and extended to form the Great Wall. The Wall we intended to follow was mainly the Ming Wall, built between the fourteenth and seventeenth centuries, incorporating sections of earlier walls. Experts estimated that there were once as many as 25,000 towers along its length. In places they are only 100 yards or so apart, although many have now been destroyed, particularly in the western part.

Up on the Wall it was bitterly cold, with an icy wind blowing off the mountains to the northwest. It was almost unbearably exciting to see the Great Wall winding up from the coastal plain into those mountains like a great grey snake, and to know that it continued westwards for another 4,000 miles to the great fort at Jiayuguan, where we hoped to end our ride.

▲ The great fort known as The First Pass Under Heaven stands guard on the open plain between the mountains and the sea at Shanhaiguan.

Mr Hou and I went to call on the Shanhaiguan Great Wall Research Institute, which was raising money in response to Comrade Deng Xiaoping's call, 'Love our motherland and repair the Great Wall.' The institute was housed in a pleasant building in the square next to the east gate. We were well received, enthusiastically so when I said I hoped our ride might raise some money for restoring the Wall. They told us that three young men from Shanhaiguan had recently returned from walking along the Wall to Jiayuguan, taking 500 days to do so. They said they were ordinary workers who had undertaken the journey without sponsorship and had simply relied on the help of friendly people and officials along the way. This certainly augured well for us. I made a donation to their work, in return for which I was presented with a gold-plated badge of the First Pass.

Mr Hou and I spent the night in the big nearby port of Qinhuangdao, as we were told (wrongly as it turned out) that there were no hotels in Shanhaiguan. In the morning our friendly policeman informed us he had had a brainwave. He thought the army might have some horses. We drove straight to the local barracks. It was a huge, rambling place with bleak buildings and cold soldiers, often bare-foot, wandering about in shabby uniforms. They all seemed to have the same rank but one was eventually identified as 'Chief of Staff'. He said that we could go and see the horses. He also said there were eight of them, but when we arrived at the stables we found that five of the animals tied up under a tin-roofed shelter were mules. Of the remaining three one was clearly hopeless, being lame, far too small and vicious; it tried to bite me as soon as I approached. I began to examine the two remaining possibles, trying to look knowledgeable and confident.

There was a bay gelding which looked quite big and strong, so I felt its legs for lumps, stroked its neck, which it did not seem to mind, and asked if I could try it out. The bay was saddled up. Chinese army saddles are quite acceptable, but, unlike our deep, comfortable Camargue saddles, they perch high on the horse's back, leaving little to hang on to. I was not looking forward to mount-ing what they warned me was quite a lively animal. The yard was rough and stony; I did not want to fall off and lose a lot of face as well as injure myself. All at once the whole idea of riding across China seemed less appealing. There was no turning back, however, so I gingerly climbed

▲ The most promising candidates of a very motley crew line up for inspection by the author.

aboard, at which the horse gave a series of little bucks and began to head back towards his friends. It was difficult to make him do anything else, as he failed to respond to the usual signals.

While I struggled to trot and walk round the yard, one of the soldiers mounted the remaining pony, also a gelding, which was black and rather hairy. As soon as he was on he walloped it into a canter and began to career around. Everyone shouted that I should follow him and so we took off out of the yard and towards the main buildings. This I guessed was the normal exercise run for the horses and it seemed that it was always done flat out. My horse seemed happier at this speed and bucked less often, so I hung on and followed the soldier, who whooped wildly and led the way round the barracks. Back in the yard I tried out the black, which was a much nicer ride, though quite a bit smaller. I decided that it would suit Louella well as she is about two stone lighter than me.

In the main barrack building we climbed stained stone staircases and went along bare, dusty corridors past broken windows and scruffy rooms with iron bed-steads to what I assumed was the officers' mess. There were blue, plastic-coated armchairs around the walls and a bunch of artificial flowers in a vase. On the walls were pictures of Victorian ladies and children in crinolines. A jolly quartermaster plied us with tea from a vacuum flask, saying 'good day' and 'goodbye' in English as he poured. Then the colonel arrived. There was no mistaking him. He wore a neatly pressed uniform instead of sagging fatigues. We explained our needs and I offered to buy the two horses I had just ridden.

'The trouble is,' he replied, 'these ones are officially members of the People's Army and I cannot dispose of them without permission from higher authority.' Fortunately, someone who had the authority to authorise the sale, General Zhou, was due to arrive the next day on an inspection visit.

Mr Hou and I at once wrote a polite letter to the general requesting permission to buy the horses, explaining what Louella and I planned to do with them and presenting him with a copy of *White Horses* as explanation for our crazy desire to ride across countries rather than go by bus. Everyone agreed that this should do the trick, and the colonel promised to look after the horses well until our return the following April. I made a little speech complimenting them on the condition of their horses, and thanked them for their hospitality and kindness. We left suppressing, with difficulty, whoops of joy. It looked as though we had cracked one of the problems which might make the ride impossible.

In a state of euphoria I suggested to Mr Hou that we should now relax and enjoy ourselves as tourists. He was as pleased as I was and our policeman and taxi

China's Friendly Monsters

▲ **An extraordinary, living sculpture of two dragons, wreathed in grass and creepers. In China, images of dragons—symbols of vitality and strength—are omnipresent.**

THE CHINESE DRAGON, according to one standard description, is a bizarre composite of physical features: it has the head of a camel, the horns of a deer, the neck of a snake, the scales of a carp, the claws of an eagle and the paws of a tiger. But unlike the fearsome dragons of so many other cultures, the Chinese version is a benevolent creature, whose 'breath becomes clouds' that bring life-giving rain. For China's emperors, the dragon had additional attributes: it symbolised power and wealth, which is why it appears so frequently as a decoration on imperial robes and palaces.

The dragon's hold over the Chinese imagination remains remarkably pervasive, even in the 20th century. After the fall of the last imperial dynasty in 1911, for example, China's new ruler, Yuan Shikai, sent teams of men into the countryside to collect dragon bones; these, he believed, would be viewed as an auspicious sign from heaven and so cement his authority.

Even today, 'dragon bones', ground to a powder, are much prized as a folk remedy in traditional Chinese medicine. Such bones are in reality probably dinosaur fossils, which are abundant in parts of China, and which perhaps have helped to reinforce the dragon myth in Chinese tradition.

driver had caught the mood, so that we were a very merry party. We decided to visit the Jiangnu Temple about four miles to the east. Here there is a statue to a legendary lady called Meng Jiang who has been venerated for more than 2,000 years. Her husband was one of the innumerable people conscripted to build the original Wall by the Emperor Qin in the third century BC. Worried that he might be cold, she travelled thousands of miles in search of him, carrying warm clothing. At last she reached a spot where she was told he had died from the hard labour. Her tears melted the Wall and the bones of her husband, who like many others had been used as ballast in its building, popped out into her arms. Carrying them back to Shanhaiguan, she threw herself into the sea with them.

▲ Old Dragon's Head— the easternmost end of the Great Wall—extends right into the sea. This photograph shows the results of restoration work which was in progress at the time of the author's visit.

We climbed up to the temple, where there is a fine view of the Wall and the mountains from the Waiting for Husband Rock where Meng Jiang is supposed to have sat and looked out for her husband. I bought a postcard of it to send to Louella and we drove to see Old Dragon's Head, the place where the Wall actually starts on the edge of the Bo Hai sea. The Wall was seen as a dragon by the Chinese, its head drinking from the sea, its tail far inland, its body coiled along the mountains. In China the dragon is a symbol of strength and energy, an auspicious presence, not a destructive one as in the West.

There was no recognised way of approaching this spot and I had been warned that it was a military zone closed to foreigners. As we approached the sea we came to a barrier across the track, guarded by a soldier. At first he would not let our taxi through, but when we explained that I was a foreign tourist and only interested in seeing the Great Wall he waved us on. We found ourselves in a large army camp with rows of huts, soldiers marching about and, above our heads, huge radar antennae rotating. It clearly was a rather sensitive place, a listening post of China's eastern defences perhaps, and I felt sure we would soon be kicked out. Trying to look as official as possible, we scrambled over the ridge separating us from the shore and emerged on to a pleasant rocky beach.

The Wall at its very end had crumbled away. Only a few large cut rocks in the sea marked the point where the final buttress must have stood in the waves. They were once joined together with molten iron poured into grooves, which were still visible. Here, in 1900, during the Boxer rebellion, a British force landed to attack Shanhaiguan from the sea, burning down a nearby town and seizing the fort and barracks behind us as their headquarters. Now I could see that the end section of the Wall was being restored. Well, I thought, if the British had played their part in knocking it down, the least I could do was to try to raise some money towards its rebuilding.

The Palace at the Centre of the World

▲ The River of Golden Water, flowing across the first great courtyard of Beijing's Forbidden City, was intended to bring good fortune to the emperor.

The Forbidden City is a veritable maze of passages and ornate gateways leading to palaces, halls, temples and courtyards. ▼

WHEN THE THIRD MING EMPEROR, Yong Le, commissioned a new palace for himself and his successors at Beijing in 1406, he gave it a grand and mysterious name: The Purple Forbidden City. The reference to colour was not, however, an allusion to the palace's appearance, but an invocation of the purple-glowing Pole Star. For the emperor believed that, just as the Pole Star hangs in the very centre of the heavens, so he would stand at the centre of the world.

In all respects, the palace was as grand as its name suggests, for in accordance with his status as the Son of Heaven, Yong Le had his residence built on a phenomenal scale. Over a million labourers and 100,000 craftsmen toiled for 14 years to assemble the hundreds of halls, pavilions, libraries, courtyards and gardens that cover the Forbidden City's 180-acre site. A moat 164 feet wide and a wall over 30 feet high enclosed the entire complex, guarding the emperor from contact with the sordid outside world. For as its name indicates, the Forbidden City was a closed community: no one could enter without express permission, and, apart from the emperor, only women and eunuchs were allowed to live within its confines.

Every aspect of the Forbidden City reflected the power of the emperor and served to enhance his well-being. The City's symmetrical layout on a north–south axis created harmony; gilded dragons and other mythical creatures protected the rooftops; bronze lions guarded the gateways; a river flowed through the grounds in order to bring good fortune. The emperor himself might have up to 9,000 concubines at his beck and call, and over 70,000 eunuchs to guard himself and them.

▲ The Forbidden City may yield a few secrets yet!

▲ The entrance to the Hall of Mental Cultivation. Behind the gateway's gilded guardian is a door studded with 81 nails—a cryptic allusion to the emperor's divinity.

◀ A fearsome lionesque dragon, with flaming mane and tail, keeps vigil in a shady garden. The Chinese dragon is an ancient symbol of imperial power.

▲ Lavish decoration and inspiring inscriptions surround the imperial throne in the Palace of Heavenly Purity, where the emperor received foreign ambassadors and other dignitaries.

Mythical beasts, some with fearsome teeth and wide, staring eyes, guard the rooftops of every building in the Forbidden City. ▶

CHAPTER 2

The Last Hurdles

▲ The Hanbury-
Tenisons' adopted
Chinese names—Happy
Guest Han (top) and Love
Baby Lou—represented
by Chinese characters.

ALMOST EXACTLY FIVE MONTHS LATER, in April 1986, I returned to Shanhaiguan, this time with Louella as well as Mr Hou. She and I had flown out to Beijing a couple of weeks before and, while all our other plans still looked extremely shaky, we wanted at least to be sure of the horses. This time we were taken to a delightful old mansion, which had just been converted into a most comfortable small hotel. It was in the walled city and in sight of the First Pass, and was once, we were told, the late Defence Minister Marshal Lin Biao's house. We were given his old bedroom, No.1, unchanged since the day in September 1971 when he was killed in an air crash in Mongolia. There was a deep iron bath on legs with plenty of hot water for an hour or so in the evening—a rare luxury in rural China—and two big, hard, double beds in our room. It was divided by a carved wooden screen and there were comfortable old armchairs and even a refrigerator in the sitting area. We were to get to know that room quite well.

On my earlier trip I had asked Mr Hou if he might be able to come with us as our interpreter. His English was so good and he had such a nice sense of humour that I felt sure we would all get on. Aged twenty-eight, he had been married for six months but, like so many others in China, was only able to see his wife once or twice a year. She was a doctor and lived in his home town of Qingdao in Shandong province. He had done his legal training in Canton.

I also asked him to help choose Chinese names for us. Our full names are quite impossible for general use in China where almost all names consist of only two or three syllables, the first being the surname. We started with my name. He asked me which three syllables I would like to use. 'I thought perhaps the Han from Hanbury, followed by Robin,' I suggested. 'Let's see,' he replied. 'Han is fine. It's about the commonest Chinese name, like Smith, so we need do nothing with that. But Robin does not mean anything in Chinese and will be hard for people to pronounce or remember. I will have to work on it.' For half an hour or so he tried out sounds and meanings, mouthing Ro, Lo, Wo and other strange noises while at the same time scribbling characters. At last he said, 'One of the meanings of Le can be "happy". Would you say you are a happy person?'

'Very much so,' I answered.

'Then if you use Bin to mean "guest", you would be Happy Guest Han. How about that?'

'Perfect,' I said. Much later I was to learn that Lebin can also mean pancake, which I found less appropriate, but Louella seemed to find funny.

It was then Louella's turn. Since husbands and wives do not have the same surname in China, we settled for Louella as her three syllables. 'Once again Lou is easy,' said Mr Hou. 'It's another common surname, but "ella" is going to be harder.' After a while he asked if she liked babies and I replied that she was mad about them, having just had her third. 'Then how about Aiwa?' he said. 'That means "love baby".' And so she became Love Baby Lou.

In Shanhaiguan's splendid old lime-green taxi, made in Russia in 1950, we entered the army barracks at Qinhuangdao in style. We had sent a cable saying we were on our way to collect and pay for the horses but had, of course, received no reply and now had our fingers crossed that they would still be there. At first it looked bad. A new unit had just taken over and was in the process of moving in so that no one knew what was going on. The stable area seemed deserted and we peered hopelessly through blackened windows into the derelict buildings. Then we saw something move and were able to make out two horses in the dim interior. The two horses I had chosen in November had been left behind with two soldiers to look after them. Their saddles and bridles were there too, they had been freshly shod and they looked in fairly good shape. We rode them and mine bucked as before, while Louella's small black one kicked out at everyone. But we managed to stay on and even repeated the circuit of the barracks at a canter, allowing them to choose the route. We decided to name them Tang and Ming.

There was, of course, no question of our turning them down now, since we had no alternative horses, and so when the new colonel appeared we would have to

◀ Tang (left) and Ming, the two People's Army horses chosen by the author for the first leg of the trip, wait patiently for their new masters.

agree to any price he demanded. However, the instructions he had been left by his predecessor were quite clear. Although the horses had originally cost 1,500 yuan each in Mongolia, we were to be charged 800 yuan each, plus another 200 yuan for their tack and keep. 'General Zhou said you were to be treated fairly and, besides, the People's Army is not a commercial organisation,' he told us. Since this came in total to less than £200 for each fully equipped horse, we paid up happily and took formal possession of them. At least one problem was now resolved. We still had many things to sort out back in Beijing but we hoped that a week or so would take care of that. We left saying we would return soon, and that meanwhile we hoped the soldiers would give Tang and Ming lots of exercise each day.

Since our train back to Beijing did not leave until midday the next day, we decided to get up early and walk as far inland along the Wall as we could. Shanhaiguan, which means 'the pass between the mountains and the sea', has always been of critical strategic significance to China. The original gate was built in AD 618, the first year of the Tang dynasty, while the present one was built under the Ming in the 1600s. Thus Tang and Ming turned out to be quite appropriate names for our first horses.

▲ An imposing watchtower guarding a particularly broad and solid stretch of the Wall.

The first few miles of the Great Wall at Shanhaiguan are among the finest and most elaborate sections along its entire length. The walls at the very start are forty-six feet high and twenty-three feet thick, made of bricks laid on great granite slabs with rammed earth inside. It was perhaps the most important defensive stretch of all, for it protected the narrow plain between the mountains and the sea; any invading army getting past was home and dry in China. Treachery by the general in charge in 1644 led directly to the downfall of the Ming dynasty and the start of Manchu rule. Since then it has been known as Traitor's Gate.

It is often said that the Wall is wide enough for five or six horsemen to ride abreast. In places this is true, but it is unlikely that horses were often taken up onto the ramparts as the passages through the numerous watchtowers were too narrow for horses to pass. There were frequent flights of steps and, for the first few hundred miles of the Wall at least, many sections are too steep for a horse to climb. It did, however, serve as an elevated highway for messengers and foot soldiers, who could rush to defend threatened sections. Messages were also sent rapidly over great distances between strategically placed beacon towers. Fires of wolves' dung were lit, as the smoke from these apparently flows straight upwards and so makes signalling easier.

We set off briskly inland along the top of the Wall from the gate, but at the point where the Wall separated from the old town walls of Shanhaiguan there was a wide gap. We had to scramble down into the town and leave by the North Gate. A rough road ran towards the mountains parallel to the Wall and we followed this. On our right, the inner mud face of the Wall was eroded and overgrown, while on the outer side most of the stone facing was impressively intact.

Just before it started to climb we crossed to the outer side and came upon a delightful rustic scene. A family of peasants in colourful clothes was ploughing behind a mule. Even the youngest child was working, busily wielding a large spade. We climbed from here along the top of the Wall. It soon became very steep, with a narrow paved surface and a crenellated outer edge. There was only room for one person at a time, but we forged ahead and came to a stop against a cliff face below the first beacon tower. Here we could go no further without returning to the bottom and detouring round the side of the hill to pick up the Wall again above the cliff. In this immediate way we found that the Great Wall is not and never was actually continuous. Natural features were used where a wall was unnecessary. We sat and gazed out over the spectacular view to the south across the plain, the walled town and the sea beyond, where many large freighters and tankers were steaming past.

In the shelter of the Wall it was quite hot in the sunshine, but a chill wind blew off the hills. The scenery around us was alpine, pretty as a postcard, with scattered fir trees under which grazed flocks of white goats, while brown cows grazed on the grassy slopes. The sounds of the plain were carried up to us: voices,

A timeless rural scene, in which a farmer and his son use a mule and an old-fashioned plough to cultivate their land. ▼

bleats and tinkling bells with only the occasional putt-putt of a mini-tractor. We returned along the outer side of the Wall, passing an old man pulling a stone roller in a wrought-iron frame behind him, then into the medieval lanes of the old town, where we bought some tea and hot muffins at a stall. The muffins were made of white flour and coated with millet seeds before being baked. Delicious and only 10 fen (2 pence) each.

Capital Consultation

Back in Beijing, meetings were inconclusive, studded with vague references to 'the relevant authority' and 'the department concerned'. We all knew who was being referred to, but it simply is not done in China to mention the military or the police. We knew that the Wall, running as it does parallel with China's northern border, passes almost entirely through sensitive military areas but we also knew that, thanks to Robbie, people were rooting for us and that there was a general feeling that letting us make the ride would be a 'good thing'.

At this point I made my first appeal to our patron, Mr Rong. I said we would need some help with customs clearance. The reason that we anticipated problems at the Beijing customs was that we did have a great deal of baggage. We

'Not for all the Tea in China'

FOR MANY PEOPLE, tea-drinking is a quintessentially British habit. Yet in the late 17th century an Englishman wrote fiercely about people 'who call for tea, instead of pipes and a bottle after dinner', referring to this as 'a base practice'. Yet the practice caught on, even though early imports of tea were outrageously expensive—the equivalent of about £300 per pound in today's terms.

By the time the British discovered tea, the Chinese had been drinking it for many centuries. No one knows exactly when tea —or *cha*, as the Chinese call it—was first brewed into a cuppa, but references to it appear in literature of the 4th century AD. And by the time of the Tang dynasty (AD 618–907), tea was the favourite beverage of cultivated people, even inspiring a book called *The Tea Classic*. Connoisseurs had by now learned to savour different styles of tea, teas from different regions, and the varying fragrances of different strengths of tea.

Chinese Buddhist monks lent tea a further dignity by giving it their approval and by developing suitable rituals for

▲ Tea pickers in eastern China. Only the topmost leaves and buds are harvested.

preparing and serving it. These were later taken up by Zen monks in Japan, where the tea ceremony acquired its most elaborate form. By contrast, with time, tea-drinking became progressively less ceremonial in China as ordinary people

discovered its pleasures, particularly in pub-like tea houses. These all-male haunts are still popular today, offering their customers a pot of tea and unlimited refills, and sometimes even live entertainment, all for one small fee.

wanted to pre-empt all practical objections to our ride by having everything necessary with us, so that we could never be accused of being a burden on the local population, and Cathay Pacific had most generously made this approach possible for us by agreeing to waive excess charges. We had a splendid three-compartment tent complete with mosquito nets in which we and our support party could sleep if there were no accommodation. (We had already announced that we would be employing a cook and a driver for our support vehicle, as well as our interpreter, although we had no idea where we were going to find them.)

Dairy Farm, one of our sponsors, had been so generous with food for the journey that reluctantly we had to turn down two thirds of it as the weight would have taxed even Cathay Pacific's goodwill, but we still had enough to feed a small army.

We had also brought the wonderfully comfortable saddles on which we had ridden across France—we had no intention of suffering daily on anything else if we could help it. These, with boots, clothes, cameras, film and forty copies of *White Horses* as presents, combined to make up a formidable quantity of baggage: thirty-two pieces in all, weighing in at just over 1,300 pounds.

At Beijing customs we fully expected all our stuff to be impounded and to have to spend the first week or so getting it cleared. Deciding to try and brazen it out, but with little hope of success, I went over to the row of baggage trolleys and paid for six. One of the nice anomalies facing the traveller arriving in China is that you are forbidden to take Chinese currency into the country, yet you cannot get a baggage trolley in the arrival hall without paying. I had learned an insight into the Chinese way of doing things first time round, when I had seen the old hands hurrying forward with notes outstretched. Many things seem impossible but there is usually a way round.

I persuaded five of the girl porters to take a trolley each and stand by the baggage carousel while Louella and I loaded a couple of heavy items onto each. Leaving Louella to stack up the rest as it arrived, I set off for the single exit, looking as confident as I could and with my attendants in tow. At that moment a fairy godmother appeared in the form of a beautiful and elegant Chinese girl we had met in London, and who was returning home to Beijing on the same flight. She offered to help. 'These are friends of mine who are going on an expedition,' she said, with a delightful mixture of charm and authority. My form was stamped and we all swept through. Outside, in the bedlam of the crowded arrival area, I found an empty space on the pavement, unloaded the trolleys, left one girl in charge and shepherded my flock back in. Twice more we loaded up and swept smilingly past the customs counters, the final time with Louella, who had been nobly grabbing, stacking and checking our belongings. Everything passed through safely and without question.

A twenty-seater minibus was barely able to carry us and all our luggage to the Jianguo Hotel, where the kind manager allowed us to take over their storeroom. For our first few days in Beijing I constantly expected to be tapped on the shoulder and told that the customs service wanted a word with me, but gradually I began to accept that we had actually beaten the system.

Being in Beijing with Louella was a lot more fun than it had been on my own. We hired bicycles and explored together. We went shopping for the children and visited all the sights. We got up very early and saw the Wall at Badaling before the first tourists arrived, and we discovered little restaurants together where we could dine out late with only red paper lanterns between us and the stars. We also made a lot of friends and were entertained generously. But none of this was what we had come for and we fretted at the delays and the expense.

Our embassy was wonderful. In spite of the fact that it was in a state of considerable upheaval because of the forthcoming state visit by the Queen and Prince Philip, the staff helped us in all sorts of ways to keep our sanity and achieve our ends. The Information Officer, John Dennis, sat in on several meetings, and while he quite properly made it clear that we were in no way official visitors, his very presence gave us an aura of respectability we might otherwise have lacked.

One of the strangest things about China at this time was that nobody knew exactly what the law was. While there was officially an 'Open Door' policy, there was also an ingrained fear of change. The same applied to the free markets, which had recently sprung up everywhere. Theoretically they were permitted, but every now and then the police would close one down. One that had recently been closed and then reopened was at the Bird Market, and we went there. The Chinese love to keep cage birds, especially hwameis, thrushlike birds which sing constantly, like an English blackbird on a spring morning. Their owners exercise them by taking them for walks, swinging their wooden cages up and down to strengthen their legs as they cling to their perches. This is said to improve their voices. There were lots of hwameis in the market and they sounded like a dawn chorus.

Just when we thought we must be breaking through the bureaucracy, another problem would be thrown at us. After two weeks of negotiations we began to feel caught in a spider's web. We presented special problems to the authorities, since much of their concern centred on who would take responsibility for us if anything went wrong on the journey. My assurances that I took full responsibility for everything fell on deaf ears. Without an overall host there would be no permission and we were at an impasse. We made another appeal to Mr Rong, our kindly patron: would he write a letter saying we were there as his personal guests? Unhesitatingly he did so and doors began to open. Everyone agreed now that probably we would get permission. It was just a question of when.

The Team Sets Out

There comes a time when a traveller has to make his own fate if he is not to spend forever planning and never doing. One way is to tell enough people that something is going to happen on a certain date, so that he will look an idiot if it does not. It is also an effective if risky way of dealing with Chinese prevarication. We announced that whether the permission had come through or not we would leave for Shanhaiguan at the weekend. On the Saturday, as we were signing our contract for our staff and paying the deposit for their wages, we heard that the military had at last agreed a route we could follow all the way from Shanhaiguan to Jiayuguan. We had, of course, asked for permission to ride the whole way along the Wall, but had by now realised that it was most unlikely that permission would be granted for this without restrictions. 'Good,' I said. 'I'll come and fetch it.' That, I was told, was quite impossible. The relevant piece of paper was somewhere in the internal security post, which was slow. It might take three or four days to emerge. Even then I would not be allowed to see or touch it

◄ Fresh air stimulates a songbird to sing its heart out—to the obvious delight of its owner.

as it was far too secret. A copy would be given to our interpreter, who would show it to the relevant authorities when necessary. Meanwhile, there was the question of Public Security: our Special Travel Permit would not be issued until they too saw the military permission. That would take more time. By now it was May 3 and we had been in Beijing for over three weeks. Another week's delay would leave us perilously short of time to get to the other end of the Wall and home in time for the children's school holidays, which began in the middle of July.

'We'll set off for Shanhaiguan tomorrow anyway,' I said, determined not to spend another day in Beijing. 'I'll come back and collect the papers when they're ready. At least we can be getting to know our horses and our team while we wait.' Everyone thought we were quite mad and begged us to stay just a few more days until it was all sorted out, but our blood was up and we overrode all objections.

Somehow we did all that had to be done on the last day. The embassy nurse gave us last-minute injections to protect us from Japanese encephalitis. This nasty malady, known in China as boiling brain disease, was transmitted by pigs, and several foreigners had recently died from it. Meanwhile, Louella rushed around in our gleaming minibus—which came with a driver, courtesy of CITIC—buying cooking equipment and bedding for our crew. We had had no choice in their selection, but they looked very promising.

Our interpreter was Mr Li. (Mr Hou was not able to come with us as his wife was having a baby and he had been given permission to join her for the birth.) Short and always impeccably dressed in a black Mao suit, Mr Li had a big round head and a serious, learned manner. Although a most unlikely candidate for the rigours we expected, he bravely stood up straight when we asked if he wanted to come, saying he was ready to take part in our 'great exploit'. 'I, too, am a man of

letters,' he said in perfect English, 'and I also plan to write a book about our experiences.'

Mr He, our young cook, had won a prize for gourmet Chinese cuisine in Beijing. Snappily dressed in a washable safari suit, his dazzling smile assured us that at least one of our party would always be cheerful. He was also a highly qualified kung fu artist. He told us laconically that if we were attacked by bandits he could kill three of them with his bare hands and feet before they reached us.

The driver was Madam Hao. Round-faced and beaming, she was quite the largest woman we saw in China. Her attitude to Louella was one of constant motherly concern. Wrapping her gigantic arms around Louella she would dare the world to molest her charge. We got on well but I suspected she regarded me as something of a brute for subjecting my frail young wife to such a journey. Actually, Louella is considerably tougher than I am in most respects.

By Sunday morning we were ready to leave, although still without a single document to show for all the months of planning; just a letter from our patron 'appreciating the significance' of our forthcoming journey. China is a very strange place. It has changed so very much this century, and yet in some ways it has not changed at all. Things still get done in the end only through the influence of powerful friends and with them almost anything is possible.

Off to the Wall

On Sunday morning the Beijing Philharmonic performed in the foyer of the Jianguo Hotel. We felt that Beethoven's Fifth was a good choice for our victorious departure. The friends who came to see us off were impressed, thinking we had arranged it all. Robbie came, of course, with his Californian girlfriend Debra. So too did Mickey Grant. He had appeared at the last moment, having been trying without success to raise financial backing to make a film of our ride. As we scurried across the foyer carrying our gear from the storeroom to the minibus, our guests drank and shouted at each other over the thundering orchestra. Suddenly we had all kissed each other for the last time, posed for final photographs, squeezed into our overloaded vehicle and we were on our way.

Madam Hao drove very slowly, which was just as well as the only really dangerous thing in China today is the traffic. Foreigners are quite sensibly not allowed to drive outside Beijing as the frequency of crashes is almost unbelievable. There are very few cars to be seen but there are endless overloaded lorries which give no quarter and drive flat out. Thousands of bicycles, even in deep country, vie for the narrow road with uncontrolled carts drawn by horses, mules or donkeys, their drivers often asleep and relying on the animal to find its way home. Through these weave noisy convoys of mini-tractors pulling vast loads of stones, sand, timber or night soil. Everyone blows his horn continuously, but the road surface is usually so bad and most vehicles rattle so loudly that few can hear anything.

We saw three crashes in the first hour, including one where a mangled bicycle still lay under a truck. When road accidents occur nothing is moved until the police have completed their investigations. This seems to include leaving the victims *in situ* as we frequently saw bodies lying among the wreckage. Mr Li told us that the Chinese are reluctant to help anyone after an accident as 'they are still so superstitious that they believe that if they do so they will be responsible for him for the rest of his life'.

A busy main road, such as the one we were following, was like a hellish river of noise, dust and danger flowing through the peaceful countryside—wide expanses of irrigated rice- and corn-fields that were always full of people ploughing behind donkeys or oxen, or pulling ploughs themselves. Hoeing, weeding, planting, rolling, channelling water: there was activity everywhere and when the land was terraced the beauty was overpowering.

▲ Rice plants are sown in special beds and then transplanted to paddy fields to mature. Here a worker carries a load of young shoots out into the fields for replanting.

We stopped at midday for lunch at a People's Restaurant. Mr Li threw his weight about, calling for the manager, telling him we were important guests who must have a private room and hygienic food. We were ushered through a big kitchen in which cooks toiled over steaming vats into a dusty courtyard at the back, where we were put in a bare room with one round table and chairs. As we sat down, Mr Li said in his precise English, 'You see, Mr He and I are now going to answer the call of nature. Would you also care to use the loo?' I went with them to a public convenience across the main road. Built of brick, these followed a standard pattern and were uniformly appalling. Behind a six-foot wall were separate enclosures for men and women. The men's consisted of a single open room with a row of four overflowing holes in the ground. The smell was beyond belief and filth was scattered over the floor, while the air was thick with flies. Surprisingly, we were to find that this is one of the few areas where foreigners' welfare does not seem to concern the Chinese. There was deep alarm that we would not find comfortable hotels, anxiety over our safety and our health, but not the least concern that we would have to visit these fetid open sewers each day. Louella assured me that the ladies' was even worse, and from then on we did our best to avoid them.

Lunch was rather good, as food usually is in China, even in the poorest places, and we all did justice to the dishes of vegetables and meat wrapped in fried dough, sweet and sour pork and omelette which were brought in steaming from the kitchen. During the afternoon we were diverted around Tangshan where, in the terrible earthquake of July 28, 1976, the old town collapsed in a shock registering 8.2 on the Richter scale, one of the biggest ever recorded.

Officially the Chinese say 148,000 people died, but the Western estimate was 800,000. We passed the rows of soulless, jerrybuilt high-rise apartments which comprise the new city. They already looked shabby and decaying, as though another small tremor would bring them crashing down too.

There were more diversions and delays, so that night was falling by the time we reached the coast at Beidaihe. Since there was still an hour or more to go to Shanhaiguan we decided to spend the night there. Our crew were alarmed at this suggestion, since in China everything is planned in advance. However, I told them that my guidebooks named several good hotels and clinched the matter by pointing out that we would be too late for dinner if we struggled on.

Beidaihe is an anachronism. A European seaside resort built in the 1890s by British railway engineers and later taken over by diplomats and businessmen from the capital, it is now being revived as a vacation spot for China's leaders. It is a pretty place, as we found next morning when we had a walk round. There are hills and beaches, solid villas set back in pine woods, and a pier. It must have been a lively place in its heyday when there were cabarets and golf clubs. Now it is full of rather determinedly happy Chinese 'working heroes' allowed to escape temporarily from the din of urban life. Mr Li told us that he had started his journal with the words, 'I awoke this morning to the sound of birdsong. This is something I do not hear in Beijing.'

On the beach we found early crowds self-consciously dipping their toes in the cold water and looking as though they felt they should be having fun but were not quite sure what to do. When two boys started wrestling and rolling in the sand, the crowd clapped appreciatively at this manifestation of the holiday spirit. The artificial atmosphere was enhanced by solemn groups of cadres (officials) in Mao suits with red badges on their chests, who had clearly earned a break at Beidaihe as a reward for their efforts on behalf of the Party. They strolled together along the shoreline like oyster catchers, with their hands behind their backs, unsure if they approved of what they saw.

Horse Trial

A long straight road through acacia and poplar woods on the edge of a wide sandy beach led to the urban sprawl of Qinhuangdao and to our horses. When the time came to try out my saddle, Tang stood stock still as I settled it on him—and then remained motionless when, in front of a large and interested crowd at the barracks, I mounted and urged him to move. He seemed rooted to the spot and refused to follow Louella and Ming who moved off easily together. Someone brought me a small stick and I struck him gently with it. At once he began a series of jolting bronco bucks, landing hard on all four feet, and accompanied by shrill squeals. I would have had trouble staying on in an ordinary saddle but was quite safe in the deep Camargue one. After a while he settled down and we decided to go for a ride to get the feel of the countryside.

This was the big test of whether our whole crazy scheme was going to be even remotely practicable. Out through the barrack gates we went and onto the verge of the main road, Tang skittering nervously at each bicycle. The first lorry to pass us blew its deafening horn from the moment it saw us until it and its astonished, waving driver were past. This was the pattern followed by almost every other lorry across China, but fortunately the horses paid little attention. They were much more interested in the far more numerous donkeys and mules, with whom they were anxious to pass the time of day. I admit to feeling very frightened at this time. It seemed inevitable that something would go badly wrong and for the first time we regretted not bringing hard hats. However, our old Camargue hats were so much more comfortable on a long journey. Tang had at last stopped bucking, but instead revealed an insatiable desire to kick all other horses, including Ming. This meant I must ride behind or alongside.

Beidaihe beach on the edge of the Bo Hai sea— once a favourite retreat for Communist Party officials, but now open to all Chinese. ▼

With relief we turned left off the main road and were soon in open country. This was more like it. Tracks led off haphazardly and their sandy surfaces were ideal for cantering. We let the horses have their heads and all went smoothly for a while. The brown fields, with vegetables planted in neat rows, were being cultivated by hand. The people looked up and sometimes smiled, but they never returned our cheerful wave nor responded to our carefully modulated '*Ni hao?*' (literally, 'You well?', the universal Chinese greeting). The sun beat down on our heads, the horses' hooves threw up dust from the parched earth and far ahead the Wall climbed up into the mountains.

▲ **China in springtime: snowy white blossoms bedeck the delicate branches of a fruit tree.**

We came to an irrigated area of apple and pear orchards, where pink and white blossom covered the trees. A clear, unpolluted stream ran through it, the first we had seen in China, since those near roads and railway lines were always full of litter. Startlingly green, lush grass grew beside it and we offered the horses food and drink. Everything around us was beautiful and our hearts were bursting with the peculiar happiness that comes when a dream is about to be fulfilled. At last we were doing what we had come to China to do, and which everyone had said would be impossible. True, we still did not have our tiresome piece of paper, but how marvellous that all our plans, which had been conceived in ignorance, really seemed to work! Only now, as we spontaneously reached out to hold hands as we rode along and revelled in the moment, could we admit how unlikely it was that so many things should have turned out all right. We were going to do it, nothing was going to stop us and it looked as though it would be great fun.

In the distance we saw a small cloud of dust and began to hear a faint approaching rumble. Thinking no evil we watched as we rode, imagining it to be a small lorry being driven fast across country. Suddenly it was on us and we saw that it was a little stallion donkey at full gallop, towing a large iron cart loaded with great rocks which were bouncing out onto the fields.

Careering straight at us he began to squeal with excitement. There was little we could do to escape this mad rush except to separate, when it became clear that the object of his intentions, which were manifestly amorous, was Ming. Wheeling around sharply so that the remaining stones were tipped off the cart, it attempted to mount Ming while Louella waved her stick menacingly at it and shouted, 'Shoo!' Fortunately his owner arrived, very out of breath but with enough strength to chase donkey and cart around Louella and Ming a couple of times before catching them. He did not seem very pleased with us, although we could hardly be blamed for the trail of boulders he was going to have to spend the rest of the day gathering up. We rode off: in China the foreigner is generally in the wrong and it was better not to have an altercation about it. We only hoped that Ming did not prove to have the same irresistible attraction for every male donkey in China.

◀ Foreigners are not alone in their admiration for the Great Wall: the Chinese themselves flock to it and are as keen as anyone to be photographed alongside it.

Heading west past Shanhaiguan, we crossed the route we had taken on our walk along the Wall and passed through a break in the ramparts. Here we had a most unexpected meeting with a middle-aged Chinese tourist. Incongruous among the toiling peasants, he wore shorts and had a camera round his neck. His reaction to seeing us was quite different from the blank stares of amazement we had already become used to. He had come to see the Great Wall and all its attractions. Clearly we were to be numbered among them and that meant a photograph. Politely but firmly he indicated that we should pose for him against the Wall. Afterwards he thanked us and hurried off, carrying the first of our explanatory handouts to be given away. These were small leaflets explaining who we were and what we were doing.

Mr Hou and I had concocted suitable wording during my November visit and a kind friend at the Chinese section of the British Museum had written it out in fine characters. With accompanying photographs of us riding the French horses, this had been photocopied 1,000 times and we planned always to carry a stock in our saddlebags. They were invaluable. Roughly translated they read as follows:

English Author and Explorer

Happy Guest Han and Love Baby Lou, husband and wife, are travelling on horses the whole of the Great Wall from Shanhaiguan to Jiayuguan. The Han Lebins, approved by the relevant Chinese authorities, are researching and exploring the whole Great Wall from Shanhaiguan to Jiayuguan. Please, all the relevant units and people along this route, give them help and support.

With the Han Lebins are an interpreter, cook and driver. We have plenty of food and drink, and a truck and tent.

My Chinese companions may answer all your questions.

Thank you.

Soon afterwards we passed a factory stuck out in the middle of the landscape, its chimneys providing a landmark but with few houses around it. As we rode past the air was polluted not only by the smoke and dust but also by a dreadful din from loudspeakers around the walls. Beyond it, we came again to a beautiful watered zone where the aqueducts and streams, which we forded, gave sustenance to tall poplars, so that for the first time we rode in the shade. We reached a low ridge

A dappled avenue of poplars gives welcome shade from the hot sun and shelter from harsh winds, whatever your mode of transport. ▶

and gazed eagerly west along our hoped-for route. It all looked possible and wonderful. We rode back to the town and entered by the North Gate. It was an extraordinary, medieval feeling to ride into an old walled town through a narrow, dark gateway. It was made all the more enjoyable by the fact that almost all the other traffic was also four-legged and no one regarded what we were doing as the least bit remarkable. The fact that we were Europeans was cause for astonishment, but the fact that we were riding was not.

We called in at the hotel, riding into the courtyard and waking up our surprised crew from their siesta, and then went out through the First Pass and back to the barracks, well pleased with life. Saddles had not rubbed and, in spite of having been ridden quite hard for three hours, our horses were not tired and barely sweating.

In order to occupy our crew and test some of our equipment we decided to put up our tent. This we did behind the stables, watched by a fascinated crowd of soldiers, with their wives and children. It was a splendid tent—the two sleeping compartments at the sides had built-in mosquito nets and the centre portion was just big enough for the round table and five chairs we had bought in the Friendship Store in Beijing before leaving. Then Louella and Mr He sorted out all the kitchen equipment and found nothing vital missing.

▲ The author and Louella in the courtyard of their hotel in Shanhaiguan after their first ride on Tang and Ming.

Final Permission

Meanwhile, there was our final problem. We still had no guarantee that we would be allowed to set off, and I was more worried than I dared admit. We had, of course, heard nothing from Beijing in spite of several faint telephone contacts by Mr Li, each connection taking several hours to come through. We decided that the time had come for him and me to return to Beijing and fight the final bureaucratic battle, leaving Louella in Shanhaiguan with Madam Hao and Mr He. Since neither of them spoke a word of English this would be a good chance for her to practise her Chinese, which was improving rapidly.

The train left just before midnight. It proved impossible to buy tickets for Beijing but we were allowed to try our luck with the train crew on arrival. To our dismay, there was no space at all on the train when it arrived. We argued and begged at the soft sleepers, the hard sleepers and even the hard seats, but we were firmly prevented from getting on. This presented us with a problem as there were no taxis and we had too much luggage to carry back to the hotel.

'Anyway,' said Mr Li, 'we cannot contemplate awakening them at this hour. We will just have to seek our destiny with the railway system.' The huge station concourse was crowded to capacity with travellers looking as though they were refugees from some disaster. Mr Li seemed quite prepared to join them and let his oriental fate work itself out. Although quite relaxed about the whole matter, as I had my Mozart and a good book with which I could cut myself off from grim reality, I also realised that we might well spend the whole night trying each train that came through. As midnight passed it became my fiftieth birthday. I suggested he track down whoever was in charge and point out that this was all a rather poor advertisement for China. Mr Li assured me he would do his best to 'charm the birds out of the trees'. Suddenly everyone became terrifically friendly and we were whisked off to the stationmaster's bare room where I was sat on a chair and given a glass of hot water. The stationmaster was a woman with a striking resemblance to an angry bullfrog, but with a sweet smile which she could unexpectedly bestow on those who, like me, miraculously found favour with her. She escorted us to the 1.30am train herself and, overriding the protestations of the train director, forced her way into one of the sleeping compartments, which proved to have only two occupants. We were bundled into the top bunks and she departed telling everyone, so Mr Li informed me, that it was done for the honour of the People's Republic.

At 5am we were woken by a loudspeaker next to my ear bursting into rousing music at full volume. There was no control knob to turn down and we were subjected to such numbers as 'Seagulls Over Sorrento' and 'Here Comes the Bride' played at full speed on an electric organ. The current pop-music hit, heard all over China on public-address systems at this time, was 'Auld Lang Syne' sung in Chinese and we had several renderings of that, too. At the same time there were repeated knockings on our door by the sleeping-car staff trying to make us get up. We all ignored them until 5.45am when we were made to get dressed and let them make our beds, after which we sat in a row, the others all smoking hard, until we arrived at 8am. Such things are not to be complained of in China.

Then followed one of the most depressing and anxious days I can remember. As it was my birthday I felt I should have been celebrating and enjoying life. Instead I found that nothing had happened and no one seemed inclined to think

The territory the author and Louella travelled through on their journey from Shanhaiguan in eastern China to Jiayuguan in the west. ▼

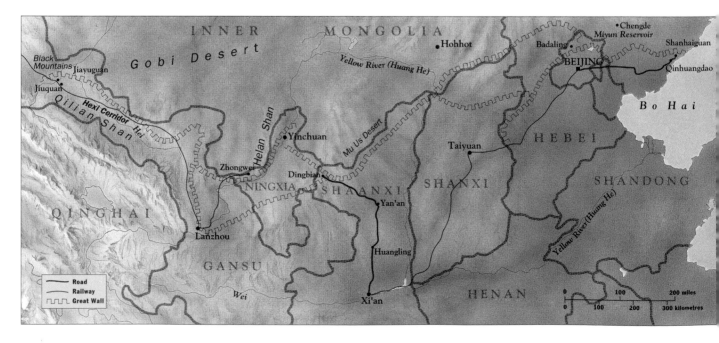

that it might. Even worse, my return to Beijing instantly confirmed everyone's doubts about whether we would ever get off and I spent a maudlin evening contemplating mortality and man's incompetence.

The next day I went to see one of our most helpful friends in CITIC, who had patiently spent hours on our behalf finding ways around our problems. I confessed to being in despair that we would ever leave. Quietly he quoted to me from a classic Chinese novel: 'The extreme of adversity is the beginning of prosperity.' It is a very Chinese sentiment, but I was grateful for his moral support. An hour later I was told that our military permit had arrived and I could take it to Public Security. There more forms were required, but finally I was handed the first ever Aliens' Travel Permit to start at Shanhaiguan and end at Jiayuguan.

▲ During China's Cultural Revolution, whole sections of the Great Wall were broken down for building materials. Today that vandalism is being redressed in an active programme of rebuilding and restoration.

Although the permitted route was not what we had requested by a long way, it would take us from one end of the Wall to the other, and for about half the way we were to be allowed to ride beside it—in three stages. For the first stage—Shanhaiguan to Miyun through Hebei and Beijing provinces—we were given leave to follow the Wall virtually as closely as we could. Only in the province of Shanxi would we not be permitted to ride at all, for 'security' reasons. A long detour by rail and road via Xi'an was indicated. In northern Shaanxi—the province to the west of Shanxi—we were to be allowed to start again on fresh horses and cross the whole of Ningxia. In Gansu we would once again have to go through the Hexi Corridor by train, but then we could ride again for the last stretch to the end of the Wall at Jiayuguan.

We hurried back to Shanhaiguan to discover that Louella had meanwhile walked back up the Wall and found that after only two days an astonishing amount of rebuilding had been achieved. She saw hundreds of men, each carrying two large building bricks, staggering up the slope in single file, in exactly the same way as the original Wall had been built. The mountains here are so steep that no horse or cart can approach the Wall, which meant, of course, that we would not be riding on, or even beside, the Wall for any of the first stage. On the other hand, travelling close to the Wall, keeping it in sight, would not present any great difficulty, even for foreigners.

Until the recent spate of coffee-table books on the Great Wall, the definitive source of information was Jonathan Fryer's book, *The Great Wall of China*, published in 1975. In the introduction he says, 'At the time of writing it seems highly unlikely that any Westerner (or Chinese, for that matter) will have the chance of making a journey along the Wall.' Times had changed and, as we lay in Marshal Lin Biao's bed on our last night in Shanhaiguan, we could hardly believe that we were about to prove him wrong.

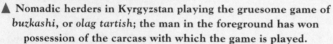

▲ Nomadic herders in Kyrgyzstan playing the gruesome game of *buzkashi*, or *olag tartish*; the man in the foreground has won possession of the carcass with which the game is played.

▲ Training for a life in the saddle starts at an early age—long before a boy's legs are long enough to reach the stirrups!

▲ This delicate painting on silk, by the 17th-century Chinese artist Li-Lin, shows Mongol noblemen enjoying a gentlemanly game of polo—quite unlike the earliest form of the sport, which involved teams of 100 players a side.

◄ A Kazakh horseman sets out for a day's hunting with a magnificent golden eagle that has been trained to hunt down hares, foxes and even wolves.

The Steadfast Steeds of the East

ON THE VAST PLAINS of East and Central Asia, horses have for centuries, if not millennia, been a necessity of life. For the nomads of Kazakhstan, Kyrgyzstan, Mongolia and parts of Tibet, horses are not only a primary means of transport, they also provide many of the necessities of everyday life: hide for clothing and utensils, hair for braiding into rope, and milk—a dietary staple consumed in huge quantities, not only in its liquid form, but also as curds, clotted cream and even a fermented liquor. In Mongolia, in particular, horses are a major form of livestock, along with camels, sheep and goats, resulting in the curious sight of mounted herdsmen rounding up, or driving to pasture, their herds of semi-domesticated horses.

Few men and women can have a closer affinity with their mounts than these people. When their distant ancestors, the Huns, first flooded into the Roman Empire in the 4th century AD, commentators were astonished: they reported that the Huns slept, performed bodily functions, and even conducted important affairs of state on horseback. No Western army was a match for the Hunnish cavalry, which owed its speed and manoeuvrability to one simple invention previously unknown in the West: the stirrup. This allowed the Huns—and the Mongols, who followed them 900 years later— to keep their balance while wheeling sharply or taking aim with bow and arrow.

From cavalry training, Asian horsemen also developed several leisure pursuits, such as the violent game of *buzkashi*, also known as *olag tartish*, in which two teams fight for possession of an animal corpse. Equally ferocious in its earliest form, polo was once played by teams of up to 100 warriors a side. However, it became more refined, establishing itself by the 6th century AD as a favourite sport among aristocrats from Persia to China, before eventually being discovered by the British during the 19th century.

▲ No one can doubt the admiration shown for the horse in this magnificent bronze sculpture, known as the Flying Horse, from the Han dynasty (206 BC–AD 220).

Przhevalski's horse—the original wild horse of Asia— once roamed the plains of the Mongolian steppe, but now survives only in captivity. ▼

◀ Mongolian horsemen gathering for Nadaam—Mongolian National Day celebrations. Some of these hardy people might have travelled for up to two weeks to get here.

CHAPTER 3

Off Along the Wall

READY TO LEAVE EARLY, we woke to the sound of heavy rain. It was May 10 and we had been in China for exactly four weeks. During that time we had not seen a drop of rain, which we would have welcomed as relief from the heat and to lay the dust. Now it looked as though we would have to postpone our departure yet another day so as not to start with all our gear wet and a demoralised crew. It was a depressing dawn, not helped by Mr Li who said he had been unable to sleep from worrying about our problems. He had had unsatisfactory discussions for hours in the evening with the local authorities, who had given him a hard time about our route and our plan to camp along it.

At 9am, although it was still pouring down, we decided that it was better to get wet than to go on talking. We went up to the barracks and groomed the horses until their coats shone in the darkness of their smelly stable, while we waited for the rain to let up enough for us to leave. We settled our final accounts with the People's Army, gave the two loyal soldiers who had been looking after Tang and Ming a Cathay Pacific T-shirt each and dressed in our full wet-weather gear—waterproof overtrousers with large army capes worn over the top, which spread out to cover the saddles.

At 11am it looked a bit lighter and there was even a patch of blue visible in the sky. We saddled up and mounted. Tang took off across the parade ground like a bucking bronco, squealing like a pig, arching his back like a frightened cat and giving a series of abrupt and very uncomfortable bunny hops. When he calmed down we rode to the First Pass, where a press photographer took pictures of us looking pretty miserable and wet. These were published quite widely in a number of countries, including Britain.

Not knowing how late we would be starting, if at all, for Yuguan, the first town on our route, we had been unable to fix a rendezvous for the next night with our crew. Chinese maps, if they can be found, are small scale and hard to follow, so we had brought with us the US Airforce Operational Navigation Charts for the whole of the Great Wall. These covered six huge sheets, from which I had cut the relevant sections and put them in protective plastic holders. They showed small country roads and tracks as well as many relief features, rivers and the Wall itself. Since we were determined to cut across country rather than follow the dreadful, noisy main road along which we had driven from Qinhuangdao, we didn't know how we would ever meet our crew again. Madam Hao had driven a short way on the rough tracks and now resolutely refused to take her minibus that way. At that moment, one of the blue-suited officials

◀ To the west of Shanhaiguan, the Great Wall climbs steeply into the mountains. Even on slopes such as these, there are strategically placed towers which acted as storerooms and observation posts.

seeing us off suggested a place called Haiyang, which he said was twelve-and-a-half miles this side of Yuguan and on the main road. We promptly agreed with Madam Hao to meet there between 4 and 5pm, waved goodbye and rode off through the town. Once out through the North Gate we felt at last that we were really on our way.

We headed off to the west, leaving the Wall climbing up into the hills on our right. At a nearby village we asked for cross-country directions to Haiyang, only to be told by everyone that we had to go round by the main road as there was a reservoir in the way. Fortunately Louella had been there while I was away in Beijing and so was able to insist that there was a way past below the Yansai Dam. Reluctantly this was agreed, but we were told we should be sure to lose our way. Realising this was likely until we became more experienced at finding our way around rural China, I held up a 5-yuan note, offering it as a reward to anyone who would show us the way. An old man on a bicycle pedalled up at that moment and, before he had time to protest, the crowd decided he should be our guide. He was sent off ahead of us looking rather cross and we followed at a canter. It was a good and happy way for us to travel, riding over ideal sandy ground. On the flat our guide was able to outpace us but when we came to hills and he had to dismount we easily caught him up. Chinese bicycles don't have gears. Through pleasant orchards and narrow village lanes we followed, greeting everyone exuberantly in our happiness to be under way and occasionally receiving dazzling smiles in return.

When we reached the wide, shallow riverbed below the dam, our cyclist crossed gingerly on steppingstones, wheeling his bike through the water beside him. We splashed through with no trouble. The mountains upstream to our right were magnificent, with trees covering their lower slopes and high, bare cliffs rising above. They reminded us of the Scottish Highlands.

When our guide left us he pointed ahead with a grin and we carried on through a succession of small villages where it was easy to imagine we were in the Middle Ages. Pigs outnumbered people, and almost everything was made of wood, clay or straw. The uniform houses had tiled roofs and white paper stuck over the glassless windows to keep the wind out. With summer coming, holes were poked through the paper to let fresh air in. Many had old entrance gates with a decorated arch on the top like a church lych gate. Dogs were still absent, but there were masses of chickens and ducks, as well as small children playing outside their houses. Each had a little garden, sometimes fenced with bamboo or rush palings, and often there was a courtyard between the house and the gate. There might also be a stable for a mule or donkey and of course an enclosure for the pigs. When these were transported, they were trussed up like chickens and lay quietly in little carts or wheelbarrows, or even across the back of bicycles. Only when their fetters were removed would a deafening squealing begin.

▲ Five little piggies going to market. They seem remarkably resigned to this undignified ordeal.

It seemed little effort had been expended to make the houses or gardens pretty. Sometimes there were a few flowers or a painted section of wall, but usually everything had an almost self-conscious appearance of squalor and decay. Yet everyone seemed cheerful and there were no signs of real poverty.

We managed to keep away from the main road until about an hour out of Haiyang. Then we followed the verge safely beside the traffic to a delighted welcome from our waiting crew. Mr Li, looking important in his white shirt, black trousers and brown patent shoes, with his black briefcase and its secret documents tucked under his arm, barked, 'Get down, please!' as we rode up.

They were very pleased with themselves at having fixed us up with a stable in a flour mill right beside the road. It was a pretty scruffy and unhygienic flour mill, we thought, just an open courtyard with rubbish everywhere and a huge heap of bones in the middle. They had been dumped there by the butcher next door, who lacked space. A crowd of about sixty people gathered to watch us unsaddle and tie the horses up for the night. There we fed them the rations they had been receiving back at the barracks: five pounds of maize mixed with three pounds of bran each per day. We had bought sacks of maize and bran to carry with us in the minibus. Hay or chopped straw for them to munch through the night we hoped to buy at each stopping place, and, as it turned out, with all the beasts of burden kept in China this was seldom a problem.

That night, what with the rain and the day's late start, we thought it easier to stay in a hotel. However, next morning, on mounting, I gave the crowd its money's worth as Tang took off across the yard, scattering the heap of bones and departing through the gate in a series of bucks before calming down and behaving well for the rest of the day. We covered the twelve-and-a-half miles to Yuguan at a good average speed of about five miles per hour. With occasional canters but mostly walking, this was about the best we could expect the horses to maintain for a whole day.

At Yuguan Mr Li made enquiries and found that there was a track through the mountains to our next night's proposed stop at Yangheying. The minibus would follow the main road via Funing to meet us in the evening.

Into a Classical Landscape

We now entered perfect riding country which we felt at the time was unlikely to be improved upon for beauty and perfection in China. A charming earthen country lane led through an avenue

▲ A great spotted woodpecker pauses on the edge of its nest, hollowed out of a silver birch tree.

of poplars beside a streambed towards dramatic mountains where we could spot occasional watchtowers of the Wall. As the land rose there were areas of terracing interspersed with open plains where we could let the horses have their heads and canter to the horizon. Birds were everywhere and their singing in the trees filled the air. Swallows, swooping low after the rain, almost passed between the horses' feet. House sparrows chirped noisily but were outdone by bulbuls and babblers. There were yellow warblers which sang very sweetly and a small, black-and-white woodpecker with a bright red flash underneath. Surprisingly, the birds seemed tame, as normally in China they are harried.

Back from the track there were apple orchards, with more trees planted as shelter belts. It was a hazy day but not too hot and everywhere there were people working in the fields. Nearly all the work was being done by hand and we learned how to recognise from people's gaits what jobs they were doing. A woman planting seed moved in a curious 'dot and carry one' way as she dropped each seed and then stamped it into the ground. A man using his weight like a roller walked slowly with tiny rapid steps, shuffling his feet along to compress the soil. Others piled earth or manure into small heaps all over their plots, to be spread later. Sometimes we saw larger mounds among those dotting a field and realised they were graves. These might have some paper stuck on top or a few stones, occasionally even a gravestone, but they seemed to be placed entirely at random and were ploughed right around.

At the head of the valley we came to a larger, rather pretty village where a stone bridge spanned the stream. Next to it was tethered an unexpectedly fine bay stallion, which whinnied and tried to escape and join us. Here we turned left up into the foothills of the mountains, through a narrow gorge between big black basalt rocks with towering outcrops above. On a grassy slope with a few young trees, beside a clear pool in the stream where there were fishes, we stopped and unsaddled the horses for their midday rest. They grazed greedily while we lay and nibbled sweet biscuits and raisins, holding the ends of their neck ropes.

▲ A haughty gaggle of geese waddles along a country lane, under the watchful eye of their keeper. The Chinese have farmed geese since at least the 12th century BC.

It was an idyllic spot. The sun shone and a breeze kept the air cool while drying the sweat on the horses' backs and their saddlecloths. Overhead a pair of red-billed choughs wheeled and turned, their familiar trilling churrs carrying clearly to us. The chough is the emblem of Cornwall, where we live, although it is now extinct there in the wild. I knew that they were to be found right across Asia but I had not expected to see them so soon. As these two flew down to us and called to each other before disappearing up the valley, they were like a signal that all would be well on our journey.

An old, grey-bearded man walked slowly up the track from the village and stopped to pass the time of day. 'We are English,' we said in Chinese, and he nodded gravely, as though he met English people every day. 'We are riding horses along the Great Wall,' we told him. He looked doubtful; so we gave him one of our leaflets to prove it, and he strolled off reading.

As we mounted and rode on, we found that it was indeed well worth all the effort that had gone into getting us here. To our left, two steep boulder-strewn mountains had groves of stunted pines and willows nestling in their valleys. On our right, a sheer rock, black on the outside, red where flakes had fallen away, stood up a thousand feet, bare of all vegetation save for a few tufts of grass and scrub clinging to the crevices. The road ahead climbed up into the hills in a series of hairpin bends between which we could dismount and lead the horses up steep short cuts while the cart track followed the contours. We were in a classical Chinese landscape and the scenery on each side could have been painted on long, hanging, watercolour scrolls. In one of my favourite childhood books, *The Box of Delights* by John Masefield, an old magician rides into just such a picture hanging on his study wall in order to escape from his enemies.

From the top we had a splendid view back through the gorge. On the far side, tightly terraced slopes led down to a fertile valley far below, which it took us another hour to reach. As we crossed a river on the edge of the village of Taitouying, a proud pair of Chinese geese swam under the bridge below us. A flock of sheep kept their heads down in the afternoon sun, huddled in a tight circle trying to share a minute patch of shade. A big watchtower on a peak marked the Wall and once again we turned left to ride parallel with it.

The landscape continued to surprise and delight us with its unspoilt beauty. Most of the time we were on a pleasant sandy track running through wild, rocky country beside a stream. Whenever we passed through villages it became muddy and narrow; life there must be pretty unpleasant in the winter when it is very cold and often wet. We were probably passing at the ideal time, before the heat and dust became too great, while the blossom was still out on the fruit trees and patches of grass and wild flowers carpeted the hillsides.

Edgy Officials

At 6pm we arrived in Yangheying. We were fairly tired. We had been on the road for nine hours and must have covered forty miles. Our crew had found somewhere for the horses, but had bad news about our own accommodation. The local authorities had been adamant that we could not stay ourselves as this was a 'security area'. Instead we had to be driven to the county town of Lulong, where there was a hotel. Too tired to argue much, we saw the horses fed and settled for the night and allowed ourselves to be led through the dark by an army jeep. Poor Mr Li was almost in tears from the constant arguments he had been having on our behalf. Although we had permission to be where we were, the whole concept of what we were doing was so new and alarming that no one was prepared to take responsibility for letting us camp or stay in remote villages. Kindly but firmly, they insisted that the only hotel suitable for foreigners was in Lulong and so that was where we must go, however time-consuming and expensive that might be. Deciding to make the best of it, we asked on arrival if they had hot water. 'Oh yes, of course,' they said, and Louella gave Mr Li a hug and told him it was all for the best.

The hotel was a grim compound with rooms leading off, a familiar design in China. Mr He was given a room to cook in and we lit his kerosene stoves for the first time. Mr Li, his sleeves rolled up as he scraped the scales off a large fish, said kindly, 'Too many cooks spoil the broth! You go and have a bath.' We did not argue. There was, however, no water in the taps and when we asked about this we were told, 'Oh yes, there is hot water in the vacuum flask for making tea. None in taps.'

When we were called for supper we found that Mr He had created an incredible feast. With the couple of pounds we had given him to spend in the local market, he had bought a huge flat fish like a turbot, which he had cooked on the bone in oil. He had made another dish of fried fish with straw potatoes and yet one more

of sumptuous, diced sweet-and-sour fish pieces. There were two pork dishes—one breaded, one with a delicious garnish—eggs and pancakes, vegetables, and an astonishing fresh fruit salad, each dish better than the last. He served them with panache, too, coming in at the last moment to sprinkle a dash of salt and pepper over the dishes with a flamboyant gesture and then joining us to tuck in with a will. His good humour and energy were infectious and it was impossible to be grumpy in his company. It was nearly midnight before we were in bed.

We were up and away at 5.30am. Now the Great Wall was visible most of the time on our right, sometimes only a mile or two away. It was exciting to see how much of it was still there. Although totally unrestored and neglected since the end of the Ming dynasty in the seventeenth century it seemed to be virtually intact. Grass and weeds grew between the building blocks, and the watchtowers and crenellations had crumbled, but it was still a massive and awe-inspiring piece of building. Once we were able to count twenty-seven watchtowers on the horizon where a great line of mountains stretched away into the distance. At other times the Wall came right down to our level before rising up into the hills again and disappearing.

As soon as we stopped in a village a crowd would gather from nowhere and we would begin to feel the claustrophobic effect of several hundred pairs of eyes

◄ Colourful wild flowers
enliven the ground beside
this semi-derelict stretch
of crenellated Wall.

fixed on us. It was tempting to prevent this happening by cantering through some villages so that we would be gone before anyone noticed how unusual we were. This made us feel like Mongol invaders and sometimes it seemed that little had changed since those days.

We were determined that we would not be forced again to drive to a hotel but would stay with our horses. In Luotun, which we reached in midafternoon to rendezvous with our crew, we told the local official that this was what we intended doing. For a couple of hours we sat and fumed in his office, while he tried vainly to contact the next county town on his hand-cranked telephone and the horses waited patiently in the sun outside. Suddenly, without any success or extra persuasion from us, he decided at six o'clock that we could camp in his compound. The horses could spend the night in a shed.

With a burst of energy we set to work. The whole town gathered on the compound wall and the hillside beyond to watch as we put up the tent, blew up our mattresses, laid out our bedding and set up the table and chairs. Mr He needed no encouragement to repeat the previous night's culinary triumph with fresh ingredients and we all had a very merry and public evening.

During the night it poured with rain, but we were warm and dry in the tent. When our crew joined us later, however, the night became less tranquil, since the

Chinese share with most Eastern people a doubtless admirable lack of inhibitions about bodily functions. Their three daily square meals inevitably resulted in the build-up of gases, which were noisily expelled for the next few hours. 'We are positively cheek by jowl,' said Mr Li. Fortunately we were both usually tired enough to sleep through anything.

We awoke to thick mist, and pottered about having a leisurely breakfast of coffee and muesli. At 7.30am the sun broke through the fog and hit the tent. At once we all sprang into action, and in no time we were off into a glorious sunny day with the clarity that comes after rain. The Wall looked close enough to touch, with little white clouds scudding past the towers. The countryside, too, was beautiful. Yesterday had been all brown parched plains with toiling peasants as far as the eye could see. It was not just the aftermath of rain that gave today a different feel. The region was undoubtedly richer and the atmosphere more relaxed and prosperous. The fields, many terraced in wide, generous swathes, ran only a short way up the hills, which were thereafter thickly wooded with pines and acacias. There were plenty of trees, fine massive poplars along the roads and orchards of ancient gnarled walnuts as well as the usual apples and pears. The soil beneath was a rich red and all the rivers and streams were running, even if sometimes they were only a trickle between grassy green banks.

When life imitates art: delicate silhouettes seem almost to float in the ethereal haze of this misty Chinese dawn. ▼

In the villages the houses were of a better quality and the gardens well tended, with wallflowers and morning glory among the vegetables. Many of the houses had wall paintings on them, well executed and charming. The standard design of house in this part of Hebei is perfect for these paintings, as the end walls have no windows and provide a wide blank space. Here we saw delicate and imaginative pictures of deer, storks, even goldfish. The tiled roofs had curled-up eaves and sometimes there were even models of storks and egrets in pairs on the ridges.

For four hours we rode through this seeming paradise and everything was good. We had lost the stiffness of the first few days' riding and the horses were going really well. We chatted happily to each other as people pushing wheelbarrows, wheeling bicycles, driving donkey carts and working on their crops stared at us in blank amazement. A few were very friendly and called out to us. When we passed a small roadside factory all the men came running out making urgent drinking gestures to us, begging us to stop and join them. But we regretfully explained we had a long way to go, and distributed our handouts.

▲ Using a plain bit of wall to excellent effect, the proud owner of this house has enhanced his surroundings with stylish wall paintings.

The road was made of packed earth, smooth and perfect for riding on. The acacia trees along it were covered in white flowers and the smell was strong and heady, like orange blossom. At midday we unsaddled the horses on the grassy bank of a stream so they could drink and graze for an hour. There had been no hay for them at last night's camp. As for us, we opened a small tin of corned beef and did not envy them.

After lunch we immediately ran into very different conditions as the elements began to do the dirty on us. We were chilled by an icy wind which became rapidly stronger until we were riding with our heads down into the teeth of a gale. Great swirls of dust were whipped up by the wind and carried off across the wide river valley we were passing. We soon had grit in our eyes, noses and teeth and inside our clothes. The horses hated it.

Several times we had to ride across low concrete bridges and felt ourselves in danger of being swept off. From here there were wonderful views leading up and down the river valleys, vistas of distant hills past groves of willows and poplars where cattle grazed in water meadows. But we could barely look up for the wind and the dust. All afternoon it continued and we began to ache for it to stop. Each time we rounded a corner or crossed a ridge of hills we told ourselves it would be better, but it never was until the evening. I tried to photograph the storm, but found that the camera was broken. This annoyed me quite unreasonably and I stayed in a foul mood for the rest of the day.

At Santunying we found our crew cheerful and deservedly pleased with themselves, having erected the tent on a hard piece of ground in the shelter of a wall with quite a pleasant stable nearby for the horses. This was owned by a cheerful and garrulous old lady who produced and sold us twenty-five pounds of hay and promised to watch over the horses during the night. While I grumpily fiddled with my camera in the tent, Louella charmed the local population by producing our Polaroid. It had been our son's first birthday a couple of days before and soon babies were being passed to her one by one for a quick cuddle. With their split trousers instead of nappies, out of which their little pink bottoms protruded, they were rather endearing, but I tended to leave this excellent method of cementing Anglo–Chinese relationships to her. Mr Li was, I think, rather shocked by the easy way she fraternised with mothers and children, communicating in the universal language of motherhood, helped by her growing command of Chinese words. The initial crowd which had gathered on our arrival never lessened: as the word spread that Louella was a sucker for babies and could actually produce instant photographs, women kept drifting in with their children, noses wiped and woolly hats on straight, hoping.

▲ Bare-bottomed babies and young children are everywhere in China! During the winter, they often wear padded aprons at the front and back of their split trousers to keep out the draughts.

Many of the people still wore blue Mao suits, but these were mostly the senior officials of the villages. Working clothes for men were usually old army fatigues, shapeless overalls in olive green. The very old were almost always dressed in black, the ladies often still in the traditional droopy trousers tied at the ankle, with a black smock over the top. Everyone wore long johns underneath at all times, whatever the temperature. These were usually bright red and often exposed up to the knee because of the peculiar Chinese habit of rolling one trouser leg up. We were never able to work out why they did this, in the boardrooms of Beijing as well as the paddy fields of Hebei, but guessed it might be a way of cooling off from the excessive heat of their long underwear.

The younger women were much more colourful and it was clear that, after decades of conformity, they were cautiously beginning to let themselves go. While blue and drab green were still predominant, a girl might have a brilliant scarlet cravat. Pink, maroon, purple and lime green were popular for scarves and we saw some outrageous straw hats and garish checked jackets, the colours in violent mixes such as green and red, puce and brown and even once orange and purple. But it was with the little children that they really went to town. Some had little lace-embroidered bonnets or brightly coloured knitted bobble caps. Many had quilted jackets in silk or cotton, well padded, on which all the pent-up exuberance of the parents and grandparents to stitch and embroider had been let loose. The colour combinations were often shattering, but the pleasure and love with which these children were dressed was very evident.

In fact, the official policy of one child per family is creating many problems, with a generation of pampered, overindulged children growing up who need to be taught at school how to behave and look after themselves. Concerned articles regularly appear in the Chinese press on this topic, where such children are referred to as 'little emperors'. One further problem is that, although female infanticide is never mentioned and would be severely punished if detected, a ratio of seventy-five male births to twenty-five female has been recorded in some areas. Most Chinese families would still greatly prefer to have a son.

Another delicious feast from Mr He finished off the evening well. This time he had acquired a chicken and, as with the fish, he had managed somehow to make three dishes from it. Every scrap was used. Eggs, too, for which we had expressed a desire, had been found and he produced two amazing omelettes, one with pork and cucumber, one with dried shrimps. While small boys sat in a row watching our every move intently, we went to bed in our tent to read for a while by candlelight, to listen to the BBC World Service news on our small radio and to feel satisfied that it had not been a bad day at all in the end.

Through the Mountains

All next morning the Wall was visible on our right again through the sunny air, now clear of dust, and we went fast along a good wide verge towards the big county town of Zunhua. As we approached, the houses became bigger, with more gardens and a general air of prosperity. It was a fertile plain we were riding through and the villages were busy with street markets selling a wide variety of

China's 'Little Emperors'

CHINA HAS, and almost certainly always has had, the largest population of any country on Earth. The first Chinese census, in AD 2, came up with a figure of some 59 million inhabitants. By 1953, when the first modern census took place, the population had increased almost tenfold to over 582 million; and in the 40 years since then, China's population has doubled again to a staggering 1.2 billion—more than one fifth of all humanity.

For years Mao Ze-dong refused to believe that there was any problem with his country's vast population, claiming that Western warnings on the subject were politically motivated propaganda. By the early 1970s, however, he had accepted that the country was heading for a catastrophe and so endorsed drastic measures to curb population growth. At first, couples were pressurised into having no more than two children; later, the limit was set even lower—to one child per family, with harsh penalties for those who disobeyed.

This policy has certainly proved to be very effective, but it has also developed

▲ **Looking quite the little emperor in his fancy dress, a beloved boy poses for a photo.**

some rather ugly side effects, not least because many parents would prefer their only child to be a boy: sons carry on the family name and have a duty to support their parents when they get old. Daughters, in contrast, leave their families when they marry and take on their husbands' responsibilities.

As a result, many unwanted baby girls have been secretly killed at birth, and in some regions the ratio of men to women has become seriously imbalanced. What is more, the policy has produced a whole generation of only children, whose doting parents and grandparents all too often indulge them excessively. The highly favoured boys, in particular, risk being thoroughly spoilt, so much so that many Chinese refer to these pampered darlings disparagingly as 'little emperors'.

vegetables. Spring onions and radishes were commonest at this time of year, but there were also apples and pears for sale, which must have been stored through the winter. We bought some of these to munch as we rode.

On butchers' tables great chunks of fatty pork were displayed, chopped into shapeless lumps and sold by weight on hand-held scales. The big white muffins we had had in Shanhaiguan were on sale, as were yellow loaf-sized cakes and rings of hard, plaited bread. Big pancake fritters were being fried at the roadside. Maize was for sale by the sack or the handful and everywhere we saw girl ice-cream vendors on bicycles. They carried a white wooden box mounted behind them and cried their wares in singsong voices which carried a long way. At first we were dubious about sampling their wares, as they were usually kept cool by being wrapped in damp old sacks which looked none too clean. But once we had taken the plunge, tasted how good they were and found that we did not instantly go down with dysentery, there was no reason not to carry on. The singsong cries were to be heard right across China and the ices were a great comfort on hot days. They cost 10 fen or 2 pence.

▲ Delicious-looking pancake fritters, the size of small wheels, being freshly prepared at a roadside stall.

Often we found ourselves being escorted by a bevy of bicyclists, who pedalled along beside us gazing curiously at the strange sight we presented. When we bade them good day they would often drop back in confusion to giggle among themselves before speeding up for another look. Then we would give them a handout and they would drop behind again while they stopped to read it. One would read aloud while the others clustered round, peering over his shoulders in a scrum. On catching us up again they would ask us where we were going and we could practise our Useful Phrases.

We had by now developed a valuable technique with these and we could slip in a couple of simple jokes to show that we were human. It was easy to say that we were English, not American, which always went down well as there is still a legacy from the days when effigies of Uncle Sam were burned in public as the big bogeyman. Explaining that our horses were good Chinese ones and not English usually brought another laugh, but the most successful ploy was always to apologise profusely for not being able to speak Chinese, and then hit them with the acutely embarrassing question as to whether any of them spoke English. This would inevitably produce a chorus of shamefaced denials. Although everyone in China now learns English in school, few in the countryside will dare to try it out without warning and the rehearsal of chosen phrases.

One of our bicycling companions for a time had a huge load of vegetables tied on behind him and draped over the handlebars. When we stopped to buy some ice creams from one of the girls, he insisted on paying and then invited us into his house for a drink. Reluctantly, we had to refuse, as we were aware that

there were barely enough hours in the day to cover the thirty miles or so we had set ourselves. But it was extraordinarily kind of him; with average incomes in the countryside at below £100 a year, an expenditure of 4 pence on strangers was generous indeed.

At Zunhua a major market was under way and we wondered if we would be able to get through the town. By the time we thought of trying to find our way round through the suburbs it was too late and we were being swept along in a tide of humanity. There was a solid mass of people as far as we could see in all directions, many pushing loaded bicycles, prams or handcarts piled with produce. Others drove donkeys almost invisible beneath their loads of brushwood. Through this, somehow, incredibly, a certain amount of traffic moved. One or two lorries, like whales in a shoal of fishes, blew their horns constantly and inched forward. We flowed along in their wake. Everyone was cheerful and busy, stopping to haggle at stalls along the sides or in the middle of the road to buy produce straight from the carts. They seemed very pleased as well as astonished to see two Europeans on horses riding through the middle of the bedlam.

It was a wonderfully colourful scene we saw over the heads of the crowd. In little tents on the roadside men were having their heads shaved by barbers. Cobblers with contraptions that looked like antiquated Singer sewing machines

▲ The bustling market crowd that blocked the author's way at Zunhua. Under Mao Ze-dong, free markets were banned; nowadays people can sell anything surplus to the state's requirements.

proffered a while-you-wait resoling and patching service. Beside them were pieces of rubber cut into the rough shapes of feet. Everything under the sun was being sold. Tobacco was on offer by the leaf, bicycle parts, cheap plastic sunglasses, strips of linoleum and all sorts of implements: trowels, shovels, sickles, spades, hoes. Then there were lengths of wire and hemp rope, steel mesh, nuts and bolts and an extraordinary lethal design of rat-trap, like a giant homemade mousetrap, which seemed very popular. Among all this was a wide variety of animal life on its way to the livestock section of the market. Sheep and goats were being dragged by ropes and everywhere pigs were tied onto wheelbarrows, carts and bicycles in the most uncomfortable-looking way. Everyone was shouting cheerfully at everyone else and there was no doubt that they were all having a good time.

It took us an hour to force our way through the town and out the other side. As we were swept out into the less congested outskirts, surrounded by a merry crowd taking their purchases home, we met what looked like a haystack coming towards us. Somewhere under the sweet-smelling new-mown hay was a tiny donkey forging stolidly ahead. On top of the load was a spectacular rosebush in full bloom.

We stopped under the Wall for a rest and a picnic beside a wide, shallow stream. It ran through a village which had been built from the stones of the Wall. Fortunately our picnic site was a short distance away from the nearest houses and so we had some time to ourselves before the crowds arrived to watch us. We

▲ Somewhere beneath this giant haystack there must lurk a cart!

unsaddled the horses and tied them on long ropes to convenient poplars so that they could graze. Ming's saddle had begun to rub him in a few places, and although the skin was not broken and he was clearly not troubled by the spots it was a worry. So, too, was some slight lameness in Tang, who had been favouring his near foreleg. There seemed to be no swelling but we had been pushing the horses hard and they were due for a day of rest.

We washed in the stream, ate some biscuits and a small tin of peaches, and lay back in the sun to rest, well pleased with life. For a while we slept. I opened my eyes to see above me an old grey-bearded sage looking solemnly down at the two strange barbarians who had materialised in his village. He had a timeless face, which could have looked just so at any travellers in any era. We were just his first Europeans.

At this point the Wall guarded the southern foothills of the mountains, and our road climbed north of it, steeply up a series of hairpin bends. The Wall here was crenellated on both sides, which is unusual: normally only the outer, northern face needed defending. The towers were closely spaced as this must once have been an important place to defend, one of the handful of strategic passes between the Hebei plain and the Mongolian plateau. Through these the Chinese emperors used to cross the Wall on their way to their hunting-grounds and their summer residence, the palace at Chengde, barely fifty miles to the north. They were also among the sections of the Wall most likely to come under attack.

The first rule observed by the Wall's builders was to follow the terrain so that signals could be flashed as quickly as possible from one watchtower to another and at the same time be seen far back behind the line of the Wall so that reinforcements could be sent up quickly in the event of an attack. The result is the

extraordinarily dramatic appearance of the Wall throughout its length. Incredibly steep ridges were followed along the crests, both because they form natural barriers themselves and also because huge boulders and sheer cliffs were used in the building to save on bricks.

Once we were on the other side of the Wall there was a marked change in the landscape. The hillsides were thickly wooded with sizable trees of many varieties, the first proper woods we had seen. Sweet chestnut was mixed with oak, pine, birch and masses of glorious flowering acacias, their great clusters of white flowers giving off a heady scent. Beside the road in terraced plantations were orchards of all sorts of fruit trees which we could not identify. Tartar horsemen must have once ridden through the forest to this ridge and looked out at the land they planned to conquer. In a few more yards we came to a much more harsh and rugged prospect. Jagged peaks stretched as far as the eye could see, and way below us was a river valley. There we could see the green trees of the little town of Banbishan, where we planned to stop and rest for a couple of nights.

▲ The Jinshan Pavilion stands beside one of the picturesque lakes in the grounds of the Summer Palace at Chengde.

The Walled Country

▲ A superbly preserved section of the Great Wall, here lit by a rosy dawn, snakes its way into the mountains along a sharp ridge.

Emperor Qin Shi Huangdi, who unified China and masterminded the construction of the first continuous Great Wall. ▼

THE GREAT WALL OF CHINA, sometimes described as the eighth wonder of the world, is one of the greatest engineering feats of all time—a gigantic monument to human endeavour, as well as to human cruelty.

The Wall that most people are familiar with is built of stone, with solid ramparts and evenly spaced watchtowers. But it acquired this form only relatively recently, under the Ming dynasty, some 350–600 years ago. Its true origins lie considerably further back in history.

As long ago as the 5th century BC, when China was composed of numerous rival kingdoms, several local rulers built stretches of mud wall for protection against one another, as well as against the Huns and other warlike peoples to the north. Then, in the 3rd century BC, China was unified by one powerful ruler, the Emperor Qin Shi Huangdi, who set about linking and strengthening many of the ancient walls, especially along his northern frontier. This was a massive undertaking: over 300,000 soldiers and up to a million conscripted labourers toiled in remote deserts, mountains and forests, often having to carry materials on their own backs, and by every account dying in droves.

However, they did succeed in building the first recognisable Great Wall, which was garrisoned along its entire 3,000-mile length and furnished with watchtowers that formed an unbroken string of communication posts: messages could be signalled from one end of the Wall to the other in less than 24 hours—an achievement unequalled until the arrival of the telegraph.

Subsequent dynasties added to the Wall, and proved no less willing to sacrifice huge numbers of people in the process: during the 7th century AD, 500,000 men are said to have perished in one ten-day period alone. In spite of all this effort, the Wall ultimately failed to daunt the formidable Mongol armies of Genghis Khan, which swept into China in the early 13th century. And yet the Wall was not abandoned; rather, once the Mongols had been expelled in 1368, the Chinese set about strengthening their Wall in a further 250-year-long construction programme. This, the greatest period of wall-building, was undertaken by the Ming emperors and resulted in a structure stretching some 4,000 miles from Shanhaiguan on China's east coast to Jiayuguan in the Gobi Desert, the very westernmost edge of the Ming empire.

A soldier gazes dreamily through the battlements of the Great Wall, just as his predecessors have done for over two thousand years. During the Ming dynasty (1368–1644), one million soldiers guarded the Wall.

From the watchtower halfway up this mountain, soldiers could quickly relay warnings about invaders to the pass at the bottom—by smoke signal, if necessary. ▼

▲ This section of Wall, dating from the Han dynasty (206 BC–AD 220), reveals an early technique of reinforcing the structure with layers of reeds.

▲ Not all the Wall was built in stone; here, a section made from rammed earth has fallen prey to the ravages of time and a harsh desert environment.

CHAPTER 4

A Beijing Picnic

AT BANBISHAN EVERYTHING WAS READY for us when we arrived. As always, Madam Hao was there to greet us, clapping her hands, with a big smile on her plump face. As we eased ourselves out of the saddle she always said, with concern in her voice, that we must be tired. Then she would clasp Louella to her ample bosom for a comforting hug. Her equanimity was only shaken when her precious minibus was disturbed by dirt, damage or other vehicles. (Dangerous drivers were threatened with a shake of her massive fist, and our sacks of horse feed were not popular as they tended to leak onto the floor.)

We were led to a courtyard similar to those we had been using to camp in, but this one, Mr Li told us, was also a hotel. We could pitch our tent there if we wished, but as the rooms were only 60 pence a night why not use them? (We knew he and the others thought us quite mad to want to sleep in tents.) We were, as we told each other, there for the riding not the camping, and so we gave in. The rooms were simple but adequate: iron bedsteads, a concrete floor covered in dust and cigarette ends, bare walls, a naked light bulb hanging from the ceiling and a wooden table. In Europe they would pass for prison cells; here they represented luxury. A rusty washbowl on a stand and a cracked mirror completed the amenities. We pulled the beds together and used our own bedding.

Mr Li said, 'This is a Chinese country hotel. Soon this area will be open to foreigners and they are getting ready.'

'We couldn't be more comfy,' said Louella bravely, but a quick look at the public latrines made us speculate how the first coachload of ladies from Denver would react. There was a well in the yard from which we drew water for the horses and for ourselves.

Mr He was allowed to cook in the corridor and as usual produced a masterpiece, this time almost entirely vegetarian. A friendly crowd came in to watch us eat, and for good measure inspected our room and our possessions.

In the middle of the night we woke to the sound of pounding hooves and realised that the horses had escaped. Dragging on our trousers we ran to chase them. They were charging wildly round the courtyard, clearly enjoying themselves and in no mood to be caught. If they had got out of the yard we really might have had a problem, but fortunately the night watchman woke up in time to close the gates. Only when they galloped into a side yard and stopped there to eat some of their hay, which I'd fetched, could we catch them, and then they were

▲ As day draws to a close, Louella helps an elderly woman draw water from the village well—a utility common in rural China.

instantly as quiet as lambs. Normally they had nice natures and we were becoming fond of them. Tang would nicker at me in the morning when I gave him a lump of sugar. Ming did not like sugar, but he was gentle and willing when being ridden. Now we tied them to a clothes line, but soon afterwards Tang was seen undoing the knots with his teeth and we had to tie special ones to defeat him.

Since the first stage of our ride would bring us back almost to the capital, we had conceived the idea of celebrating with a picnic for all our Beijing friends at a delightful cove on the Miyun Reservoir north of the city. It now looked as though we would make it by the following Sunday, barring accidents, and we were anxious to get word to the long-suffering John Dennis, our friend the Information Officer at the British embassy, who had been given a list of people to invite. There was a telephone in Banbishan, but getting through to Beijing took several hours and when finally the embassy was on the line, they could not hear us at all. Shouting myself hoarse I yelled, 'Miyun Sunday,' again and again until I got what sounded like an acknowledgment and we were cut off.

Now we were free to enjoy the rest of our day off. Taking our books we headed north from the village on a track leading up a promising valley. After a couple of miles we came to an even better view than those of the previous day. Climbing up through pine woods, we found a shady place where we could sit in dappled sunlight and observe the wonderful valley below us. In a great bowl in the mountains lay a cultivated hill, surrounded like an island by a wide loop of

A breathtaking view down a fertile valley lined with terraces glowing with their flowering crops. ▼

river. On either side, bridges led to small villages nestling in their trees and all over the hill the work plots and crops were like a patchwork on the fertile soil. It looked to be an idyllic place. We were at least 1,000 feet above the valley floor, but voices carried up to us and every now and then the frogs in the river would set up a chorus of croaking. A cuckoo, which the Chinese call *buku*, was calling from across the valley and yellow swallow-tailed butterflies drifted past. As we lay and read it was impossible to imagine anywhere we would rather be.

The valley seemed to represent China at its best. Virtually self-sufficient, prosperous by most Third World standards, it was as neatly and artistically laid out as a painting. There was a palpable air of contentment. Even the large black ants which climbed all over us and investigated us failed to bite.

After a couple of hours we climbed to the top of the nearest hill, where the sun beat down on baking rocks, and sunbathed for a while. When the heat became too great we climbed down by a steep path through some terraced fields, where a friendly man with a large yellow dog was inspecting some recently planted fruit trees.

As we neared Banbishan we fell in with three charming schoolgirls walking home. They told us in quite good English that they were sixteen. We invited them to come and call on us later and they left us giggling uncontrollably. Back in the yard we washed in buckets of cold water from the well and felt a lot better for it. Afterwards we went for an evening stroll through the village. Perhaps because we had been there for a whole day, and by then everyone knew who we were and what we were doing, we felt that we were stared at less. But the moment we went into the village shop we realised how wrong we were. It was quite a large store and completely empty when we entered. By the time we had walked the length of the long counter and looked at a few items we did not need, the shop was full and we had to fight our way through an eager crowd. We hoped for the shopkeeper's sake that perhaps they bought something.

▲ These happy, laughing schoolgirls clearly prefer bright, colourful clothes to the drab uniforms that were ubiquitous only a generation before.

During supper, for which Mr He had obtained some small river fish which he cooked whole, our three schoolgirls arrived with eight friends. They watched us eat for a while which they found hilarious and then we showed them pictures of our baby, which reduced them to a state of total collapse. Eventually Madam Hao lost patience with them and sent them home. We then gave the horses some exercise, as they had been standing about all day. We walked and trotted them round the compound and were relieved to see that Tang was no longer lame.

The hotel proprietor was a charming old boy with whom we had a long session settling up our minuscule bill. His one unredeeming feature was that he was a master spitter. Suddenly, in the middle of an amiable conversation, he would clear his throat ominously, roll the resulting phlegm around his mouth for a bit and then carefully drop it on the floor next to his chair. Later, when we were sitting with our crew having a mug of tea before turning in, I felt a sneeze coming on and pulled a big red-spotted handkerchief from my pocket. After sneezing I blew my nose loudly and as I did so I caught sight of Madam Hao's face. In her appalled expression I saw exactly the same disgust which had been on Louella's face when the old man spat. It was salutary to realise that my actions were just as offensive in Chinese eyes and there are no absolute or universal standards of behaviour.

On to Miyun

The road west from Banbishan was terrible. Often it consisted of nothing more than piles of unbroken boulders, and the only other traffic we saw was an occasional heavy lorry carrying stones. I feared for the van's suspension and Madam Hao's peace of mind.

We climbed steadily up into the mountains beside a rocky river, now low but clearly at times a mighty torrent. The scenery became wilder as we gained altitude. From a distance the mountains could have been anywhere, but once we were in among them there was a peculiar cragginess, with wild, mad pinnacles of rock and eccentric, beautiful pines leaning into space from unlikely crevices, which stamped them as unmistakably Chinese.

The rocks of the cliff faces were very strange. Riddled with horizontal and vertical cracks of a reddish brown, they looked like slabs of dried cork. A lot of quarrying was going on, as it seems to all over China, the stone being used for the road, for terracing and to build groins in the riverbed. A couple of times dynamite exploded without warning quite close to us. The horses were good and calm; perhaps as military horses they had heard loud bangs before. Apart from these disturbances we saw few people during the day. For once there were no donkey carts and often we were alone for long periods without even a cyclist.

High up, where the river was dry and such water as there was flowed underground most of the time, Louella saw a perfect place for our midday rest. In a patch of vivid green marsh a cool, fresh spring welled up and flowed for a yard or two before vanishing again below the rounded boulders of the river. We and the

▲ Tree and stone—
components of an
archetypal Chinese
landscape, and subjects
of countless paintings.

horses drank from this, and then, because they were so clearly enthusiastic about grazing the lush grass, we let them loose, hoping they would not try to escape. For once we had no visitors and could sleep peacefully in the sun.

At the top of the pass the road went through a tunnel, and I wondered how the horses would react. But they were quite unafraid of the dark and even when, inevitably, one of the rare lorries came through just as we were in the middle, they paid no attention and kept to the side. Outside in the sunshine again we began a steep and zigzag descent towards Xinglong. This was one place specifically mentioned in our military permit that we must ride around and not through. Of course, we wondered what we were not supposed to see and looked around all the more keenly. As we approached the town we saw some very strange buildings high on a hill to the north and surrounded by a high wall. There were two gleaming observatories, their domes shining in the sun, and next to them a tall tower. Perhaps that was it.

In an outlying village we paused to watch two young women having a noisy and quite violent fight, surrounded by an interested crowd. One was screaming abuse at the other at the top of her voice while trying to grab her hair or punch her. But the moment we were noticed everything stopped and all attention, including that of the two combatants, was directed at us. At that moment a

The Gentle Art of Fighting

▲ A Tai chi session in the tranquil grounds of Beijing's Temple of Heaven.

TAKE AN EARLY morning stroll through any Chinese city, and you will stumble on little islands of tranquillity in the midst of the hustle and bustle—quiet corners in which groups of men and women of all ages seem to be rehearsing some slow and solemn ballet. In fact, they are preparing for the rigours of the day by practising Tai chi, an ancient form of keep fit—one aimed at relaxing the mind as much as at tuning the body.

In spite of its slow and gracefully flowing motions, Tai chi was originally a serious form of self-defence. According to legend, its inventor was a Taoist monk of the 14th century, who witnessed a battle between a crane and a snake and then developed a set of movements inspired by the adroit manoeuvres of the snake—the victor of the duel.

Revolutionary as this idea may sound, it was but a further development in an already venerable tradition. Almost a thousand years earlier, in the 5th or 6th century AD, the founder of the Buddhist Shao Lin monastery, near Luoyang in north central China, created a system of exercises, based on the movements of various animals, to help his monks improve their concentration when meditating. These exercises developed, so tradition has it, into all the eastern martial arts, from judo in Japan to kick-boxing in Thailand, as well as China's own speciality—kung fu.

The martial arts are deeply embedded in the culture and philosophy of the Chinese and other eastern peoples. Kung fu and Tai chi alike lay great emphasis on mental or spiritual training, alongside the physical. In both fighting and everyday life, the aim is to reach a state in which body and mind work together in perfect harmony.

small motorised tricycle with a cab pulled up and two important-looking military men got out of the back. The senior one waved his blue identity card at us sternly and signalled that he wanted to see ours. Although we did not have our passports on us we did fortunately have the Aliens' Travel Permit, which named all the places on our route. He scrutinised this carefully, found Xinglong on it, to his evident surprise, and returned it to us. When we showed him our handout he became positively friendly, saluted and waved us on. This was the only time on the whole ride that we were stopped and asked for our papers.

The road went past Xinglong and as we rode along we could see a large, grim camp with wooden towers at the corners, barbed wire and rows of long huts. A labour camp or top-security prison, perhaps, we thought. But when we asked Mr Li what there was in Xinglong that was so secret, he said that the only reason we had been told to avoid the centre of town was because it was being rebuilt and so was in a dreadful mess.

We camped a short way beyond the town, and that night Mr He demonstrated his kung fu skills to us. He had extraordinary control over his body as he performed the balletic ritual associated with this martial art. He was able to fall to the floor like a log and he could lie rigid between two chairs, supported only by his neck and ankles.

▲ Workers on the march during the Cultural Revolution (1966–76), with placards showing Mao Ze-dong.

Mr Li was forty and therefore still a student when the Cultural Revolution broke out in 1966. He had been a Red Guard and forbidden to study for nine years. Instead he had rampaged round the country with a group who harangued the people with extracts from Mao's Little Red Book. 'We were gripped by a kind of madness,' he said. Nonetheless, he had studied English secretly, rightly thinking it might come in useful one day. Most of the rest of his generation are totally uneducated. The skilled and those in authority today are nearly all much older or younger.

We asked Madam Hao how she had fared at that time and she replied that as her husband was in the army they had not done too badly. The military stood apart during the Cultural Revolution and they were virtually the only section of the community safe from the attentions of the Red Guards. Now everyone seemed to talk quite openly about those dreadful days, comparing notes on their sufferings, vying with each other over stories of being sent to live in caves or being separated from husband or wife for the decade. Many are still separated.

That night we slept fitfully, disturbed by the horses stamping restlessly outside. A very long and tiring day lay ahead of us.

During the morning Tang began to go lame again and both horses needed constant urging to prevent them walking slower and slower. After a time the road was metalled and there were few stretches where we could canter along the verge. Our bones ached and we devised ways of distracting ourselves from painful reality. One was to test each other on Chinese words and phrases. Fortunately we both talk a lot and are never bored in each other's company.

We also tried hard to observe and identify the birds, trees and flowers we saw along the way. Here larks were nearly always present, singing their way up into

Central heating with a difference: a *kang*—a platform with a built-in stove—makes a very snug bed or, as here, a cosy place to play with Grandma. ▶

the clear blue sky or feeding on the ground beside us. They were bigger than the ones at home and had pronounced crests. Sometimes, as we approached a village, one of the less attractive features of modern China would compete with their song. Even in the remotest villages loudspeakers were mounted on a water tower or other high point, and when music or exhortations to work harder and love China were broadcast through them the din could be heard for miles. Often the distortion was so great that it was hard to tell if the music was Chinese or Western.

Most villages had some electricity, usually just a handful of forty-watt bulbs, but few had more than a single tap to supply water, and mostly this was fetched from the river or a well, in buckets suspended across the shoulders. The communal latrines were always dry and with a pigsty alongside. The houses had floors of beaten earth or sometimes concrete, and the inhabitants usually slept on *kangs*—brick platforms with a stove underneath, which could, in the depths of winter, be fired with twigs, straw or animal dung. Sometimes a heating flue led inside the house from a cooking stove outside.

▲ The black-naped oriole is known in Chinese simply as 'yellow bird'. Its melodious song has long been considered a harbinger of spring.

Some of the time we walked to spare the horses, as the road climbed and dropped through a series of ridges. Once again the most memorable moment of the day was our midday rest, when we were simply dazzled by a brilliant little meadow of splendid buttercups in a grove of poplars. The horses were too exhausted by the heat and the steepness of the ascent to do more than roll and then stay lying down, barely bothering to graze. We lay and munched on biscuits and dried prunes while bright red ladybirds with no spots landed all over us. Thinking that the colours were almost too good to be true we looked up into the shimmering green and silver of the poplars and saw two lovely yellow orioles mobbing a magpie which had dared come too close to their nest. A tiny, grey-and-black-striped squirrel, no more than six inches long, flicked its tail over its back and sat up to eat a nut held in its front paws. Grey wagtails bobbed and dipped on the rocks and a cuckoo called persistently from the hills. It must be said that most of the time the landscape was dry and brown, which only made these rare, lush midday moments all the more memorable. Also spring is, I suspect, the only time of year when there is much colour to be seen in these hills.

We thought the afternoon would never end as we dragged ourselves and our tired animals towards Miyun. By the time we arrived, met up with our crew and then managed to get lost, we had covered forty-seven miles and we had been on the road for over thirteen hours. We spent the night in a billet owned by the local work brigade, where they provided accommodation for farmers and drovers coming into town with their produce. It was like a Middle Eastern caravanserai: a spacious yard where a great many mules and donkeys were being fed and watered while their masters lounged about smoking or cooked in their cell-like quarters around the sides. There were good mangers and sturdy hitching posts and it was a relief to be staying somewhere where our mode of transport at least was not considered extraordinary. In the morning we were woken by a cock crowing. There was a great bustle as teams were harnessed to their carts and departed to loud cracks of whips and cries of 'huh', which with only the slightest tonal variation meant either right or left.

Triumphal Celebrations

It took us less than three hours to ride by the side of a busy highway from Miyun to our planned picnic site by the reservoir on the fringes of the city. On the way we passed an amusement park, which had just been completed for the entertainment of the people of Beijing. In it was a huge roller coaster with its first screaming passengers of the day being terrified, right next to the road. Nothing could have been more incongruous after the wild landscape we had been riding through. There was even a papier-mâché Great Wall around the entrance, with the real thing only a couple of miles away.

At the reservoir, a vast and beautiful lake with islands and a backcloth of mountains, where the Great Wall is silhouetted along the horizon, we found our secluded cove and set about cleaning up our picnic site. There was a rusty old iron boat to which we tied the horses and an amazing amount of litter, but we soon had it looking pristine. We made the crew, who clearly had no faith in the whole crazy affair, put up the tent and start cooking delicious titbits for our guests. We groomed the horses, cleaned our tack and our boots, and wrote a sign saying BEIJING PICNIC. This we nailed to the tree where the track to our beach led off the road.

By midday we were convinced that our message had not been understood and that no one would come even if it had been. We sat in our chairs feeling ridiculous, while Mr He piled more and more food up in front of us. Then Mickey Grant walked round the corner and said, 'Hi, welcome back!' He told us Robbie Lyle had hired a Cadillac and was on his way down. A huge black limousine with a futuristic television aerial on the back inched itself onto the beach and out poured people carrying bottles of champagne, beer, white wine and *mao-tai*—the Chinese spirit with which toasts are given. Soon afterwards the British Ambassador, Richard Evans, arrived with his family in the embassy Daimler, followed by several more cars, until a very noisy party was under way.

With the relief of having arrived, and after downing our first alcoholic drink for some time, we were soon both pretty merry, but we energetically saddled up the horses and gave virtually everyone present a go. This included many of the Chinese officials who had helped us get permission for the ride. Tang and Ming behaved themselves immaculately, plodding up and down the hill beneath riders of all shapes and sizes. I gave a rather incoherent interview to Mark Brayne, the BBC man in Beijing, and then I sold Tang to a good friend called Peter Batey. This was the end of the first stage of our journey and we would need to buy new horses at the point where we were to be allowed to start again. We gave Ming to Robbie in gratitude for all he had done. He said he would keep both horses on a farm just outside the city, where all were welcome to come and ride them. It was a very good party and the afternoon slipped by as the drink which everyone had brought was consumed and Mr He's food was much appreciated.

John Dennis had even arranged a truck to take the horses into Beijing. This was just a small open lorry with a couple of bits of scaffolding tied along the sides. When it backed into a bank and we led the horses round, they just walked straight on without protest. During the fast drive along the motorway into town we followed behind, astonished at how calm they were. Side by side in the open air, they ignored the traffic hurtling past and only revealed their nervousness in the way they leaned into each other for security and companionship.

Our triumphal return to the Jianguo Hotel, where we had spent so much time worrying if we would ever leave, was great fun. The staff were not used to travel-stained guests arriving in their elegant lobby wearing riding boots and carrying large saddles. The senior staff took it all in their well-trained stride and welcomed us back, but the porters, who were not used to handling sacks and saddles, were supercilious and allowed us to manhandle the trolley along to the storeroom ourselves.

However, we were in far too good a mood to allow anything to deflate us and the party continued as different friends came and went. Later, we all dined together and celebrated until the small hours in Charlie's Bar.

Much the hardest part of the journey lay ahead; but we had proved it was possible to ride in China and we now felt confident that we would reach Jiayuguan and the end of the Wall.

▲ The first appearance of silk thread, as a humble silkworm starts spinning a cocoon in which to undergo a miraculous metamorphosis into a pupa and then a moth.

Using a technique that has probably changed little in hundreds of years, a peasant woman spins a reel of silk on an outsize spinning wheel. ▶

▲ Intensive silkworm farming: the insects live in large trays, where they are provided with a constant supply of mulberry leaves.

Silkworm cocoons being sorted according to shape, size and quality at a busy silk factory in eastern China. ▶

◀ The finished product: this sumptuously embroidered fabric demonstrates clearly why the Chinese guarded the secret of silk with such care.

▲ Once dyed, the silk is ready for weaving into a lustrous fabric, sometimes—as here—incorporating complex designs and even gold or silver thread.

The Secret of Silk

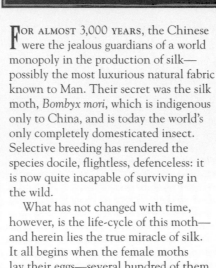

For almost 3,000 years, the Chinese were the jealous guardians of a world monopoly in the production of silk— possibly the most luxurious natural fabric known to Man. Their secret was the silk moth, *Bombyx mori*, which is indigenous only to China, and is today the world's only completely domesticated insect. Selective breeding has rendered the species docile, flightless, defenceless: it is now quite incapable of surviving in the wild.

What has not changed with time, however, is the life-cycle of this moth— and herein lies the true miracle of silk. It all begins when the female moths lay their eggs—several hundred of them apiece. These hatch into tiny white caterpillars, commonly known as silkworms, that are endowed with a gargantuan appetite for mulberry leaves. After six weeks of steady munching, each silkworm has increased its weight ten thousand-fold and begins to spin a protective cocoon in which to undergo a remarkable metamorphosis, first into a pupa and then into a moth—its fully adult form.

And here the silk farmer, or sericulturalist, intervenes, for the silkworms have served their purpose: they have spun their cocoons out of pure silk filament created within their own bodies. Leaving a few pupae to emerge as moths and so continue the cycle, the farmer unravels the remaining cocoons, releasing from each a single, continuous strand that can be up to 3,000 feet long. This thread, at once very fine and very strong, is then spun with several more threads to form a fibre, which in turn is woven into the sumptuous fabric that is still a byword for delicacy, opulence and sensuousness.

No one knows exactly when the silk industry began, but according to ancient tradition the Empress Xi Ling Shi, wife of Emperor Huang Di (the Yellow Emperor), was its first patron in about 2700 BC. For this benefaction, she was eventually accorded semi-divine status as 'goddess of the silkworms', and was venerated in annual public ceremonies. Ironically, legend charges another high-born lady with the betrayal of China's secret. In about 140 BC, so the story goes, a beautiful Chinese princess betrothed to a foreign prince smuggled silkworm eggs out of her homeland on the flowers decorating her hair.

CHAPTER 5

Detour to Xi'an

B URSTING WITH ENERGY to sort everything out and be on our way again, I jogged with Robbie before breakfast and swam ten lengths of the hotel pool. There was a lot to do and every reason to delay for further protracted negotiations and more permissions, but I insisted that we would catch the train to our next starting point in three days. My most fervently observed rule of travel is that the longer a traveller stays in a city the more things will turn up which he will have to sort out before he can leave.

We talked to the press and bought our train tickets to Xi'an. We collected a pile of letters and wrote replies. We had my camera repaired and decided to buy a spare for Louella to use as her own. We whizzed around the town on bicycles, shopping and seeing people. I had lost a filling and was given the name of a lady professor at the dental hospital who was highly recommended by the embassy. It was a huge place where no one spoke English, and explaining one's needs by sign language was alarming. Through countless doors off endless corridors were rows and rows of dentists' chairs, where men and women in white coats and masks

were hard at work on open mouths. It was like being in a hall of mirrors. A kind nurse took me under her wing, filled out the necessary forms from guesswork and delivered me to the professor, who drilled and filled expertly.

Back at the hotel we met Mickey Grant, who was deeply depressed at having received in writing a definite refusal of permission to film our ride. Our disappointment was eased, though, by the fact that he had seen an item about our ride in *Reference News*, which everyone thought should help us greatly. *Reference News* is a tabloid containing selected items of news about international and Chinese events filched from the foreign press. It is claimed to be the most widely read paper in the world, with ten million copies printed daily, and each copy seen by perhaps fifteen people. Now we learned that it had picked up a Reuters report of our departure from Shanhaiguan.

Our last evening in Beijing provided the ultimate in Chinese contrasts. We dined on the terrace of the embassy residence by candlelight. Above us glowed red lanterns and a moon; we were served exquisite food by silent and efficient Chinese staff. The guests were cultivated and cosmopolitan. They made witty speeches. But we had to leave before the end to deal with our baggage, which had to be sent by goods train to Xi'an. There were twenty-three pieces, all our supplies and equipment for the rest of our time in China: far too much to go in the compartment with us. We had been told that the quietest time for checking it in at the station would be 11pm and that was when we arrived.

There were slightly fewer people than when we had bought our tickets earlier, but the scene which greeted us still resembled the aftermath of a nuclear holocaust. Bodies lay everywhere, singly and in heaps. One group of ten lay like

◀ One of the ways in which newspapers are read in China—pinned up on large, public notice boards. Others are bought and then carefully passed around among friends.

the spokes of a wheel, their heads resting on their baggage piled in the centre. We had to park a long way from the freight hall and pick our route through. Then our troubles began. There were no porters or trolleys and the official in charge was extremely unfriendly. We had to carry each item by hand over the sleeping crowds. When we finally had everything stacked up in the hall, he said it was improperly packaged. The trunks must have padlocks, the sacks must be stitched and the boxes tied with stronger cord. The people who could be paid to see to the packaging had gone home. It was now 11.15pm, the office closed at 11.30pm, and quite clearly we were in an impossible predicament where disaster loomed. These situations occur all too often in China; in fact, travel seems to revolve round them. The traveller—and to be fair it seems to make no difference if you are Chinese or foreign—is driven to despair by insuperable problems and it is tempting to rant and rave. But it is essential to stay calm and polite, outwardly determined against all odds to succeed somehow. Then, suddenly, in a flash, everything changes, and from being surly and unhelpful those around are transformed into the most friendly, inventive and helpful people on earth.

Sure enough, a glimmer of light now appeared at the end of the tunnel. A girl in a blue uniform produced a needle and began stitching up our sacks. Next,

three new padlocks appeared and were paid for by me without a murmur. Sixty-nine labels (three for each item) were written out and stamped at the speed of light. A couple of items we had been told at first were quite unacceptable were passed. The office did not close and by midnight all was finished. As we shook hands all round and thanked everyone for their kindness, the formerly surly boss said with a grin that he had read all about us in *Reference News* and hoped we would have a good ride.

For the twenty-four-hour journey to Xi'an we shared our soft-sleeper compartment with a serene old general of temperate habits, who neither smoked nor spat. Messrs Li and He, who were to stay with us the whole way, were in the next compartment and so we saw them only for meals. Madam Hao had driven us to the station for our morning departure and promised to collect us whenever we arrived back. We hoped to arrange fresh transport and a new driver in Xi'an.

▲ This rugged terrain in Shanxi province does not look particularly well suited to agriculture, but the dusty soil here is actually very fertile.

The weather was now very hot both day and night, and we sweltered as the train made its way across the plains of Hebei. It was a chance to read, write and sleep. Once we started to climb up into the mountains of neighbouring Shanxi province, the scenery became much more interesting and the train wound along the edge of deep valleys and passed through numerous tunnels. They were rugged, dry mountains, but with lots of terraces irrigated from clear rivers, groves of poplars and dirt roads.

◀ A different province, a different landscape—the lusher, gentler colours of Shaanxi offer a soothing contrast to those of neighbouring Shanxi.

When we woke, Shanxi was behind us and we were in Shaanxi province. Here the landscape was completely different again: lush, undulating hills and river plains, where rich market gardening was being carried out on the farmland. The fertile Wei river valley, through which we approached Xi'an, was the cradle of Chinese civilisation, populated as early as 5000 BC, in Neolithic times. Some of the first agriculture in the world was practised here.

We were met at the station by contacts arranged through our friends at CITIC and by an official of the railway, who guided us across the tracks, between four big steam engines, to a special exit. This was, he said, 'to avoid the crowds and some reporters'. It was a welcome change not to be pushing and fighting our way through the throng and we followed him docilely. Our contacts put us in the Bell Tower Hotel, which is right in the centre of town. The view from the window was the hotel's only redeeming feature. Described in the guidebooks as a compartmentalised aircraft hangar, it was perfectly adequate, but nothing worked, everything was very dirty and the staff seemed to have been specially trained in the art of unhelpfulness.

The Emperor's Bodyguard

We had planned to spend two nights in Xi'an but, due to further delays over permits and a resolute refusal all round to let us move until they came through, we were doomed to be stuck for eight. There are many worse places to be stuck than Xi'an, as there is a great deal to see, but we fretted because our time in China was running out and we still had a very long way to go. Meanwhile, our transport was produced and a reasonable price agreed for it on the first day. It was a twenty-seater bus, which comfortably took all our baggage. In it we could visit the sights at our leisure and in our own time, thus avoiding the coachloads of foreign and Chinese tourists.

Most important for us were the tomb of the Emperor Qin Shi Huangdi and the terracotta figures guarding it. Everyone now knows the story of how, in 1974, peasants digging a well uncovered what is now recognised as one of the greatest archaeological finds ever made. Thousands of life-size figures of warriors and their horses drawn up in battle formation were buried a mile or so from the tomb, a whole army ready to protect their emperor. These are gradually being excavated. Over the main site a roof has been built to protect it from the elements. Other sites have been filled in again with soil to protect them for future excavations.

Under the roof 6,000 life-size figures stand or kneel in ranks. Each has different features and clothing, clearly modelled from life. Some smile, some scowl; some have loose scarves around their necks, others what look like cravats. They wear loose-fitting robes or, in the case of horsemen, short coats of chain mail and wind-proof caps. Many still lie buried under the yellow earth. Heads and torsos emerge from test holes which reveal the size of the site. The first thing that struck me was how amiable they looked: good companions and loyal friends, gentlemen who enjoyed life rather than representatives of one of the most power-ful armies ever. It is a scene too grandiose for the mind to grasp. We gazed and

Archaeologists couldn't believe their eyes when they began excavating the vast terracotta army, buried over 2,000 years ago to protect the Emperor Qin Shi Huangdi in the afterlife. ▼

wondered, unmindful of the other tourists, the garish notices, the prohibitions in English against taking photographs, the noise of engines and voices.

We were delighted as well as appalled by what we saw that day. Some workers, mostly women in padded overalls, were hacking away with pickaxes at the central terraces and loading soil into a dumper truck. As it chugged off up a ramp we could feel the vibration it caused under our feet and clods of earth fell down into the pit where the immaculate soldiers stood. Other women smoked and rested on their shovels, chattering and flicking their stubs away. It all seemed so casual. We felt that there must be more sophisticated techniques now for sucking dust and dirt away gently, rather than the crude methods being used.

The figures are wonderful, but they are, however, only an appendage of the real treasure house. It is the promise of what is yet to come that is most exciting about the place. When the emperor was crowned King of Qin in 246 BC at the age of thirteen, work began on his mausoleum, 700,000 castrated men labouring on a construction over four miles in circumference. This continued for the next thirty-six years of his reign, during which he conquered and unified China to become its first emperor. His tomb lies beneath a man-made hill a mile from the site of the terracotta army. It has not yet been excavated and may never have been looted. If so, unimaginable treasures await archaeologists underneath the 150-foot-high mound which covers the tomb.

▲ Every single figure in the terracotta army has individual features, said to represent the physical characteristics of people from the different regions of China that had been unified by the Emperor Qin Shi Huangdi.

The walls of the tomb itself are said to have been lined with bronze plates to keep the water out. Liquid mercury was pumped in to create underground rivers and oceans, which could be made to flow and surge. Pearls and jewels studded the ceiling to make galaxies of stars, while gold and silver ducks and wild geese were placed on the floor among jade pine trees. An entire imperial court, with palaces and pavilions filled with treasures and utensils for the afterworld, was reproduced to accompany the emperor for eternity. It is also said to be guarded by crossbows set to impale intruders automatically. Since the bronze weapons held by the terracotta figures were found to have been forged from a special rust-resistant alloy, so that after more than 2,000 years they were still sharp, the first archaeologists to penetrate the site should be wary.

What worries me about the whole future of the site is that the Chinese find it hard to accept that any modern barbarian could have anything to contribute to their excavation. We were told that no foreign scientists have been allowed to take part in the work, in spite of offers from universities around the world who would be happy to contribute money, personnel and expertise in return simply for the interest of being there. Doubtless the Chinese do have good archaeologists, though their numbers must have been depleted during the Cultural Revolution when such occupations were considered bourgeois and 'revisionist'. They say they will excavate slowly and it may be decades before the whole complex and the tomb itself are uncovered, and this sounds sensible, except that the memory of that dumper truck impacting the soil and the labourers hacking away with pickaxes inches from the terracotta figures haunts me still.

The museums around the site were quite well done, with clear signs and a lot of interesting information. The models of horses that had been restored were also excellent. A beautiful bronze chariot with four horses and a kneeling coach-man had recently been unearthed. Everything was in astonishing condition, the trappings, reins and decorations gleaming brightly.

We climbed through pomegranate bushes, their flowers a gaudy red and orange, to the top of the hill above the emperor's tomb. Behind the tomb towered mountains with dramatic terracing and high alpine meadows. Below, the lush countryside with fields of green wheat, some just beginning to turn yellow, was broken by copses and gave a surprising feel of Wiltshire in the summer.

At the foot of the hill was a double row of stalls run by delightfully aggressive ladies. They looked and behaved like gypsies, thrusting their wares under our noses, shrieking with laughter at our bargaining, a marvellous contrast to the usual dour state stores. The goods on offer were also astonishingly varied and colourful. There were lots of dazzlingly embroidered children's clothes, as well as old silk garments in need of some repair but of excellent quality. We bought our baby son a padded scarlet suit covered in dragons and a beautiful antique waist-coat. Everything was ridiculously cheap. Accurate scale models of the terracotta soldiers had been for sale in the museum at £7–£20. Here they were 50 pence or so and just as well made.

We later discussed this phenomenon with our crew, who had at the time seemed rather shocked by the aggressive commercialism displayed by these traders. I tried to explain how refreshing I found their cheerfulness and enthusi-asm after the surly salesmanship in state shops. To our surprise they agreed, saying, 'No competition, no progress.'

Making the Best of the Delay

The sights of Xi'an kept us occupied for the next week as we tried not to let the delays exasperate us. It is a city with a cheerful, relaxed atmosphere, where one can stroll among the street vendors. Food, ice cream and trinkets of all sorts are sold from handcarts by pedlars. One man had his bicycle almost concealed under cages of budgerigars. In the Muslim quarter, around the Great Mosque, enter-prising shopkeepers displayed their colourful wares outside for visiting Chinese and the occasional foreign tourist. The mosque itself, one of the largest in China, was a haven of peace in the bustling city. Sedate gentlemen in turbans strolled among the roses and the birdsong looking pensive, and for the first time in China we felt that here were people who were not afraid of being devout. Before the Cultural Revolution there were fourteen mosques in Xi'an; now there are three or four, but Islam is regaining ground.

Our visit to the zoo was a far less agreeable experience. It was fortunate that we went alone, as our disgust was such that we would not have been able to restrain ourselves from being uncivil to our hosts about the conditions in which the animals were kept. The site was attractive enough, with water, willows and low hills, but almost all the enclosures were mean and bare, the animals miserable. Mangy wolves and foxes, their ribs showing and with sores on their legs, paced around slatted cages, their feet slipping between the bars. They stank and looked wretched, while the shouting Chinese visitors threw stones at them and flapped their arms for a reaction. It would have done no good to intervene. Everywhere we looked there were injured animals and birds. The camel house was a bedlam of hysterical, filthy beasts, moulting great mats of hair and galumphing insanely about. The deer stared into space, emaciated and sick, some with diarrhoea, others dying. Between the animals were noisy circus and funfair exhibits, a round-about with blaring music and a wall of death where motorcycles roared about.

A Formidable Empress

Avenues or 'spirit ways' of giant stone animals and human figures leading to tombs, some with accompanying museums, abound within driving distance of Xi'an. With our own transport we were able to visit several and to see a lot of the countryside at the same time. Of all the tombs we visited, we had two particular favourites. One was the tomb of Princess Yongtai, where deep underground in a cool, dank tunnel were wonderfully vivid paintings of life at the Tang court. Comely ladies in stylish gowns, whose pure colours were still bright after nearly 1,300 years, were carrying offerings of fruit and food in bowls and cloths. Life at the Tang court must have been very civilised but also very dangerous. Princess Yongtai had been executed by her grandmother, Empress Wu Zetian, on suspicion of having criticised one of her cronies. During the seventh century China was ruled, as happened quite often, by a powerful, scheming woman. Wu Zetian had been a concubine of Taizong, the second Tang emperor. After he died in AD 649 she managed, through palace intrigue and murder, to dispose of both the rightful empress and two of her own sons. Eventually, she seized the throne to rule as the Empress Wu until she was over eighty, when she herself was finally deposed.

One of her sons was the heir apparent, Prince Zhanghuai, whom she forced to commit suicide. His tomb, the second of our favourites, also contained beautiful

◀ Stone effigies of animals, warriors and courtiers stand to attention in long lines in front of many ancient imperial tombs. These 'spirit ways', as they are called, were probably intended to provide the deceased with an eternal guard of honour.

murals. These were of horsemen playing polo and hunting, a marvellous assortment of animals riding with them. Perched behind them or clasped in their arms were hawks, owls, dogs and even a leopard, as they careered through the trees having a tremendous time.

It was a golden age. Chang'an, the old capital close to modern Xi'an, was the most enlightened city in the world, rivalled only by the Baghdad of Harun al Rashid. China already had a population of about fifty-three million, of whom over one million lived in the capital, where the streets teemed with travellers. Persian influence was strong and religious freedom was allowed, with Nestorian Christians vying for congregations with Manichaeans and Zoroastrians. Buddhism was, of course, dominant, with dozens of great monasteries, and Islam was just arriving.

▲ Peasants spread grain on the road so that passing vehicles can thresh it for them.

Although it was still May, the harvest was well under way and the roads were being used for threshing. Everywhere we drove, grain had been spread out so that the passing traffic would do what otherwise had to be done laboriously by hand. The vehicles still all drove flat out and the peasants winnowing with pitchforks between them had to leap clear. Beside the roads bullocks were pulling large carved stone rollers round and round, threshing more grain, while the ears of barley or millet were crushed by heavy hand-operated millstones. We saw rape seed being milled also, and rice grew in paddy fields close to the rivers.

Back in Xi'an we climbed the two astonishing pagodas which still tower over the ancient walls and modern buildings of the city. They are in such good condition that it is hard to believe they were built in the seventh and eighth centuries, but the views from the top over the smog-ridden industrial sprawl are depressing.

We were taken to a silk factory, doubtless a showpiece, where rows of girls stitched busily, making embroidered kimonos, tablecloths and cushion covers. Louella, who is a talented patchwork quilt-maker, was impressed by their skills, especially the hand embroidery using silk thread. Small samples of this work, about six inches square, were for sale. Louella decided that if we could collect enough of them in suitable matching colours they could be made up into a fantastic quilt when we got home. After some calculations she explained that we wanted thirty different designs in four colours: gold, blue, green and red. They began to enter into the spirit of the thing, and we pulled out drawers, piling up and separating silk pictures of birds, flowers, butterflies and people. At last we had the correct set of 120 pieces and it was time to discuss the price. The manager was sent for. He seemed appalled by the mess we had made of his factory; then he said we could have the lot for 150 yuan—about 30 pence for each piece of embroidery.

As time dragged on and we were still not allowed to continue the journey, we decided we needed exercise to take our minds off our situation. We asked our nice

new driver, Mr Bo, a sturdy, reliable man, to drive us up into the mountains south of Xi'an so that we could go for a long walk. Embarrassed, he told us that only Xi'an itself and the tourist sites around were 'open' to foreigners. There was, however, one beauty spot we could visit and so we agreed to go there. It was a lake on Mount Cuihua, the foot of which was about an hour's drive south of Xi'an.

We left Mr Bo to go in search of some lunch and climbed up a well-trod path alongside a clear, tumbling river. There was birdsong and an increasingly magnificent view as we gained height. Trees shaded our trail and under them sat entrepreneurs selling homemade squash, ice creams and even hot meals of noodles and soup. The sun beat down and there were few other people except occasional parties of noisy schoolchildren. It was steep and it took us an hour to reach the top. There we found a Buddhist shrine and a pleasing hill village of old houses. An old man sat in the sun puffing on his pipe, his two grandsons turning a millstone beside him, while chickens pecked at the fallen chaff. Beyond was the lake, and it was peaceful and silent until suddenly a truly dreadful noise rent the air. A long-worn-out needle on a scratched record was relayed through a distorted loudspeaker to produce nothing but noise. It was, after all, a beauty spot and someone was determined to prove it in the Chinese way. We had to walk for another hour along the shore until we were out of earshot. There we found a plashing stream where we could bathe, scooping the cold water over ourselves, and a patch of sand where we could lie in the sun.

The Buddhist monastery at Xingjiao, which we visited on the way back to Xi'an, was the most active we had seen, and the refectory, which was laid ready to accommodate more than a dozen monks, was decorated like a Rotary Club dining room with fraternal Buddhist flags from all over the world. Set on a hill among pines, Xingjiao's seventh-century pagodas and twelfth-century pavilions faced back towards the mountains we had just left. Their summits looked like clouds above the hazy plain.

That evening we received a faint telephone call from Beijing telling us we could leave Xi'an and return to the Wall. To celebrate we went out to dinner at the luxury hotel which caters to the 'terracotta tourists'. Chinese food is wonderful, but it always comes all at once and has to be eaten as messily as possible,

The well-tended vegetable garden of a Buddhist monastery near Xi'an, with a flower garden and one of its pagodas visible in the background. ▶

leaving gristle and bones scattered all over the plastic table top, and no temptation to linger. The Golden Flower is Swedish-owned and superbly run by the Norwegian manager and his Swiss wife. We dined with them on outstanding French cooking, the last non-Chinese meal we would enjoy until our journey was over. Their Austrian chef had discovered quantities of freshwater crayfish in the market; crystal finger bowls with scented rose petals came with them. We savoured every minute of eating at a table laid with a clean, white cloth. Fresh strawberries and a lot of French wine left us feeling ready for anything.

Back to the Wall

The drive to northern Shaanxi took three days. We were all in high spirits at being off again. Mr Li, who had taken the brunt of our impatience at the delay, said, 'This lightens my mental burden considerably.'

We left Xi'an through a fine gateway in the massive walls and plunged at once into a ghastly industrial suburb. I found that my mood, my whole attitude towards China, often changed just as swiftly, so that I sometimes alternated between awestruck admiration and outright disgust.

I am constantly amazed by China's very real success story. Nearly everyone looks reasonably well fed; there is a dynamism and an enthusiasm in the air which one can practically feel. Crops grow, factories produce, there is next to no unemployment and all is rush and hustle. But progress has been bought at a heavy price. China today appears to have lost its soul and with it all aesthetic sense. Everywhere we looked the buildings were not just utilitarian, which was understandable in a poor, developing country, but hideous, badly furnished and appallingly maintained. We barely saw a large building in China which had not at least one broken windowpane, some of the roof falling off or streaks of dirt down the walls. Inside, the decor was always atrocious, lacking the faintest colour or design sense, and nothing was ever properly finished. Carpets curled at the corners, stains were not removed, pipes were exposed and leaked.

These shortcomings cannot be excused on the grounds that the country is poor. India is a much poorer country, but grace and beauty shine among the squalor. Malaysia and Indonesia have many regions where life is not dissimilar to that of the mainland Chinese, yet there the women are elegant, buildings are cared for and there is a sense of quality. It seems such a pity that a political philosophy, justly credited with having removed the oppression and regular famine suffered previously, should have to have such a disastrous effect on the finer things of life. In the end history remembers and admires eras and dynasties more for producing pyramids, poetry, paintings and porcelain than cement, coal, cars and cuckoo clocks. Man cannot, and should not, try to live by rice alone.

Driving in China is always interesting, but our journey back up to the Great Wall was exceptional. It was the only part of our trip when we were in real and constant danger of death. Mr Bo was an excellent, fast and quite aggressive driver, a necessity in a country where no quarter is given to the weak. The problem, as my Aunt Madge used to say, was the other damn fool drivers. There were no cars on the road, just an endless procession of lorries driven by maniacs. Heavily loaded with coal or rocks and dragging equally heavy trailers behind them, they spewed acrid black smoke and swayed dangerously from side to side. When empty they drove flat out, overtaking on blind corners, bouncing wildly in and out of ruts and potholes, and blowing their air horns constantly.

Louella and I had chosen to sit in the front of our minibus, next to Mr Bo, so as to see as much as possible. This meant that there was nothing in front of us except the large glass windscreen. It was good for taking photographs, but fatal for us if we hit anything, since seat belts were unknown in China.

After we left the outskirts of Xi'an we passed through beautiful farmland where the harvest was being gathered amid scenes of bucolic contentment. For a time these alternated with towns which were archetypes of industrial pollution: terrible dark satanic mills surrounded by slums, where factory chimneys discharged clouds of pitch-black or sinister white smoke, which fell on the road and caused noxious dust. In between the towns the landscape became more and more lovely, making another Chinese contrast.

This was loess country. Loess is fine yellowish soil, the dust of Mongolia which blew down into China thousands of years ago and now covers the land to a depth of hundreds of feet. Rivers have cut deep ravines through the loess and so the landscape, which appears to consist of a series of great beige plains and softly contoured hills, is actually full of sudden sheer valleys, at the bottom of which lush bushes and trees crowd the narrow streambeds. The soil can be quite fertile where it is possible to cultivate and irrigate it, and terracing continues right up to the edge of terrifying brown cliffs. We could see distant men and donkeys ploughing within feet of vertical drops.

Some of the hills were covered in a white flowering shrub, and the acacia, too, was in bloom. All along the road migrant beekeepers were out in force, living in tents beside their rows of hives. A few wore hats and veils, especially when working on the hives, but we saw no honey for sale. Perhaps it was too early in the year.

At Huangling, where we spent the first night, there was a hotel. We skipped dinner and instead climbed through cobbled streets up to the wooded hill above the town, to the tomb of Huang Di, the Yellow Emperor. Huang Di is the legendary father of the Chinese people and is said to have lived some 4,500 years ago. He has always been revered as the inventor of almost everything useful and important to China, such as weaving, writing, the wheel and the compass. Today his tomb is guarded by a surrounding wall and a great many lovely old twisted cypress trees. We strolled peacefully in the shade, passing an elderly shepherd watching over a herd of cows with bells round their necks. It was a wonderfully tranquil place of magic glades, from which we glimpsed—through the trees—inspiring views of terraced hillsides far away. As Louella said, it felt quite unlike China, more like the background of a Renaissance painting.

▲ The unmistakable arched façades of cave houses in central Shaanxi province. These cave dwellings make such comfortable homes that their design has been adopted by the authorities for local housing projects.

Next day, as we approached Yan'an, conventional houses became rare and almost everyone lived in caves. In the loess this made good sense, especially as the winters are bitterly cold and the summers very hot. Rooms the shape of small Nissen huts are dug into the side of the hills; the fronts are bricked up, a door and window are built in, and a chimney is poked up to emerge through the soil above. Two or three of these rooms side by side make a good house, well insulated and relatively easy, quick and cheap to build. They reminded us very much of the shelters underneath the arches below London railway lines. Some had a short stretch of quite grand castellation along the top of the front or intricate trellis work around the door and window. We also saw several modern cave 'condominiums' outside the town: two- or three-tiered rows of caves clearly built as a municipal effort.

Yan'an is a famous place in Chinese Communist mythology, as it was Mao's headquarters after the 'Long March'. The cave he lived in is preserved and there are museums visited by the Party faithful. The rest of the town is a sprawl of factories squeezed into a narrow canyon along the Yan River, into which all the town's effluent flows.

The Long March ended at a place called Wuqi in October 1935. During the previous year well over a hundred thousand people had died as the Red Army fought its way across China. Fewer than 10,000 ragged survivors had staggered into Wuqi, then a village of only seven families. We stopped there to find a rather ugly town on the edge of a muddy river. While our crew went off to see if they could find a restaurant for lunch we were told not to leave our bus. 'You must not get down. This is a closed area,' said Mr Li. They returned having failed to find anywhere to eat. 'This place is not clean,' they said.

The land became progressively poorer and drier, until at last we emerged on the third day of driving to see a hazy plain stretching away northwards, and the Great Wall again quite clearly marking the boundary of cultivation. Here it was a very different Wall to that in Hebei province. The original scale and design must have been broadly similar but, because there was little or no stone here, the Wall was made of mud and much of it had melted away over the centuries. Once again it was the watchtowers that stood out, now shapeless lumps of pitted adobe. Between them often only a mound, like a low ridge, marked where the Wall had once been.

Mao's Long March

▲ **Mao Ze-dong (on horseback) and his bodyguard during the Long March of 1934–5.**

OF ALL THE REMARKABLE EVENTS that have taken place in China this century, the Long March of 1934–5 has acquired a special place in the nation's consciousness and seems destined to be enshrined in its folklore.

In the early 1930s, two major adversaries had reached a state of all-out war for control of post-imperial China: the Communists, under the leadership of, among others, Mao Ze-dong, and the Nationalists, led by Chiang Kai-shek.

By October 1934, the Nationalists had routed the Communist Red Army from its base in Jiangxi province, in the south of the country. Rather than surrender, however, the Communists—comprising 80,000 troops and 20,000 ordinary Party members, a mere 35 of whom were women—began an arduous retreat to the north in the hope of finding safety and a chance to regroup.

And so began the historic Long March—a gruelling 12-month journey of over 7,500 miles across 18 mountain ranges and 24 rivers. By the time the weary marchers found refuge at the village of Wuqi in Shaanxi province, they had endured starvation, disease, extremes of physical hardship and constant attacks by Nationalists. The toll on human life was enormous: more than 90,000 had died, including two of Mao's children and his younger brother. Yet in the eyes of China's vast peasant population, the Communists had achieved a spectacular victory and Mao's reputation as the champion of the people was ensured.

As we drove down onto the plain we looked out for horses, but saw none, although we were not far from the borders of both Inner Mongolia and Ningxia, regions once celebrated for their horses. Even worse, at Dingbian the 'relevant authorities', who were supposed to have been warned about our arrival and our pressing need to find some horses, had heard nothing and we had to start from scratch. They were friendly and willing, though pessimistic, as they said that mechanisation was making horses scarce. We were taken back eastwards along the Wall to a village called Zhengjingbu, where we were told there was a horse market.

A Wily Horse-trader

The village was quite small, just one dusty street between single-storey mud houses, and it lay right against a massive, crumbling fort where a garrison must once have been housed. As soon as we stepped down from our bus, we were surrounded by a jostling, staring crowd of all ages, the teenage boys pushing their way to the front. Mr Li told us that we were the first foreigners they had ever seen, this being a closed area.

We all walked through to the market, a wide, sandy space enclosed by a mud wall. There were several mules and donkeys, but at first no sign of a horse. Then a very small, thin chestnut gelding of barely twelve hands was led up. It appeared most unpromising, but I had a look at its teeth, which were long in front, implying considerable age, but clean and white under the muck it was chewing lugubriously. I suggested that it was very old. Its owner assured us it was five. On my expressing doubt this was amended to eight. It looked a hundred, but when its owner leapt on to it bareback and careered around the crowd it seemed quite willing to oblige and appeared to have a nice nature.

The crowd was very pressing and so we retired to the relative peace of our bus. A splendid character, the local horse coper, now joined us, as well as a couple of 'local authorities' to see fair play. The coper said he would send for some good horses, which would be there by the evening. We suspected we were being manipulated, but there was little we could do about it. After the delays in Xi'an we were desperate to be off and had decided we would take anything we were offered just so that we could be in the saddle again.

That evening the coper arrived with the two 'fine specimens' he had promised to procure for us. One was a slightly larger chestnut than the one we had seen in the morning, with an ugly cropped mane and a nasty skin disease which made its head and neck scabrous. Its head was mulish and plain, but it had good legs and neat feet, and its ribs hardly showed at all. I put my saddle on it and managed to persuade it to canter up and down the village street while the crowd gaped, clapped and parted like the Red Sea. We agreed that it would have to do for me as there seemed no prospect of doing any better. The second horse, which Louella tried out, was a little black foal. The coper assured us it was four years old, but it had little spindly legs and it nearly fell over when she put her saddle on it. We told him it would not do and asked if he could get us another. This, it seemed, might be possible, but would involve a day or two of waiting while the surrounding countryside was scoured. 'Are there no other horses here?'

we asked. 'None,' he replied. At that moment a cart trundled past with an old man asleep in the back. Between the shafts was the chestnut horse of the morning. 'We'll have that one,' we said in unison, and soon Louella was mounted on it and succeeded in urging it into a reluctant canter.

The discussion about the price now began. Horse dealing is the same all over the world. It is a matter of character, humour and bluff as much as a business transaction. Mr Li now showed an unexpected and admirable side of his nature by entering into the spirit of the negotiations with the enthusiasm of an old hand. He and the old rogue of a coper began to nudge each other in the ribs and exchange secret signals, and I was suddenly transported back to the Irish village fairs of my youth, where much the same sort of nudging and winking would accompany a deal. The coper was wearing a straw hat like a solar topi, an old cardigan and extraordinarily old-fashioned dark glasses. Mr Li was, as always, in a spotless white shirt, and he, of course, had to refer to us from time to time to see how far he could go.

We settled at 750 yuan for my horse and 600 yuan for Louella's. This represented about £150 and £120 respectively. It was, we suspected, a good bit more than the local market price, but any horse dealer worth his salt knows when he has the opposition over a barrel. When the deal was concluded Mr Li told us proudly that the coper had made a special price for us because of the significance of what we were doing. 'He was working for the dignity and honour of his country when he sold us those horses,' he said.

The chances of dignity and honour alone getting us safely over the next three or four hundred miles seemed slim to us as we looked at the wretched creatures we had been landed with. Optimistically, we decided to call them Yang and Yin after the two forces that maintain harmony in the universe.

▲ Evidence of cruel burial customs from a bygone age—these chariots and skeletons of chariot horses were excavated from a royal tomb of the Zhou dynasty (1027–256 BC).

▲ By the time of the Tang dynasty (AD 618–907), sacrificial burials were a thing of the past; miniature terracotta effigies had replaced real people and animals as companions for the dead.

Other guardians, in the form of stone effigies, often stood in silent tribute, forming so-called 'spirit ways' outside the tombs of royalty and nobility. ▶

The burial suit of Dou Wan, a Han princess who died in the 2nd century BC. The suit is made from 2,156 pieces of polished jade, beautifully joined by gold ribbon and gold thread. ▼

▲ This life-size terracotta archer, buried over 2,000 years ago to guard Emperor Qin Shi Huangdi, once held a real bow in his hands.

Treasures of the Tombs

MOURNERS AT CHINESE FUNERALS TODAY often perform a ritual that has its origins in customs reaching back thousands of years—they burn paper money, miniature paper houses and even some of the deceased's possessions in a symbolic gesture to help that person in the afterlife. Some 3,500 years ago, however, the earliest forms of these practices were not nearly so emblematic: the emperors of China's oldest dynasty—the Shang (c.1600–1027 BC)—had themselves buried with everything they might need after death, including their chariots, servants and horses, and even their wives.

During the next dynasty—that of the Zhou (1027–256 BC)—this macabre custom was on the wane: tomb figurines, of various sizes and materials, gradually replaced living victims, probably because of the absurd profligacy of the old rites. And by the time that Emperor Qin Shi Huangdi came to the imperial throne in 221 BC, the process of substitution was complete. All the more shocking, therefore, that this despotic emperor decided to revive the custom of sacrificial burial for his own funeral: his childless wives and the builders of his tomb are all said to be interred with

him in his great mausoleum, which has yet to be excavated.

And yet Emperor Qin Shi Huangdi was clearly also a practical man, for he spared his trusted soldiers and cavalry, ordering instead that a vast army of terracotta replicas be made. These were life-sized and exact in the most minute detail, and they were all meticulously accoutred: horses were fitted with bronze bits and leather reins; archers carried wooden bows in their hands. Altogether, some 8,000 individual figures were buried in three sites around the emperor's mausoleum in perfect military formation.

With the coming of the Han dynasty, soon after Qin Shi Huangdi's death in 210 BC, the rite of burying household members ended forever. Instead, precious objects accompanied the dead, some of whom were encased in spectacular jade burial suits bound with gold thread. Then, in about AD 25, the Han decided to discourage people from placing items of great value in their tombs: earthenware replicas were to be buried instead of real treasure. Later dynasties, however, to the delight of historians and archaeologists, often ignored such pleas for thrift.

CHAPTER 6

The Plains of Ningxia

T O OUR SURPRISE, everything was ready early in the morning and we were
away for the start of stage two of our journey by 8am. The whole village saw
us off. Yang and Yin were very good and tripped along merrily. Yang had a
rather faster pace and Louella had to urge Yin to catch up from time to time, but
he did so fairly readily. He had a pretty head with a sweet expression but he was
very thin and his feet were a mess. We had asked Mr Li to find a blacksmith to
shoe both horses that evening if possible.

We rode north of Zhengjingbu along a sandy lane between old mud-walled
houses until we came to the remains of a great fortress. A fine stretch of Wall,
with arches still remaining in places, surrounded a patch of cultivation. The track
passed through what must have once been a grand gateway but had by now
completely vanished and at once we were in wonderful
country outside. The Wall stretched away to the horizon
while ahead lay the great Mu Us Desert. We turned west
and followed a level sandy track beside the remains of the
Wall. There was no mistaking the substantial mound which
marked where it had once been. It was much eroded, with
sand blown up against it, but the continuous low hummock
crested at times to make a ridge one could not ride over,
and most of the regular watchtowers were still there as
squared-off lumps of mud twenty or thirty feet high.

It was pleasantly cool, a nice hazy day, and the ground
was carpeted with wild flowers—yellow blooms like
cowslips, purple convolvulus and another creeping plant

▲ These bizarre salt
flats arise from the
evaporation of landlocked
water containing a high
concentration of soluble
minerals. After the USA,
China is the world's
largest producer of salt.

like a clover, as well as lots of smaller white flowers. Pale fawn lizards, about five
inches long with pointed tails, scurried away from the horses' feet, and there
were butterflies everywhere. Sometimes whole clouds of white ones enveloped
us. There were yellow ones, among which I saw some swallowtails, and some
very pretty tiny blues. With larks overhead, flocks of sparrows chirping as they
raided the crops and white, presumably tame, doves flying past us to perch on
the Wall, it was all quite magical.

For some hours we rode along on top of the remains of the Wall itself. This gave
us a good view over the sand dunes to the north, where we could see salt flats
shining white, and across the plain to the south backed by the high yellow
mountains of loess. We put up a large hare with a black spot on the tip of its tail,
which lolloped absent-mindedly away from us, not in the least afraid. There were

◀ A little pig enjoys his slops outside a cave house built into the side of the Great Wall in northern Shaanxi. As this photograph shows, the Wall in this area was made of compacted earth, rather than stone.

lots of small holes in the ground, which we had to watch out the horses did not step in. They were made by small, stout rodents, which sat up to whistle at us before diving into them. I took them to be marmots, but they may have been pikas.

We also saw cave houses built into the Wall itself. These dwellings tended to be on the inner side of the Wall, so that often all we saw of them as we passed along the outside or on top was a stovepipe chimney incongruously sticking up out of the ground. The soil looked unpromisingly poor and the crops, where they were being attempted, were thin. But the occasional people we saw working on the land were friendly and waved to us as we rode by.

One little boy ran off screaming hysterically as though we were about to kill him. Fortunately his parents were nearby, ploughing behind two donkeys. They laughed, seeing we meant no harm, and we gave them an explanatory handout to pore over.

Later, as we approached Dingbian, we came to slightly more fertile soil, where the land was divided up by long, straight double rows of poplars and willows. They made lovely, shady glades to canter along, grassy underfoot and cooler than being out on the plain.

We had arranged to meet our crew at an exceptionally large fort, which could be seen from the road some way out of Dingbian. We arrived there before them in the early afternoon and looked forward to a good rest to stretch our limbs. I tied my reins up so that Yang could graze and suggested to Louella that she should do the same with Yin. She was doubtful about letting him go, but I assured her that it was quite safe as they were both tired and Yang had proved that he had no desire to escape. Once released, they looked at us, then at each other and, before we could move or speak, took off at high speed.

'It's all right,' I said, 'they'll stop in a minute and carry on grazing.' But they

failed to do so, and instead galloped off the way we had come, their stirrups flapping and their heels kicking in the air as they disappeared over the horizon. I have seldom felt more foolish or more furious with myself. All the magic of the day evaporated and I cursed ceaselessly for several minutes. Louella waited patiently for me to finish and then we set off in pursuit, trudging glumly along through the soft sand in our riding boots.

As we passed a farm several large and angry dogs rushed out barking. We felt defenceless on foot but managed, by walking determinedly on, to avoid being attacked. At the same time a dust storm hit us. It was not particularly severe, but the warm, thick, swirling cloud depressed us further as we plodded on.

At last we met our bus and crew back on the road, and soon after Mr He spotted a group of people in the distance. They were holding a horse, which proved to be Yang. Saddle and bridle were undamaged and he seemed fresh as a daisy. Filled with renewed energy, I thanked them and leapt on, galloping off in the direction they said Yin had gone. Thundering back down one of the long glades of trees, I cast about among the windbreaks and after half an hour or so met up with Louella, now riding Yin and accompanied by a boy riding bareback. It seemed that an old man, who had watched us go by during the morning, had seen our riderless animals gallop back again. 'Those must belong to the Foreign Guests,' he had said. 'You, Number Two Son, must go and catch them for them,' and he had done so. We were, of course, very grateful, took Polaroid pictures of all the family and pressed them to accept a reward, which they tried hard to refuse. 'There is no need to be grateful,' they said to Mr Li. 'It is the duty of every Chinese person to help Foreign Guests.'

Having added a good nine miles to our day's ride, we continued into Dingbian, where Mr Li had arranged lodging for the horses in the courtyard of a delightful extended family. Elderly grandparents presided over a number of married sons and daughters and several small babies. The horses were tied to a pile of logs and we were taken indoors to be fed on hot orange juice, made from crystals, and glutinous rice which we dipped into a bowl of sugar while we waited for the blacksmith to arrive.

He was old and grizzled, irritable and stone deaf, but clearly a considerable local character. He had with him a string of improbably shaped iron shoes tied in a bundle and some very primitive tools. There was no question of a forge, but he hammered away until they more or less fitted each horse and then he banged them on cold with his homemade nails. I could see daylight in places between shoe and hoof, but he assured us they would stay on for 1,000 miles. Everyone said he was a wonderful blacksmith, who had shod the horses of Marshal Peng Dehuai, one of the greatest heroes of the Long March.

A Hermit on the Wall

We managed to leave Dingbian before dawn next morning, before the strident lady on the loudspeakers all over town roused the workers with inspiring slogans. We had spent much of the night packing and sorting our supplies, since we were about to head out into country where, we were told, we were unlikely to find anything. We were pretty sure Mr He would always manage to find food in local markets, but we had to be ready to come up with meals from our packaged resources if necessary.

It was good to be on our way again. The family were only rubbing the sleep out of their eyes as we rode out of their courtyard, cocks were crowing and the sun was catching the top of the town wall. The Great Wall makes a right-angled turn to the north at Dingbian and we managed to get lost trying to ride round the outskirts of the town instead of through the middle. At last we picked up the Wall again and were once more able to ride along a very broken stretch across a grassy plain until we crossed the road. Here we had to make a decision. Ahead

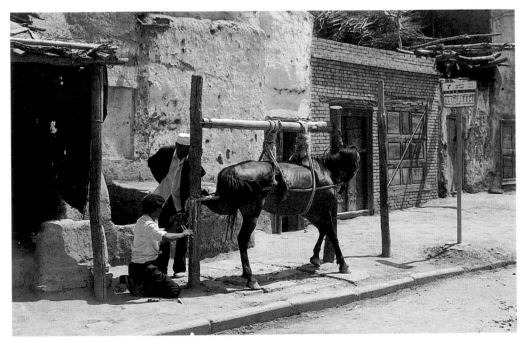

◀ Some horses hate being shod and refuse to keep still. As a result, blacksmiths in many parts of China rely on a harness capable of taming the wildest stallion.

the Wall disappeared into the dramatic sand dunes of the Mu Us Desert, patently inhospitable country. To our left the road made a wide dogleg to the west—safe, easy to follow and rather dull. We decided to risk it, cantered across the last mile or so of grass, and rode up across the sand into the dunes.

It was like being transported into the heart of the Sahara. The sand was surprisingly stable and once we stopped worrying about quicksands we began to enjoy ourselves and make good time. There were no other tracks of man or beast but, with the remains of the Wall running straight and true through shifting sand hills, we were unlikely to get lost. It was not even too hot to begin with, and right out in the middle we came on a pool of clear water from which both horses drank.

At the highest point in the dunes, a spot marked as being 4,648 feet on my US Airforce map, we saw ahead the remains of a large, square fort commanding a fantastic view in all directions. To our surprise there seemed to be a house built in it, and an old man was hoeing an unpromising piece of sandy garden nearby. He stopped work and came up into the fort to talk to us. The house proved to be a simple little square temple. We dismounted and entered, to be astounded by a large poster of a richly dressed man on a fine, white horse. We assumed that it was the Emperor Qin Shi Huangdi on the horse which, legend has it, showed the builders where to build the Wall, but what an unlikely place to come across it.

Next to it was a small brass Buddha, and below it a carved stone container in which incense sticks had been burned. The old man, when he saw our interest,

Louella riding Yin among the dunes of the Mu Us Desert, with the eroded remains of the Great Wall on one side. ▼

reverently brought out two more Buddhas, which were wrapped in cloth. He also produced a box of incense sticks, some matches and a candle. We each lit a stick from the candle, salaamed reverently to the Buddha and stood for a moment peacefully together as the scented smoke curled upwards. It was a totally unexpected moment of sheer enchantment. The old man must have been a monk who had escaped persecution and chosen to live far from the rest of mankind.

Next to the temple was a cosy cave house dug into the wall of the fort and beside it a pen for his animals. There were chickens and a family of large white rabbits, which had just had a litter of tiny, fluffy white babies. To complete the magic for me there were four choughs nesting in holes in the wall above. A tranquil place, miles from anywhere, on top of the world. The old man cordially invited us to stay and sup with him, but we thanked him and declined.

▲ The old man discovered by the author and Louella living in one of the Wall's ancient forts. He was probably a monk who fled here during the Cultural Revolution, when a great many monasteries and temples were forced to close.

As we crossed the border between Shaanxi and Ningxia we saw big salt lakes with piles of white salt being extracted. Yanchi was the first town in Ningxia, and as we rode in we found that Yang had cast one of his shoes and was going quite lame. We walked up the main street, with me leading Yang, and the inevitable crowd gathered round us. It was stiflingly hot, the crowd hemmed us in, leaving no air so that we felt claustrophobic, and it was depressing being unable to continue. We needed another blacksmith and it took an age to find one, while we waited with the horses tied to a telegraph pole. Beside us was the town bank and after a time the manager came out and kindly invited us in to rest, offering his premises as a haven from the crowd. We accepted gratefully and found it much cooler inside, sitting on the long wooden counter. Unfortunately the populace followed us in, and soon the crush and heat were as bad as before.

At last Yang's problem was sorted out and we were able to be on our way again. Now we were riding along beside a road. It was exactly what we had expected Ningxia to be like: a wide open country of shepherds grazing their flocks on poor grass growing in sandy soil. It was perfect riding country and there were even trees planted on either side of the road to give a dappled shade.

As we cantered merrily along a lorry approached, the driver as always tooting his horn and leaning out of the window to stare at us, while his companion whistled and ogled from his side. Seconds after they passed there was a loud bang and we looked back to see that the driver had been so captivated by the sight of us that he had driven straight into a tree. It was a large tree, and the lorry had snapped it in half. At the same time it had shed its load of crates and bottles. This poetic justice was beyond our greatest expectations. No one was hurt, but the mess was appalling and the loss of face acute. We snatched a couple of

Sheep graze contendedly on a plain in Ningxia province, while behind them rise barren, brown mountains. In such a landscape, it is difficult to remember that China is the world's most heavily populated country. ▶

photographs and cantered away. This being China, we were likely to be blamed for the accident if we lingered.

We stayed in a good mood for the rest of the afternoon, waving to shepherds as we passed, the only figures in the wide, rolling landscape except for occasional beekeepers. It was evening as we came to the hamlet of Niumaojing, where our crew had arranged an excellent camp site: a roadmenders' compound, which was clean, with a deep well from which pure, cold water was drawn for us and for the horses. The horses had a sandy enclosure under some trees and plenty of chopped straw, as well as their maize and black beans. We had been unable to obtain bran but they seemed content, if rather prone to wind, on this diet.

After supper we went for a starlit walk out into the desert beyond the walls of our compound. The cluster of flat-roofed mud houses lay in the centre of a great bowl of space with a horizon that stretched right round; it was like being at sea. A single tree was silhouetted against the paler western sky and there was absolute peace and quiet. It was cool and serene under the stars, all was well and

we had a comfortable mattress and warm sleeping-bags waiting for us, lit by the romantic glow of a kerosene lamp. We felt a sense of great contentment that we were achieving what we had set out to do.

Along the Edge of the Desert

The tranquillity of awakening to a cool, clear morning with no loudspeaker sent us off in a happy mood. The roadworkers were friendly and proud to have entertained us, though in truth it was we who had entertained them with our strange ways. The high point of our performance had been when I pumped up our inflatable mattress. The whole community of a dozen or so watched entranced and speculated on what on earth it could be for. Laid on a concrete floor it made all the difference between sound sleep and aching bones and we found it well worth the effort.

We cantered away waving farewell. Our route was unmistakable, as the only road and the Wall both stretched away to the northwest as far as the eye could see. A dangerous euphoria overcame us as we sped hand in hand over the surface of gently undulating grassland. We felt confident that nothing could now go wrong. Of course, it immediately did.

As we were at our most ecstatic and irresponsible, urging our horses faster, we plunged side by side into an invisible quicksand. Louella was pitched right over Yin's head and we were both immediately struggling to drag the horses clear before they sank in too deeply to be able to scramble out. The morass was caused by water from an apparently dry streambed, which had seeped under the sand to create a trap. Fortunately the surrounding land was firm and we were soon safe, but both Louella, who had knocked her ankle, and Yin were lame for some time.

It was a day of following a long, straight, empty road across featureless country, enlivened only by a series of quite unpleasant dust storms. Fortunately the wind was from the east and so in our backs, which made things more bearable, but the grit swirled into our eyes, noses and mouths, while the surface of the ground was a constantly shifting film of eddying, wind-blown sand and dust. There was a kind of tumbleweed, too, which blew past us, adding to the sense of desolation. In spite of the poor visibility in the storms, when it was like being in a thick fog, we were never in danger of being lost as there were almost always rows of poplars planted along both sides of the road.

In between the storms we could see that the ground was carpeted in places with pink and white convolvulus or perhaps a type of morning glory. Other wild flowers stood out among the sedges and the tamarisk. Several seemed to be

The Perils of Quicksand

DESERT TRAVELLERS have always had to be on their guard against one of Nature's cruellest disguises—a patch of sand that looks like any other, but which behaves like a viscous liquid, engulfing the unwary person or animal that blunders into it. This is quicksand—a bed of waterlogged sand that can be anything up to several yards deep.

Quicksand forms when a subterranean layer of clay or rock prevents water from fully draining away. Instead, the water remains just below the surface of the ground, saturating a layer of sand and giving it the properties of a dense fluid. To make matters worse, a thin, dry crust often forms on top, further disguising the morass lurking underneath. This process can happen almost anywhere that sand and water occur: in the middle of a desert, long after rains have passed, beside a quiet stream, and even on a beautiful golden beach.

Quicksand is often lethal for animals, largely because they panic and struggle to free themselves. Yet with each desperate tug on their trapped limbs, these unlucky creatures merely speed their own doom.

◀ In this lurid 19th-century depiction of the perils of quicksand, an unhappy traveller sinks away to a gruesome fate.

This is because quicksand flows very slowly and has to be given time to fill the space left when something is pulled out of it. An impatient heave merely creates a vacuum, which sucks back with equal, and eventually exhausting, force. Victims are therefore swallowed up as a result of their own exertions—though to an observer the sands may seem disconcertingly animated; hence the name *quicksand*, deriving from the old sense of *quick*, meaning 'living' or 'alive'.

Fortunately, quicksand is not nearly as dangerous as popular fiction writers have made it out to be. The density of quicksand is greater than that of a living body, which can therefore float on it, exactly as a log floats on water. Experts advise victims to fall gently on their backs and spread their weight as widely as possible; then to extricate any trapped limbs with infinite patience, and eventually to roll to safety.

members of the pea family, with both yellow and red flowers like snapdragons and small curled leaves to resist the extremes of temperature found in those northern deserts. Others had spiky leaves and yellow flowers, making them look like gorse or broom. There were purple, yellow and white daisies, pale anemones and a delightful, small white flower with a yellow centre, which we recognised from our garden at home in Cornwall. We also saw for the first time the rare red willow of Ningxia. At this season only the stems were red but in the autumn the leaves also turn. Hares were quite common, springing up under our feet and bounding away.

For hour after hour we trudged on, Yin refusing to move from time to time so that Louella would have to lead him. At last we reached our rendezvous, a straggle of poor homesteads on a blighted wasteland. Our minibus was nowhere to be seen and the people, not having been warned of our arrival and understandably fearing that we might be robbers, turned their dogs on us. We were too tired to try to explain and instead huddled behind a low wall out of the worst of the wind and driving grit while we waited.

When our team did turn up they were cheerful, having secured another excellent billet for us, once again in a roadmenders' compound a few miles further on beside the village of Dongwa.

The population here were Muslim and very relaxed and friendly. The disadvantage of all this goodwill was that they hated to be parted from us and burst into our quarter—a simple bare cell furnished with two iron bedsteads. On these they sat and watched in rapt attention as we washed ourselves and our socks, cleaned our cameras and wrote up our notes. They were so amiable that we could not object to them curiously handling our possessions, trying on our watches and looking through our books and photographs. But when they spat with great deliberation and no less volume on the floor beside our beds, it was harder not to ask them to leave and in the end we did so. Our team slept cheerfully on the ping-pong table with which this well-equipped compound was provided, and they were up and ready early in the morning. 'Laziness is the enemy of us all,' said Mr Li.

Our hardest day now lay ahead. The road made a big detour to the south via Lingwu, crossing the Yellow River (known in China as the Huang He) by the only bridge for many miles before turning north again for Yinchuan, the capital of Ningxia. We planned to cut across country marked as empty on the map, following the Wall to a point on the Yellow River where we understood there was a ferry.

The horses seemed sluggish. Worse, Yang set off dead lame. I thought we would have to postpone this potentially dangerous stretch for a day, until I found a stone lodged in his hoof. With this removed he was fine and Yin became the problem, lagging behind and exhausting Louella as she constantly had to urge him on. For the first hour a kindly man on a bicycle insisted on showing us the way across a trackless waste until we were in sight of the Wall again. Here, he reluctantly left us. How could we go wrong? There was the Wall on the skyline, its watchtowers stretching to the west, where the Yellow River lay some thirty miles away. All we had to do was follow it.

▲ Colourful flowers and their attendant butterflies become all the more spectacular in an arid, desert setting.

▲ The Gobi Desert—where the ferocity of the climate has reduced a substantial river to a mere trickle of water in a valley of parched sand.

We rode all the way to the Wall, finding ourselves in one of the most dramatic pieces of country imaginable. A meandering dry riverbed, with occasional pools of water where a horse might drink, lay beneath sheer sand cliffs. A steep path down through patches of sagebrush led us to the floor of a canyon where we dismounted to give the horses a rest. It was still and windless, a romantic place which we could be fairly certain no European had ever seen before. Knowing this is one of the minor pleasures of travel in remote places.

High above us clear remains of the Wall teetered on the edge of the cliff. Much had been washed away but enough remained to impress us once again with the incredible scale of the operation. To build, without any stone, a wall which would still be there 500 years later must have demanded a vast amount of labour.

Onwards to the Yellow River

Our problems began when we tried to follow the canyon downstream to the west. The Wall was on the northern side and the cliffs there were far too steep to attempt. While it looked as though it might go fairly straight, the riverbed curved and meandered like a snake, so that our distance would be doubled if we tried to follow it. Up on the plateau we should be able, we thought, to go in a straight line towards the Yellow River, and so with luck arrive that day.

Unfortunately, once we had climbed up again we found that what appeared to be a level plain was networked with impassable gullies which were invisible until we were on them. Time and again we headed for a fort marking a point on the Wall far ahead, only to be stopped after a few hundred yards and forced to make a wide detour to the south. We were becoming frustrated and rather desperate, when we came on a mule pulling a little cart, in which sat a smiling elderly couple, the woman with a red shawl over her head. The man was intelligent and kind. 'Huang He,' we said, pointing towards where the Yellow River lay. '*Women yao qu* Shiba *he* Yinchuan.' ('We want to go to Shiba [where the ferry crossed] and

Yinchuan.') He shook his head and climbed down to draw a map in the sand. We must go back, he indicated, and pick up a cart track which avoided the canyon.

Now we made better time, cantering through herds of donkeys, which we thought at first were wild until we spotted shepherds watching over them. Once the small distant figures proved to be two very small boys of about five years old. If we had been in danger of feeling that we were pretty tough to be travelling in such a wild and inhospitable place, the sight of those two little mites resolutely rounding up their wandering flock soon put things in perspective.

From the top of the plateau we could see the contrast this particular stretch of country presented. To our left was the great plain of central Ningxia, brushed with the green of thin grass in parts, relatively fertile, watered by occasional streams. To our right, beyond the river canyon and the Wall, lay Inner Mongolia, yellow with sand dunes, barren of all life. The Wall here really did seem to mark the edge of civilisation. Inner Mongolia, where we were not allowed to venture, looked dreadfully hard country. The few houses we saw had been abandoned and there were seldom signs of modern man attempting to cultivate the land. What we did see were traces of past occupation. There were dried-up canals and aque-

ducts, ruined garrisons for the troops defending the Wall, and bare, long-abandoned fields. Once we found ourselves riding along an ancient brick road which could have been Inca or Roman, but was, in fact, Ming.

There were flocks of choughs here, too, wheeling and tumbling above our heads, and nesting in holes in the Wall. Also, there were several varieties of hawk hunting over the plain. The smallest had scimitar wings like a peregrine and sped low over the ground. Another sort would hover briefly before stooping on its prey.

Unexpectedly, after we had been riding for some hours, we followed a track which led to the edge of the main river canyon and there came on a totally different scene. Below us the minimal flow of water in the riverbed had been channelled and gathered to create a fertile oasis. Lush grass grew, tall poplars lined neat square fields where bright green wheat grew tall, and a low dam had been built to make a small lake. There was a mud village built into the side of the gorge, its street silent as everyone was working in the fields. Crossing the valley at a point where the stream trickled busily over pebbles, we stopped to cool the horses' heels. We sensed they were near to giving up.

For a time we were able to ride along the bottom of the canyon again, where there was flat, level sand and a few grassy meadows. We passed traces of a series of abandoned dams, showing that the valley must once have been fertile and well populated. The troops guarding the Wall would have welcomed the back-up of a farming community to supply them with fresh produce. For a time, after we had

▲ Some of the desert's most efficient predators are birds of prey—such as this splendid goshawk perching on the hand of an Uigur falconer.

been forced out of the riverbed when the going became difficult, we were able to ride along a shelf between the Wall and the cliff dropping down to the river. Once we crossed through a gap in the Wall to ride briefly into Inner Mongolia.

From time to time the Wall and river separated and the terrain between them became impassable. Then we had to use the compass to work out the best route. It was spectacular country, through which we would have liked to dawdle, but the horses were tired and the Yellow River still far ahead. When Yang lost his shoe again and became quite lame, we began to be worried if we would make it. On the hard surface of the plateau he suffered. And this was the moment when we had to leave the river and head across the plain to our destination.

Both of us were now on foot most of the time, Louella dragging a reluctant Yin and exhausted by the effort. She hated herself for having to be beastly to him, was cross at constantly lagging behind and having to hurry to catch up, and obstinately determined to deal with the problem herself and not ask me to help. I was worried too about Yang, who became exaggeratedly lame when we mounted to canter across open stretches of good ground. The bleak plain seemed interminable. When we came over yet another low ridge, only to be faced by another stony waste with no sign of our goal, Louella burst into tears for the only time on the whole journey. We sat down, treated ourselves to a couple of slices of dried mango and some Marie biscuits and decided to swap horses, since we were both so fed up with our own mounts. Surprisingly it worked. Yang, with Louella's lesser weight, cheered up and stopped limping. Yin responded well to my fresher heels and right arm so that for a time he kept up. We began to suspect that they might have been putting on a bit of an act.

We came over a final ridge and there, far below us, across a gently sloping stretch of desert, lay the Yellow River. We fairly rollicked down to it to find our minibus and crew waiting by the little ferry. The Yellow River was wide, turgid and full of silt. The water, like that of China's other great river, the Yangtze, starts in the melting snow of the high mountains of Qinghai province, bordering Tibet. As the Yellow River passes through the loess plains it collects thirty times as much silt as the Nile, although it is about 750 miles shorter. It has been the cause of endless flooding through the centuries, so that it has been given the name 'China's Sorrow'. Several times it has drowned a million people at a time through natural disasters or the actions, sometimes deliberate, of man.

Far downstream in Henan province the peasants regularly build higher dykes, so that today the water is in places as much as twenty-three feet above the surrounding fertile plain. When the banks burst in a flood, disaster follows over a wide area. In 1938 Chiang Kai-shek had the dykes blown up in order to halt the Japanese army's advance. A million peasants drowned and another eleven million were made homeless and starved. After that, it was hardly surprising that the people chose the Communists in preference to him.

We walked the horses onto the ferry behind a gravel lorry and our minibus, and we chugged off into midstream. There we hit a sandbank and were stuck for a time as the current swirled us round and boys with poles tried to push us off. This gave us a good chance to see the dramatic contrast between the two banks

◀ Huang He, the Yellow River, snakes through Ningxia province on its incredible journey from the Tibetan Plateau to the Bo Hai sea—a distance of some 3,400 miles.

of the river. Behind us, all was yellow and pale brown desert and bare hillside. The Wall came proudly through this barren land to stop abruptly at the water's edge. Ahead was a land of milk and honey, green from the irrigation of dozens of canals and well wooded.

The plucky little horses stood steadily through all the bumps and jolts of our crossing. Ashore, we rode them through some scrub country along the bank, with long grass and lots of trees, to a rough road leading to Yinchuan, the capital of the province, ten miles away. Now paddy fields stretched away on either side and it was as though the desert had never been. Here, thanks to the fertile alluvial soil and the network of canals, the finest rice in China is grown.

At the first village we reached we found the very model of accommodation for our tired and sore animals. A pretty little farmhouse had an enclosure for a mule next to it. Part was roofed over, the mule was friendly and there was plenty of room for two more occupants. Quantities of good green hay were stacked nearby and the young couple who lived there seemed to know about and like horses. They helped us unsaddle and rub them down before readily agreeing to feed and care for them for two or three days. They even said they would get the local blacksmith to come and check their feet and replace Yang's shoe. It all seemed too good to be true, but better was still to come. Mr Li had booked us into the best hotel in Yinchuan, grandly overriding the predictable objections that it was full and getting us a suite usually reserved for senior officials. We were in no mood to argue as we wallowed in a hot bath and washed all our clothes. The decor left a lot to be desired: plush, red, overstuffed armchairs with lace antimacassars, pink nylon pillows, a hideous patterned carpet and green walls, but it was luxury, and above all it was private.

Wearing bright silks and studded leather waistcoats, a pair of wrestlers concentrate intently on unbalancing each other.

For the Mongols of the plains, life has hardly changed over the centuries. Here, herders round up their sheep and horses. ▶

Horses, rather than cattle or sheep, provide the Mongols with milk—an essential component in the traditional herder's diet. ▼

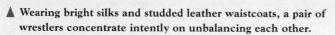

Genghis Khan is surely alive and well in the minds of these modern Mongols re-enacting the deeds of their ancestors.

◀ The life of a Mongol herder is notoriously tough, but it is not bereft of pleasure. Here, a number of families enjoy the music and dance provided by a group of travelling players.

The Mongols—Heroes and Horsemen

FEW EASTERN PEOPLES can have experienced such great swings of fortune as the Mongols. At the beginning of the 13th century they could hardly be called a nation: more a collection of scattered nomadic tribes led by petty warlords. But within a few decades they had united under the brilliant leadership of Genghis Khan to establish the greatest empire the world had ever known. By 1242, the Mongols had pushed south into China and westwards into Russia, Poland and Austria, until almost a third of the known world lay at their feet.

In 1279, Genghis's grandson, Kublai Khan, completed his family's conquest of China, but less than a century later the Mongols' power was on the wane, and in 1368 they were driven back across the frontier. Some 300 years on, they were themselves conquered by the Chinese and their territory was divided into two regions: Outer and Inner Mongolia. The

Winter on the Mongolian plains is long and harsh, with night-time temperatures dropping to lower than –30°F. ▶

former won its independence in 1921, only to become a virtual protectorate of Communist Russia, while the latter has remained a province of China—the country's fifth largest.

In both Mongolias, Communism has brought many changes to the inhabitants' traditional nomadic way of life. In Inner Mongolia, in particular, where Han Chinese migrants greatly outnumber the Mongols themselves, the authorities have

succeeded in forcing most of the populace to settle on farms or in towns. But in the great open plains of the region, many ancient customs have survived, often unchanged by the centuries: herdsmen and their families can still be found living in large, circular, portable, felt houses called yurts, and gathering with other families to enjoy open-air dances and traditional sports such as wrestling, archery and horse racing.

CHAPTER 7

Islamic Hospitality

▲ During the Song
dynasty, craftsmen
reached new heights in
the production of
ceramics, as this
exquisite glazed vase
from that period shows.

THERE ARE NINE VAST GROUPS of mausoleums spread across the desolate plain to the west of Yinchuan. No one lives there now and the eroded remains of the tombs are dotted about like big brown jelly moulds on the brown plain, with the brown Helan Shan mountains rising behind them.

We went out to look at them, simply driving our minibus off the road towards them until gullies stopped us going further, and then walking a mile or so up to the nearest group. Close to they were like the pyramids of Egypt, poignant in their solitude and silence. In the eleventh century a mysterious kingdom called the Western Xia was set up in what is now Ningxia. It lasted for 200 years, conquered a large part of northern China and gave the Song dynasty (AD 960–1279) a lot of trouble. The kingdom was finally obliterated by Genghis Khan, and the area named Ningxia, meaning 'Peaceful Xia'.

Very little is known about the Western Xia, but its first emperor was supposed to have had seventy-two tombs built to deceive grave robbers, as his remains were to be hidden in only one. Around these tombs were masses of shards of broken green, blue and white glazed tiles, which led us to believe that they must once have been roofed or coated. Perhaps they looked like mosques, with their very un-Chinese shapes. Nobody seemed to know, though one has been excavated and we saw later in the Yinchuan museum some nice carved stone horses and bronze bulls, as well as lots of complete tiles which had been saved.

Yinchuan means 'Silvery River', a name supposedly derived from the deposits of salt which are left behind on the land whenever it is flooded by the Yellow River. The region is also famous for the huge canals built by successive dynasties, the Han (206 BC–AD 220) and Tang (AD 618–907) canals being the main ones used today. Yinchuan itself is quite an attractive city, with some of its walls still standing and a bell tower in the centre. There are also two fine, tall pagodas. The 177-foot-high North Pagoda has bells hanging at the four corners of each tier. These are supposed to sound like the music of heaven when a breeze blows, but we were there on a still evening and heard nothing. It is a wonderfully elegant and light building and we were astonished at how well preserved it was. So many glorious treasures in China were destroyed during the Cultural Revolution, but the pagodas seem to have been spared. Perhaps they were too hard to knock down, or they may have been useful for displaying Big Character banners bearing political slogans.

In Yinchuan we suddenly found ourselves being treated as heroes. The local paper carried a picture and story about our arrival on its front page two days running, and a banquet was given in our honour. The day chosen was the end of Ramadan. As Ningxia is a Muslim province, this was regarded as a signal honour.

The occasion was to be hosted by the Chairman of the province, the equivalent of governor. Fifty years before, Peter Fleming had written that 'the death rate at banquets is appalling'. Although our expectations were not that gloomy, we did not imagine that the evening ahead of us would be great fun. We were wrong, although it started slowly. We were received in a large reception room with antimacassared armchairs all round the walls. Mr Hei Boli, the Chairman, and I sat at one end with his ministers next to him and Louella next to me. Like heads of state we each had our own interpreters behind us. While we made polite and formal remarks to each other, television cameras recorded the scene and photographers took pictures.

Hei Boli looked a nice, jolly man, but I found it difficult to sparkle as I was saving my best remarks for the speech I knew I would have to make at some point in the proceedings. Louella saved the day by leaning across me and asking him how many children he had. 'Seven,' was the answer. 'Why, you dirty old man,' she said. 'That's why everyone else in China is only allowed one now!'

There was a nervous moment as this was translated and we waited to see how he would take it. Then he roared with laughter and the general mood began to be more relaxed. Soon afterwards, his interpreter was translating some lighthearted remarks of his about how lots of children would contribute to the prosperity of

The Protecting Pagoda

Rising out of the ground like a gigantic petrified tree, or a bizarre skyscraper from another age, the pagoda is an essential element in the popular image of the traditional Chinese or Japanese landscape.

Yet the origins of the pagoda lie not in China, or even Japan, but in India. When Buddhist missionaries brought their religion to China in the 1st century AD, they also imported the notion of a stupa—a building for housing holy relics or scriptures, or for marking a sacred site. In India, such buildings are dome-shaped, but those that were built in China, and later Japan, evolved into a new design: inspired by the architecture of watchtowers, they became tall and narrow, stretching 15 storeys or more high.

Not all pagodas were built in the service of Buddhism, however: a great many were erected purely to ensure good fortune. According to the ancient Chinese system of *fengshui* (literally 'wind and water'), all buildings must be carefully located in order to ensure harmony between Man and Nature. But a well-placed pagoda could do more: it could exert protective powers. As a result, pagodas were often built on auspicious sites, such as hilltops, just outside towns to placate destructive spirits of nature and avert disasters such as earthquakes or floods.

The largest of the so-called Three Pagodas of Saintly Worship at Dali dates from the 9th century and stands some 226 feet high. ▶

his small province when he was, for a moment, lost for a word. In perfect English the Chairman said, 'The word you are looking for is "development".' 'But you speak English,' cried Louella. 'How wonderful!' 'Not for fifty years, I'm afraid, so I'm rather rusty.' After that there was no holding us all. He took a distinct shine to Louella, gallantly escorting her into the banqueting hall on his arm and swapping jokes all through the delicious feast which had been prepared.

There were triple-coloured eggs, chicken, cabbage with cherries, duck, whole fish, lotus fruits and a host of other delicacies. We also had a chance to sample three of the five 'Treasures of Ningxia'. *Facai* is an edible black moss, translated unromantically on the menu as 'black, hair-like vegetable'. The subtlety of its unique flavour was lost on us but we smacked our lips appreciatively. Easier to relish were the wolfberries, small, bright red, sweet, dried fruit, and the liquorice root, both of which are supposed to be powerful aphrodisiacs, or so the Chairman told Louella. He also managed to make her eat all of the four foods which, until then, she had baulked at in China. She had been very brave about eating whatever we were given, accepting in general terms my theory, which has seen me safely through many strange meals in odd parts of the world, that if the locals are eating it it is unlikely to do you any harm.

But she did still tend to reject certain items. I sympathised with her about sea slugs and 'tendon', although with the eyes closed both slipped down easily and the aftertaste was pleasant. Mushrooms and yoghurt were two peculiar dislikes which she

▲ The Chinese are experts in the art of food sculpture. Here, a peacock made entirely from vegetables graces an important banquet.

claimed to have had all her life. The charming Chairman offered her each of the first three on his own chopsticks and her prejudices melted in a flash. At the end of the meal ice-cold yoghurt was brought in stone jars. 'This is one of the great specialities of our region,' said the great man, and again she succumbed.

While this valuable flirtation was progressing, we were plied with local wine and toasted in *mao-tai*, the potent, colourless alcohol used only for this purpose. It is quite revolting and lethal, going straight to the legs. After half a dozen glasses the strongest find it hard to stand up. I had to do so towards the end of the meal, long after I had lost count, in order to make my speech. I said how honoured we were to be the first foreigners for fifty years to be allowed to arrive in Ningxia by horse. This produced a satisfactory round of applause. I then got thoroughly confused commenting on the three Treasures of Ningxia we had tasted, but had more success when I outlined my own special interest in the fourth—the famous, soft, long-stapled lamb's wool from the Ningxia tanyang sheep. As a sheep farmer myself at home I could appreciate the fine quality of this and said that perhaps we could do business together one day. This was not such a far-fetched idea as it must have sounded at the time, as my farming partner and I had plans to start the first stud in Britain of Angora goats, whose fine mohair is of even better quality.

The fifth Treasure of Ningxia is the special stone from the Helan Shan mountains which is considered the best in China for making ink blocks, an essential part of traditional writing and painting. I had nothing useful to say about that, although we had been round an exhibition of them that morning and were aware how highly prized they were by the Chinese.

I presented Hei Boli with a copy of my French book and promised to send him a copy of the one I intended to write about China. In return we were given a book about Ningxia and two fine, scented medals, with the white horse symbol of Chinese tourism on one side and a map of Ningxia on the other. They were impregnated with a really strong aroma of ladies' talcum powder, which the Chairman said would last for at least two years.

▲ Traditional tools for the Chinese arts of printing and calligraphy: a bowl for dissolving solid ink in water (left), an ink block made of stone, and a large brush for mixing the ink to the correct consistency on the block.

By the time the evening ended we were all bosom friends and barely able to stand. Anglo-Ningxian friendship had been toasted to death, Louella had shown the Chairman pictures of all our children and we had taken Polaroid pictures of each other. We did feel very honoured as we staggered up to our room.

The next day the Director of Foreign Affairs and the Director of the General Office of the Ningxia People's Government, the two senior officials at the dinner after the Chairman, arrived bearing two huge bunches of red roses from Hei Boli to Louella. There was also a charming letter from him wishing us a successful completion of our journey. In it he said, 'Your visit has left a memorable impression on us,' and he praised us for 'the brilliant contribution you have made to the friendly relations between China and Britain'.

We went back to the farm to find that the horses had been well looked after. The blacksmith had been to sort out Yang's feet and after four days' rest they both seemed quite a bit stronger. Crossing back over the Yellow River on the ferry, we spent the day gently exploring the countryside. At midday, Mr He prepared an outstanding feast which he laid out in a sheltered spot out of the wind. Unfortunately, none of us was able to do justice to it due to the great midday heat, and afterwards we lay panting and sweating in the sun. Cold drinks would have been nice, but such luxuries are not yet part of the Chinese picnic scene. Even persuading the dining room in the hotel in Yinchuan to put a couple of bottles of orange in their kitchen refrigerator for the evening was a major battle.

Before leaving our pretty picnic site we cleared up all the rubbish and put it in bags to take home. The concept of litter being a bad thing had, we found, been omitted from the Chinese rules of correct behaviour. Even educated and otherwise quite sensitive officials we met chose to smash empty beer bottles against rocks rather than keep them; we never succeeded in training our own crew not to do this, although they tended to do it out of our sight.

In the cool of the evening we rode back along the riverbank towards the ferry. This led us past the attractive walled village of Shiba. The walls must have once enclosed a large fort, and indeed this must have been a vital strategic place. Perhaps it was the very spot where Genghis Khan reached the Wall to bring about the destruction of the Western Xia kingdom. Now there were just a few houses inside the fortifications, with generous gardens and vegetable patches. The great river ran past just outside the walls, leaving a narrow strip of land along which we could ride, looking into the village through gateways. Beyond there was a brilliant green stretch of water meadow where a few donkeys and cows grazed peacefully in the sunset. It was a pastoral scene of great beauty. Half-a-dozen wild ducks flew up as we cantered past their hidden reedbed and large hares bounded off into the desert from which they had come to nibble the rare lushness.

▲ Musicians dressed in costumes of the Tang dynasty give a concert on traditional instruments.

On our last night in Yinchuan a concert of folk dancing and music was laid on for our benefit in the hotel theatre. There was an excellent eighteen-man orchestra playing an extraordinary collection of Chinese traditional instruments. As well as familiar mandolins and double basses, the string section had peculiar long-stemmed fiddles with oddly shaped sound boxes, from which a noise like a Swanee whistle was produced. There were also various wind instruments, mouth organs and flutes, including some with multiple bamboo tubes, on which virtuoso solos were executed. Brilliant, tiny children performed astonishing acrobatic contortions and there was a troupe of mature local dancers, the boys behaving in a camp way which would have brought the house down in Europe but seemed not to shock the audience. The singers were very popular, belting out what sounded like Chinese versions of Gilbert and Sullivan. The compere was a girl in blue velvet with a bunch of yellow chicken feathers at her bosom, who introduced each act in a demure singsong. At the end we were invited up onto the stage to shake the cast by the hand and share in the plaudits of the audience.

Back on the Road

Next day we rode off past Yinchuan's smaller version of the Tiananmen—the Gate of Heavenly Peace—at the entrance to the Forbidden City in Beijing, and then south along the Huang Canal, one of the network of canals irrigating the plain south of Yinchuan. It had a good and uninterrupted towpath, so we had a peaceful day together in refreshingly cool and pleasant surroundings. The packed earth of the towpath was an ideal riding surface and there were mature poplars between us and the water all the way.

Canals are always relaxing to ride along after the frustrations and hazards of cross-country travel. There are no hills or gullies and it is impossible to get lost. There is also usually a lot of wildlife attracted by the water. That day I saw, for the only time in my life, flocks of hoopoes. They are usually rather shy and solitary birds, seldom seen in more than twos or threes, but here they were all over the place. With their black-tipped orange crests, like South American Indian head-dresses, and their moth-like flight, they are the most exotic of birds, and they are surrounded with legends and superstition. In the Middle Ages, adding parts of them to witch's brews was said to restore eyesight and loss of memory. Like pork and shellfish they were proscribed as unclean food in the Old Testament, probably because of their filthy nesting habits—they do not clean out their nests, which become very smelly—and they even appear in ancient Egyptian tomb paintings. We had them for company all day.

Flocks of Ningxia sheep were driven alongside the canal to graze its banks. There were also tree frogs, calling noisily and invisibly from the leaves above us, as well as their terrestrial cousins, sounding like a dawn chorus in the paddy fields. These stretched away on either side of the canal, the groves of silvery poplars dividing the fields reflected in the still flood waters. Now we were for a while in the more familiar countryside of China, where peasants planted and weeded rice up to their knees in water, shaded by wide, conical straw hats. It was a colourful scene, as the women wore bright red, blue and green woollen head-scarves and vivid red shirts that stood out among the usual drab clothes. There were also small patches of a brilliant blue-flowering crop which we took to be flax for linseed oil. These were often covered by a cloud of hovering white butterflies which made a pretty sight. So too did the yellow water lilies in the canal, which, it seemed, was purely for irrigation, as we saw no boats on the water.

◀ **Yinchuan's small-scale version of Beijing's famous Tiananmen—the Gate of Heavenly Peace.**

We lodged the horses that night at the veterinary department of the Ningxia Agricultural College at Yongning. There were two young English teachers there, on Voluntary Service Overseas, whom we had been told about by the embassy in Beijing. Theirs was a lonely life. There were no other foreigners in Yongning and only two Americans and a German couple in the whole province. The authorities in the region were especially sensitive to the possibility of spies, probably because of the fear we heard expressed all along the Wall of invasion from the north by the Russians. It seemed likely that the Helan Shan mountains, which guard Ningxia's northern border and whose name, incidentally, means 'Horse Mountains' in Mongolian, were heavily defended. We had hoped to ride that way but had been firmly refused. A Canadian couple, who had innocently broken down near the ancient Western Xia tombs at the foot of these mountains, had been the cause of a major anti-foreigner scare. As a result, no Chinese were allowed to invite the teachers into their home for a meal, and their movements were strictly controlled. Nonetheless they said they enjoyed teaching at the college, found the students eager to learn and planned to extend their stay.

We were glad to meet the resident vet at the college as we were becoming very worried about our horses. Yin was now lame most of the time, and Yang had started to develop an extremely unpleasant saddle sore on his withers. This I had treated with an antiseptic spray I had brought from England, and a clean lint dressing, which I changed each day. But it was a nasty sight and I was beginning to wonder if it was fair to make him carry on, although it did not seem to hurt him. The vet was reassuring, saying that the horses should make it to our destination near the border of Gansu, but when he looked at their teeth he confirmed our suspicion that they were much older than the rogue horse trader in Zhengjingbu had told us. Yin was, he said, well into his teens, probably sixteen, and Yang only

a year or two younger. This was an added worry, not least because it would make them even harder to sell.

We carried on south and west across Ningxia towards Zhongwei, which was as far as we were to be allowed to ride on this stage. From there we would have to go by train until permitted to mount up for the final stretch.

Much of the time now we were unable to avoid the long, straight roads of China. At least they had good soft verges for the mule and donkey carts, which still greatly outnumbered the heavy lorries thundering past; but much of the time the scenery became monotonous and we needed distractions. When conversation flagged and we found ourselves riding in silence, we rather shamefacedly dug out our Sony Walkmans, placed them in our saddlebags and plugged ourselves in. It was extraordinary what a difference Mozart made to my spirits. Instead of slouching along thinking about my own aches and pains, while worrying about Yang's increasing reluctance to move, I happily conducted away, humming loudly to myself. Louella bopped along to her own collection of pop music. This made the Chinese stare at us a little more intently as we passed, and some now even smiled in sympathy. If you look happy enough, even the most dour of people are usually forced to look happy back.

There was a nice moment when, on the outskirts of a small town, we passed two telephone engineers, with headphones on, poring over a box of coloured wires at the foot of a telegraph pole. I grinned at them, pointed at my own ear-phones and asked, 'Good stuff on your set, too, is it?' Even in English my meaning was unmistakable and they laughed heartily. Moments like that bridged the cultural barrier that tends to surround all foreigners in China, and compensated for all the utterly blank stares.

We were riding parallel with the Yellow River and occasionally one or other of the canals came close to the road and we could follow a towpath again for a while. At midday we were able to rendezvous with our crew and share a better picnic than we could carry with us. It was always a huge relief to flop down on the grass and stretch out for a time, while the horses grazed and the sunshine dried their sweaty backs. We swapped saddles, as Louella's had a higher bridge which rubbed Yang's sore less. We were by now both so hardened to sitting in a saddle all day ourselves that we hardly noticed the difference, although we would probably both have objected to the idea at home.

A Downpour of Frogs

At night from now on we stayed in transport compounds. These were where lorry drivers and muleteers stopped overnight. The accommodation was extremely basic, but there was no need to put our tent up as we were always given a couple of bare, cell-like rooms, in one of which Mr He would prepare our supper. As always, the loos were the worst part, the smell hitting us as we rode through the entrance and the flies buzzing excitedly around identifying their location. Being on or near roads all day made it harder to find convenient lonely patches of scrub to visit, with the result that we became scatologically preoccupied. It is a long-standing preoccupation of foreigners in China. In 1793 John

Barrow, the virtual founder of the Royal Geographical Society, complained, 'There is not a watercloset nor a decent place of retirement in all China.'

One evening, Mr He revealed a new and most welcome talent when I complained of a stiff back. Firmly laying me down on one of the hard beds he gave me a wonderfully strong and confident massage, manipulating my limbs painfully but effectively. How could we complain of discomfort when we had not only our own cook but also a personal masseur?

There was a noisy game which some of the rough customers staying in these lodgings played at meals and during the evenings. It was a variation of 'scissors, paper, stone', but done with fingers extended and numbers barked out in a crescendo of shouts and counter-shouts, which became confused and deafening. There seldom seemed to be an actual winner, just one player who outshouted the others, although we gathered that it all depended on quick mathematical reflexes, so that the players never shouted numbers which, added to the previous one, made ten. The background noise of these games, the constant stream of the curious coming to peer through the barred window of our cell, like visitors to the zoo, and the smell coming from across the courtyard were the only minor inconveniences we found. Certainly there was no danger to travel in China. Surprisingly, and thankfully under the circumstances, we neither of us ever suffered from a single upset tummy, in spite of all the strange and certainly unhygienic food we ate; another tribute to Mr He's skills in the kitchen.

Just south of the town of Qingtongxia we stayed in a small place called Lixin, close enough to the Yellow River for us to take a stroll along its banks after supper. The massive quantity of water was controlled here by a series of sluice gates, through which it churned frighteningly. Canals led off, taking foaming torrents at high speed into the countryside. Upstream was a huge dam which controlled and tamed the river, preventing at least in this region the floods for which the river is notorious. It also supplied the energy for an industrial area, the chimneys and gaunt buildings of which we could see all around us.

Next morning it was raining as we rode out in the early hours through this forbidding landscape. I think I have never seen a more terrible prospect, making me think of the ugliness of Britain's own industrial revolution in the nineteenth century. The smoke belching from the innumerable factories coated the ground and filled the air with noxious substances. The air was gritty and there was a strong smell of sulphur. We tied handkerchiefs over our faces, feeling like bandits in our waterproof capes and funny hats, and we rode through glum crowds of workers trudging or cycling dutifully to their toil. At the edge of the factory complex we were greeted by another totally unprepossessing view: a bleak countryside crisscrossed with

A spontaneous card game on the street attracts a large crowd of spectators. The Chinese love playing games, many of which are thousands of years old. ▼

◄ Children and adults
alike watch entranced as
itinerant performers in
elaborate costumes enact
a scene from a folk opera.

giant pylons leading to generating stations. The grit was so pervasive and painful here that for a time we had to ride with our eyes closed, trusting the horses to follow the road.

After a few miles of scorched earth and industrial nightmare, we noticed some adobe walls and the remains of ancient buildings among the pylons. Could these be outlying watchtowers from the Wall in this unlikely setting? The theory was proved soon afterwards by the sight of a line of towers clearly marking a section of Wall along a ridge far to our right. It was good to feel we were back with the Wall again, and from then on it kept us intermittent company. One section, which came close to the road, was made of stone; not fine-cut blocks as at the Wall's start, but definitely stone rather than mud bricks.

The main railway line also joined us for a time, and we had the pleasure of watching a succession of handsome great steam locomotives pulling strings of goods wagons past. Gradually the soil improved and we rode through an assortment of villages surrounded by irrigated land. Here we would usually give away one or two of our handouts to people who came out of their houses to watch us. We felt that the more people who knew what we were doing, the more likely we were to get help if we should need it. Sometimes a whole school would come pouring out into the road and we would be surrounded by little children.

Once we overtook a group of young men walking along the road with sacks on their shoulders and two performing monkeys on leads. They must have been a group of strolling players who went from village to village putting on entertainments. They would certainly not have been allowed to earn their living this way during the Cultural Revolution.

We also passed a very serious bicycle race, with the military in charge using official jeeps. Important men in uniform were sending off four-man teams of bicyclists in shorts and crash helmets of different colours, who pedalled furiously into the distance to reappear still going at the same speed half an hour later. Some of the teams were friendly and waved to us, but most were too preoccupied with the effort of pedalling, and for once we were largely ignored by participants and spectators alike. We almost felt slighted not to be the centre of attention.

Much more satisfactory was the occasion when a smartly dressed official in a rare black limousine travelling down the main road stopped ahead of us to take our picture. An ordinary peasant cyclist riding past us was so taken by the sight that he continued to look at us over his shoulder, ran straight into the photographer and they both tumbled into the ditch in a heap.

With irrigation and cultivated fields the bird life increased. There were still lots of hoopoes with their exotic crests, but these were now joined by terns, which dived into the flooded paddy fields to catch small fish, and once we saw a refreshingly English moorhen paddling about. There were swallows as well as sand martins nesting in a cliff, more crested larks, cuckoos, feral pigeons and quantities of sparrows in the roadside trees. There was also a plague of frogs one day; we found ourselves riding through shoals of baby ones hopping across the road. It would have been easy to believe that they had dropped out of the sky in the shower of rain we had just had, and I almost convinced Louella that this was the case; after all, such events are spoken of in the Bible. But when they continued to hop out of the wet fields at the side she realised I was teasing.

People in Ningxia were noticeably more friendly than they had been in Hebei. Often a family, riding together on one bicycle or piled into a diminutive donkey cart, would ride with us for a few miles, chatting amiably about the handout we had given them. Although our conversation was still extremely limited, this never mattered. Ice-cream girls were plentiful and the time passed pleasantly.

On the last day Yin began to cast a shoe and at our midday stop we asked if there were a blacksmith nearby. None could be found; so I removed the loose nails and tried to hammer in two of the spare nails we had with us. I was hampered by not having a proper hammer, only a piece of iron pipe, and I am always nervous of doing more harm than good at such moments. In the end an old man in the crowd, watching my efforts, took the pipe from me and did it firmly and efficiently. He seemed more than happy with a Polaroid picture of himself as payment.

▲ The hoopoe, with its distinctive barred plumage and black-tipped orange 'headdress'.

Interlude at Zhongwei

Four days' hard riding from Yinchuan had brought us to Zhongwei—a strongly Muslim town with a thriving mosque. The imam wore dark glasses and a turban, and had a long grey beard. He and all the elders, both male and female, were extremely friendly. Although Islam seems to have fared better than other religions during the Cultural Revolution, it was still a very bad time and perhaps that was why they were so uncharacteristically welcoming to infidels. There

◄ All aboard: an entire family has managed to balance on one bicycle. Judging by their relaxed expressions, they must be accustomed to this precarious mode of travel.

were, we were told, 1,800 mosques in Ningxia, or the Ningxia Hui Autonomous Region, to give the province its full name. The Hui are the descendants of traders from the Middle East who married Chinese women and settled down in northwest China. They now form one of the major nationalities of China, together with the Hans, the Tibetans, the Manchus, the Zhuang and the Uigars. Most of them are Muslims and about a fifth of them live in Ningxia.

The elders had wonderful faces: the men bearded and hawk-nosed, the women wearing white coifs over their heads like nuns, framing beautifully lined features which crinkled into the most amiable expressions imaginable.

After tying our horses up in the courtyard of the mosque we were led into the bathhouse, where water was ceremoniously poured over our hands from fine brass pitchers. The building provided a perfect example of how the pride and reverence which were beaten out of most of the population during the Cultural Revolution are needed in such simple things as making a bathroom pleasant. Instead of peeling walls, chipped receptacles and a nasty smell, everything was pristine. A fine advertisement for religion and one of the most sensible aspects of Islam: the active association of cleanliness with godliness.

We were entertained in the imam's quarters, which led off the mosque court-yard. There, seated in comfort, we had sweetmeats pressed on us and were urged to eat our fill.

Taoist monks perform the rituals of their faith to an accompaniment of cymbals, a drum and a huge, ornate bell. ▶

The mosque itself was a plain but handsome modern structure, unlike the incredible Buddhist temple we also visited at Zhongwei. That was an astonishing, romantic building of high galleries, towers, turrets and upturned eaves, like a wooden fairytale castle. We rode up and tied our horses to two trees outside the walls. There, an old monk greeted us and led us in to see the main statue of Buddha, where we lit joss sticks and salaamed politely.

We were able to wander through the inner courts, up flights of steps to high terraces, and see the careful restoration work that was being undertaken. The paintwork on the red pillars and ceilings was being patched up where it had flaked and a man was modelling a clay figurine of a devil guardian in a side pavilion. The temple is called Gao Miao and is unusual in that it represents three different religions. Over an archway is a sign which reads: 'At this place Confucianism, Buddhism and Taoism release souls from purgatory. Within these confines nature and man cultivate themselves.'

This admirably ecumenical sentiment disguises the fact that the religions of China have always been something of a blend. Confucianism is as much a political philosophy based on the virtue of education as it is a religion. As a code of behaviour it rejects the supernatural, concentrating instead on a stable social order. Buddhism was introduced from India and gradually changed as it absorbed local superstitions and traditional beliefs, especially those of Taoism, the only truly indigenous Chinese religion.

At the heart of Taoism lies the desire to merge with nature. *Wu wei*, meaning 'do nothing', is its motto—the concept that action comes from inaction, like water dripping on a stone. Beginning to understand this helps the foreigner in

China to cope with the frustrations of the instant *mei you!* and the bureaucratic genius for prevarication.

Our horses were at first lodged in a coalyard on the edge of Zhongwei. We had to sweep the ground and remove some broken bottles so that they could lie down, but we managed to obtain some straw and there was shelter, so that they were not too badly off. The black beans and maize on which we had been feeding them had to be thoroughly washed to remove the dust, and they were still eating well, but their condition was beginning to deteriorate rather; Yin too was now developing a saddle sore, while Yang stumbled frequently.

After a few days' rest, we rode them through the centre of the town, past the inevitable bell tower and out the other side. A lane through pleasant, mud-walled villages led us to the edge of a wide, shallow lagoon beside the Yellow River. It was one of the most beautiful places we were to see in China, an idyllic scene of rural peace and prosperity. There were no intrusive overhead wires and pylons, nor any modern buildings. Against a backcloth of rugged mountains across the river and a fringe of trees along its bank, a fisherman was paddling a raft made from inflated sheepskins. These craft are still used as the main form of local transport on the river, for fishing, crossing, carrying loads, cutting weed and for finding the famous *facai*, the edible black moss, which is gathered at night because it vanishes by day. We tried one out for ourselves. The skins are blown up like balloons through one of the legs, until the other legs and the tied-off neck and rear end stick out obscenely. A dozen or so are then attached to a light-weight frame made of poles and the whole thing is dropped on the water where it floats well enough to carry two or three people for some hours. Propulsion is quite easy, using a paddle dipped over the front from a kneeling position.

Next to the lagoon was a pretty farmhouse with a courtyard and outbuildings where the farmer said we could leave our horses in a fine stable. He and his family were hospitable and cheerful, and after feeding and grooming the horses, seeing to their feet and drawing water from the hand pump in the yard, we ate with them and chatted in our fractured Chinese.

It was a pleasant and wonderfully restful interlude and gave us the chance we had been missing to experience at leisure the daily life of a Chinese peasant. Our main impression was how good it was. Certainly the work was hard and there were few luxuries, but there was an excellent feeling of content-ment and family life. Two married daughters lived with the family, and there were four young grandchildren; the daughters and their constant stream of visiting friends wore pretty and colour-ful dresses.

The floors of the courtyard and most of the rooms of the low buildings round it were of packed earth, warm and mellow in the sunshine. There was also a television set and, during our stay, a new washing machine arrived and was

Rafts such as this, made from inflated animal skins tied to a wooden frame, are a common sight in parts of rural China. They are exceptionally buoyant and remarkably sturdy— provided there are no sharp objects about. ▼

placed incongruously next to the hand pump in the yard. Young poplars grew against the walls, and there were flowers in pots and a small patch of vegetables. A wooden ladder led to the roof, where maize was spread out to dry. They had two cows and a donkey in one of the outhouses next to the stable.

We now set about negotiating to sell the horses. Mr Li spread the word and several potential buyers came to view. The offers we received were not encouraging and we were not in a strong bargaining position. Everyone knew we were due to leave shortly by train and so would have to take what we could get. After rejecting the first few sums mentioned as insulting and 'derisory', more for saving face than because we hoped to push the price up very far, we gladly settled for just under half what we had paid for them.

I have to admit to few regrets when we finally said goodbye to Yin and Yang. The constant effort of keeping them moving had soured our relationship, so that our feelings as their new owner led them off were more relief than grief.

Our last visit was to a major desert reclamation scheme at the town of Shapotou. All the way along the Great Wall we had been aware of the existence of the desert to the north of it. The regions through which we had been riding in Shaanxi and Ningxia, and would soon be riding through in Gansu, represented the very edge of cultivable land. The battle for those living along the Wall was no longer to keep out raiding Mongols and Tartars but to hold back the sand. The single thing that had impressed us most as we rode through this barren land had been the huge efforts being made everywhere to plant trees.

The mud-walled farmstead near Zhongwei where a farmer and his cheery family gave refuge to Yin and Yang until they could be sold. ▼

After Liberation in 1949, projects were started to conserve water and plant trees in the northeast. Along what came to be known as the Green Great Wall, shelter belts were planted beside roads and between fields on the edge of the desert. During the Cultural Revolution, however, shelter belts were considered revisionist and most of the trees already planted were felled. Even much of the remaining natural forest was cut down, as were the poplars and red willows growing wild in the desert and holding the fragile ecosystem together. As a result, the dunes began to encroach on a strategic railway line, blocking it with driven sand. The only solution now was to find some other way of holding the dunes back and this the inventive Chinese had succeeded in doing.

To the west, the Yellow River made a great sweeping curve to the south and it was here that the railway was most threatened, where it squeezed between the desert and the river. We drove out along a rough cinder track beside the railway line. There was desert on both sides, but close to the railway it was covered in light vegetation and had a curious chequered look to it. At Shapotou we saw how it was done. Straw is dug into the sand in metre squares and then left to rot. This both binds the sand for a time and provides some humus. The idea originally was that trees would be planted later in the squares, but the system proved to work spontaneously once the heavy labour of digging in the straw was completed. Scrub vegetation, taking advantage of the marginally improved conditions, began to sprout and a benign circle of growth slowly commenced.

What we saw was the result of more than fifteen years' work in places, and the work was continuing. Where it was possible to irrigate, crops were being grown, and elsewhere the land was turning green spontaneously as weeds and scrub invaded the strawbound sand. It was clearly a slow process but an effective one, and a possible solution to the worldwide problem of encroaching deserts. Here was something for China to be truly proud of, a model and a lesson to be shared, especially in Africa.

The view over a steep hill of sand to the bend in the river was magnificent. Down by the river I could see some tall trees and I ran down to look at the little oasis where there was a small modern house beside a freshwater pond, part of the research project. I heard laughing voices and was surprised to see a group of young Chinese tourists arriving down another steep slope. Waiting for them at the bottom were two gaily caparisoned camels. Looking at the young people's clothes, I guessed that they must be a party of students from Hong Kong; they were much too smart in their shorts and colourful T-shirts to be local.

One of the girls was being helped onto a camel amid much laughter. I asked if anyone spoke English. Her friend said, 'Yes, I do. Where are you from?' When I told her, she said, 'Oh, I live in Hemel Hempstead.' We chatted for a time and I learned that they were on their way by train to a folk festival in Hohhot, the capital of Inner Mongolia. When I rejoined Louella I enjoyed being able to say laconically to her, 'Sorry I took so long, but I just met a rather pretty girl from Hemel Hempstead.' She didn't believe me.

▲ Two men animate this fanciful costume of a lion, prancing to the accompaniment of cymbals during a traditional Chinese festival.

▲ Acrobats on stilts put on a colourful display as part of Chinese New Year celebrations.

China's Great Performing Tradition

THROUGHOUT THEIR LONG HISTORY, the Chinese have been great lovers of all the performing arts, from music to theatre to the circus. Practically every large town in China still has its own troupe of daredevil acrobats and costumed dancers who parade the streets during New Year celebrations and other important festivals throughout the year.

In ancient China, the performing arts were a favourite entertainment of the emperors. Music, in particular, formed an essential component in court rituals, primarily because it was believed to have heavenly qualities. Since the emperor's official title was Son of Heaven, music expressed his divinity as well as the exalted nature of his court.

Music still plays a vital part in China's cultural life, especially in traditional Chinese opera—now dominated by the style known as Beijing opera. This is quite unlike opera in the Western tradition, being a curious amalgam of song, dance, instrumental music, acrobatics and mime. The performers, originally always men, use bizarrely garish make-up, elaborate costumes, high falsetto voices, and heavily stylised patterns of movement. There is no place here for avant-garde productions: everything has significance according to ancient symbolic codes. So a red costume represents a character's bravery and loyalty, and a subtle shrug might indicate a crucial change in mood or plot. Experienced opera-goers pride themselves on their expert knowledge of the codes— no easy acquisition, considering that an actor has at his disposal as many as 50 different ways of moving just his sleeve!

▲ In this delicate 18th-century painting, elegant ladies play traditional Chinese instruments in the imperial court, where music was central to many rituals.

◀ One of the most unusual-looking of traditional Chinese instruments is the *erhu*—a two-stringed fiddle, which still enjoys widespread popularity.

▲ A performer with the Beijing opera, his face a mask of highly symbolic colours, waits for his cue to go onstage.

◀ *The Monkey Creates Havoc in Heaven* is a well-loved opera. The bearded figure is the monkey, his impudence symbolised by his bright yellow costume.

CHAPTER 8

On the Edge of the Gobi

WE NOW HAD TO MAKE another infuriating detour. In spite of all our efforts in Beijing we had been unable to obtain permission to travel through the Hexi Corridor of Gansu province other than by train. The road and the Wall appeared from our maps to run side by side for most of the way, but the authorities were adamant. Only Chinese citizens could travel on the road. Our crew therefore set off in our bus while Louella and I went by train to Lanzhou, the capital of Gansu, and from there through the Hexi Corridor to Jiuquan, where we would all rendezvous. We then planned to backtrack as far as possible, acquire new horses and ride to the end of the Wall.

As the big steam engine pulled out at three o'clock in the afternoon we were comfortably installed in a soft-sleeper carriage. We puffed our way past Shapotou and round the bend in the river. From the train the reclaimed desert looked like a hessian carpet. Soon we were passing through barren hills, looking from habit for glimpses of the Wall, which should have been out there somewhere.

We saw little of Lanzhou, except for the fine range of mountains towering over the end of the main street. It reminded me of a large-scale Innsbruck. We had no time to explore as we had to buy tickets. We managed once again to secure a compartment to ourselves for the nineteen-hour onward journey. On the way I walked along the platform at a wayside station and looked into the hard-sleeper carriage. On three tiers of narrow, tightly packed bunks sprawled half-naked figures, smoking and drinking beer out of bottles, which were then of course thrown out of the window. The scene reminded me of an old-fashioned opium den to which I was taken in Bangkok in 1957. With all our luggage we would have had a tight squeeze if it had been the only option, while the hard seats, always jammed full of passengers, would have been physically impossible. There are times when I am glad I am no longer a student.

Once again we were pulled by a steam engine and it was a fine sight in the sunset as the train wound like a snake through high, desolate mountains. Although we would much rather have been on horses, there were certain advantages in being on a train. We could look down onto villages and see that here they seemed less spoiled than elsewhere. Several were still surrounded by a full wall and inside we could see temples and towers—once a whole series, like a miniature Forbidden City. Still completely closed to foreigners, it looked good country to visit. Beside a fast-flowing stream there were clumps of wild irises in flower and a young shepherd playing on a flute. There were good-looking horses grazing the valley grass, too, and watchtowers in the hills.

By dawn the Wall was there again right next to the line—packed earth, about twenty feet high, with traces of ramparts occasionally, and some fine, well-preserved enclosed forts. Sometimes it would simply vanish for a time but when there it was impossible to miss, as the Hexi Corridor was much narrower than we had expected. The road and railway line in the middle ran through largely bare ground with the only cultivation near the intermittent villages. To our left were the incredible Qilian Shan mountains, catching the first sunlight on their snow-capped summits. At first they looked like a frontal system of white cumulus clouds, only a few miles away it seemed, soaring straight up out of the plain to over 18,000 feet.

In spite of the spectacular view to our left, we were more interested in looking out to our right, where there were some low hills through which we had glimpses of endless desert. There were patches of green in these hills and we knew from the map that the Wall would soon vanish behind them. We hoped the land it then passed through would be good riding country. First, though, we had to wait for our crew to catch us up at Jiuquan, see the local authorities and get permission to go back along the Wall and start riding again.

While waiting for them to catch us up and for the authorities to recover from the shock of our arrival, we asked the Cultural Department representative to show us some of the local sights. There is not much written about Jiuquan, or Suchow, as it used to be called. Marco Polo mentions Muslims and Christians there, as well as rhubarb, for which the region is supposed to be famous.

Jiuquan was the last major town on the Silk Road before the Gobi Desert and it has been a strong point and administrative centre since the Han dynasty. It was founded by the legendary 'Swift Cavalry General', Huo Qubing, whose tomb

◀ The author's steam train chugs its way towards Jiuquan through an empty mountainscape bathed in glorious, late-afternoon sunshine.

we had visited at Xi'an. The Martial Emperor Han Wudi sent him to fight the fierce northern nomads in about 111 BC and presented him with a special jug of wine for his personal use. After a great victory Huo Qubing decided that there was not enough wine for his army to celebrate with and so he poured this jug into a clear spring, from which everyone then drank.

Today, the site of this legendary event—from which Jiuquan, meaning 'Wine Spring', derives its name—has been made into a municipal park. We went there and found it to be a pretty place, with a wild feeling still. There were islands with rushes and willows where birds sang, there were dragonflies and the water was clear, with lots of small fish. Once it must have been a perfect natural oasis, a rare habitat in the bleak desert, fed by underground water from the snowy mountains. Now there are stone bridges and pavilions, as well as rowing boats for hire; but for once there were no crowds and we felt that it was all done with pride.

▲ Colourful frescoes dating from the 5th century adorn the walls of the Wenshu Shan Buddhist cave temples. Sadly, they have suffered from mindless vandalism, much of it very recent.

The only other place of interest we could find a reference to in our guidebooks was the site of the Buddhist cave temples at Wenshu Shan. We asked the Cultural Department representative if we could go there and transport was arranged. It took over an hour to drive over very bumpy roads towards the mountains, until we came to a military area with a barrier across the road. The soldier guarding it was reading a comic and barely glanced up before letting us through. We found ourselves driving past rows of tanks, guns and barrack buildings. After being made to travel by train through the Hexi Corridor so as not to see anything we shouldn't, we were now in the middle of a major combat establishment defending China's border. We had a distinct feeling we should not have been there, but it was too late to turn back and we could see the caves in a cliff ahead.

The Wenshu Shan cave temples must once have been part of a great and beautiful monastery. There were traces of buildings, arches and staircases all over the hill. Inside the caves, which were surprisingly cool and pleasant, though only one or two rooms deep, there were frescoes painted on the walls and pedestals where Buddhas had stood. However, today it is a sad and rather dangerous place. The hot dry ground had been eroded so that it was hard to scramble about on, and everywhere the Buddhist remains, which date back to the fifth century, had been vandalised disgracefully. Much of this seemed to have been done recently, the paint hacked off the faces of the figures on the walls, leaving fresh chips of plaster on the ground. No Buddhas remained and everywhere there were broken beer bottles, which indicated that the soldiers from the camp had free access to the place. The tragedy of a country which has lost all respect for the old and the beautiful again depressed us.

From the top of the small brown mountain on the side of which the cave temples lay there was a fine view across the flat plain to the white-topped Qilian Shan range. There were tank traps all over the plain and another squadron of twenty-one tanks was parked at our feet. An eagle soared overhead; the dry furrowed hillsides around us looked like elephants' skin.

Although there were soldiers everywhere, no one accosted us and we were able to walk through the village spread out along the valley next to the barracks. There were a couple of small temples with painted wooden panelling, which seemed to be in good condition. One appeared to be lived in, having glazed windows.

We drove back to Jiuquan to find our bus arriving with the crew exhausted after their three days' drive. They had been caught in a sandstorm and had had to hire a gang of navvies to build up the road with boulders along one stretch in order to get the bus through. Once they had recovered, negotiations began for our final stage. It was a bit like horse trading all over again, only before we could go and look for horses we had to obtain permission. We wanted to backtrack as far as possible along the Wall, which was clearly marked on the maps at this point, so as to be able to ride as far as we could along it. There was an interesting-looking river called the Hei, which flowed down from the mountains and out towards Mongolia, where it died in the Gobi Desert in some lakes. I would have liked to drive there to make a start, but was assured that on either side of the river lay empty dune country in which horses would be unlikely to survive.

The Pitiless Gobi Desert

WHEN MARCO POLO, the intrepid 13th-century Venetian explorer, reached the edge of the vast Gobi Desert, a daunting sight confronted him: a stark, empty wasteland, which locals warned he would need 'a year and more' to cross. Skirting the southern edge of the desert, Marco and his party were terrified by its dramatic mirages—'evil spirits', they called them, which easily lured unwary travellers to their deaths—but they kept their heads and eventually reached the safety of Kublai Khan's summer palace at Shangdu, near the modern town of Duolun.

The Gobi, Asia's largest desert, covers an incredible 500,000 square miles of northern China and southern Mongolia. Its terrain varies from flat, stony plains to undulating sand dunes; from sparse grasslands to mountains over 12,000 feet high. The climate is desperately harsh: in some areas the rainfall is less than three inches per year, and temperatures can range from −40°F in winter to over 110° in summer. No other desert on Earth experiences such extreme variations.

▲ A traveller with three Bactrian camels amid the stony plains of the Gobi Desert.

Remarkably, in spite of these apparently intolerable conditions, some areas of the Gobi support wildlife such as antelope, gazelles, wild asses, sand grouse and vipers. In certain areas there is even sufficient grass for Mongol nomads to graze their herds of camels, sheep and horses. Other, if temporary, residents are traders who, since time immemorial, have braved the Gobi with their camel caravans, tracing fragile routes between the desert's sparse water holes. Theirs is a tradition that survives even today, with twin-humped Bactrian camels continuing to provide an indispensable means of transport across the Gobi's severe terrain.

Indeed, we were now in country where there were as many camels as horses, and for a time we considered using them instead. Outside our room in Jiuquan, a noisy camel pulling a cart delivered coal daily to the hotel and we knew caravans still supplied outlying oases. But we would not have been free to travel alone on camels as we were on horses, nor could we have used our good saddles.

The authorities were at first quite unhelpful, but in the end, as always, a compromise was reached and we were allowed to go to a village an hour's drive northeast of Jiuquan, called Gu Cheng. It was near a place called Sandong, meaning 'Three Towers', and some good bits of Wall were not far away. We decided to go there, find some horses, and then explore the surrounding countryside and the last sections of the Wall in a leisurely fashion.

Marco and Polo

The name Gu Cheng means 'Ancient City', though the village itself was built only in 1982. It lay on the very edge of the desert, on land irrigated via a tree-lined canal. Between the village and the first dunes lay an open area of meadowland through which a stream ran. After rain the grassland flooded and shallow lakes formed; without rain the stream dried up.

On the meadow flocks of sheep and goats, some cattle, horses and camels grazed. There were good stretches of mud Wall beside and through the dunes, and stark water towers were silhouetted on a high ridge. Beyond the dunes there was another grassy plain, less fertile here, the vegetation struggling against the sand. Beyond that there were more sand hills and then nothing but empty stony plains and dunes as far as the eye could see.

Looking back towards the village all was green and lush. Poplars had been planted everywhere around the houses and fields, so that the countryside seemed wooded. Above rose the southern mountain barrier, which made the community's existence possible. The water from the huge perpetual snowfields was not far below the ground. Every house had in its yard a hand pump from which beautiful ice-cold water was drawn.

We based ourselves on a family called Han, who were extraordinarily kind to us. Mr He borrowed their kitchen to cook our meals, which we ate in their courtyard. We stored our saddles and other equipment in one of their rooms, we washed at their pump; the only thing we did not do was sleep there, although we were invited to do so. We thought it easier all round to commute from Jiuquan.

The layout of the Han house was much the same as that of the one we had used beside the Yellow River. Although here in the far northwest the lifestyle was simpler, there being no electricity, television or washing machines, it seemed in some ways even more comfortable and well organised. The yard was swept immaculately each day and a good crop of vegetables grew in the centre. Chickens and pigs—these people were not Muslims—were kept either in pens or in the back yard. I wandered through into this on our first day and was greeted by a scene straight out of a Bethlehem nativity play. In a thatched stable against the mud wall were a donkey, a cow and two goats eating from a manger. A sheep with two young lambs lay at their feet, next to an old-fashioned wooden

waggon with long shafts. A pitchfork with wooden prongs was stuck in a pile of straw where chickens scratched. Beyond was an arched gateway, through which there was a view of poplar trees in rows leading to the plain: Leonardo da Vinci's dream background.

Feeling safe in such familiar surroundings, the subject of innumerable Christmas cards, I strolled on. Suddenly a small boy who had followed me began to shout and gesticulate urgently. I turned, and there was such terror on his face as he pointed at something behind me that I leapt towards him without even looking over my shoulder. At that moment a large black dog jumped out from behind the archway and flung itself at me, snarling and snapping, to be brought up short by its chain inches from my retreating back. Everyone laughed when my young saviour and I returned to the front courtyard and told them about it, but it could have been nasty and I was grateful to him.

The people here being considered a 'minority', the one-child rule did not apply. Three children were allowed, though children born beyond the permitted three were considered 'non-people' and were given no papers. We were told that every-one hoped that the rules would be changed by the time they were grown up.

Ever since we had reached Ningxia we had been seeing an increasing number of people with relatively non-Chinese features, such as curly hair and hooked noses, clearly the product of interbreeding with Turks and Uigurs. The minorities who traditionally inhabited the northwest have had a very tough time over recent centuries and many were wiped out. Yet Gu Cheng seemed to be a happy and contented village. The main street, which was lined with young poplars to

▲ **Looking every bit an oasis in a barren wilderness, this farm is typical of the area around Jiuquan.**

shade the courtyards along it, was swept daily. The villagers could buy their houses for 2,000 yuan (about £400)—perhaps two years' total income. They told us that although it was quite cold in winter there was sun most days in which the old people could sit for a while out of the wind in their courtyards. They knew whether it was going to be cold enough to warrant lighting the fires under the *kangs* by watching the snowline on the mountains. When it dropped below a certain point that meant it was time to start the central heating.

Our first task was to find ourselves some horses. We walked to the far end of the village and stopped outside a house where a man was having his head shaved. Down an alley next to the house we saw a nice-looking grey tied up. Louella, having drawn the short straw with Yin last time, took a liking to it and claimed it for her own. It appeared to have an amiable character, though I thought it rather long in the tooth and put its age at fourteen or so. The young

Louella, mounted on Polo, chats with a peasant girl leading a tiny donkey and cart through a shady avenue of poplars. ▶

wife who owned it assured us it was eight. We seemed to have heard that before, but accepted it nonetheless. On his left flank the Chinese character for 'middle' was branded. This is the same character as that used for 'China', deriving from the country's ancient name, The Middle Kingdom.

A quite frisky bay with dark eyes was then led out and tied to a tree. I walked up to him and gently laid my hand on his neck. He threw his head up, snapped the rope and escaped. So much for impressing the locals with my way with horses. Fortunately, he did not try to run away but allowed himself to be caught at once. I put a halter on and led him up and down the street. This he accepted, though the sight of me clearly alarmed him. I was not sure if my being a European had anything to do with it. I asked his owner to bring some food, and a bowl of black beans and maize was produced. He accepted this from the bowl but would not take it from my hand. He was very nervous of fast movements, but he was definitely much younger than the grey and I accepted his owner's claim that he was seven years old as not being a huge underestimate. Both horses were in far better condition than any of our previous mounts. We decided they should be able to stand the two weeks' hard riding we had in store for them and agreed to hire them and bring them back later.

The next move was to try them out. Both horses behaved sedately and Louella was delighted to be riding something again which did not feel as though it were about to collapse beneath her. We called my horse Marco and hers Polo, and agreed to hire them at 10 yuan a day.

We then set off for our first proper ride on our new mounts. Marco loped along quite well, although he was not as fit as I had expected and worked up quite a sweat. Polo made a lot of fuss about stopping, throwing his head about and nearly falling over if pulled up sharply. They both had very bad mouths, but since most of the time we were giving them their heads that did not matter much. The village street ended at the edge of the open grassland with the dunes and horizon beyond. We cantered across, past grazing animals, stopped at a stream to let the horses drink, and rode up into the dunes. We felt free at last of the problems of needing permission to do everything. Our spirits lifted and we were tempted just to keep going across the Gobi to whatever lay beyond. Instead, we let our horses race each other home, only slowing up to walk the last mile or so into the village. There, as soon as they were unsaddled, they both rolled in the dust, which we felt was a good sign, showing that they were feeling well.

Young Pioneers and a Birthday

From now on we were free to explore a different bit of the countryside around Gu Cheng each day; to follow half-hidden stretches of Wall and ride to distant watchtowers.

The shaded lanes surrounding the villages, where rows of trees gave a distinctly French feel to the landscape, were perfect for riding along in dappled sunlight. Decorative peasants in straw hats and headscarves, looking more like fashion models than the labouring proletariat, led little donkeys pulling carts. Others headed for the fields with hoes over their shoulders, chatting merrily as though on their way to the shops. There was little sense of toil. Even the bearded old men smiled at us and the little rosy-buttocked babies positively squealed with glee when Louella cuddled them.

One day we passed the school while talking to Mr He, riding up just as the teacher, who happened to speak good English, was marshalling his class at the entrance. We all greeted each other and the teacher prevailed on us to dismount and visit his class. There were thirty children aged between eight and ten, most of the children of both sexes wearing red Young Pioneer kerchiefs. Millions of primary-school pupils belong to this organisation, which is similar to the Boy Scouts in that it undertakes community projects. Selection is supposed to be by ability, and during the Cultural Revolution they were known as 'Little Red Guards'.

Seated at uncomfortable little desks below walls bare of decoration, they were perfectly behaved and chanted dutifully, line by line, a story about giant pandas, international friendship and conservation. It seemed oddly appropriate in view of our fundraising efforts for the World Wildlife Fund.

Then it was our turn. Mr He turned out to be a natural with children, full of unexpected talents. First he sang them a song and then he made the children join in. He was so funny and so good at making everyone relax and laugh as he conducted and clowned about that they loved it, and we were all sorry when anxious parents started arriving to collect their offspring for lunch.

It was Louella's birthday on June 25. We spent most of the day pottering about the countryside on our horses, and found a nice man living in a small hut guarding a fishpond. He told us people would come and steal the fish if he were not there. We could see the fish moving in the water when he threw a bundle of weeds in to feed them. They seemed to be about six to eight inches long. In the Han family's courtyard Mr He was preparing a surprise feast for Louella. There was a huge communal chicken stew and endless side dishes. Everyone in the village came and went to see how the foreigners behaved and to sample the Beijing cook's creations.

▲ The rare sight of a young giant panda enjoying its natural habitat. This individual seems to have taken its clownlike appearance to heart, leading it to act the part as well.

In Jiuquan I had managed to get a revolting pink sticky cake and to find thirty-five tiny candles to go on it. This caused a lot of interest and there was a resounding cheer when Louella blew them all out in one go. They all tried a bit of cake and congratulated her. Everyone in the village was smiling and ready to make friends. The teenage boys were particularly forward, even a little cheeky at times. There was one boy who had become a special friend. He had a sensitive, squashed face and regularly called me by my name, Lebin. Mr Li told me that his name was Liu Binxian, which sounded much like my name at the start, and that he was a talented painter. We went to visit his home and he produced his collection of works. They did show talent but were, as he said himself, quite unskilled as he had had no training. He insisted I choose one for myself and he gave Louella a picture of Jiuquan Park which he had done especially for her birthday. There was a message in his good calligraphy along the side which read: 'Wishing Mrs Han Lebin a Happy Birthday.'

I promised Liu Binxian that I would keep in touch with him and that I would try to see if he could get a scholarship of some sort. It seemed such a pity that a boy like that, clearly desperate to develop his talents, should be unable to do so. There was not much we could do, but we told the British Council in Beijing. They do have scholarships to help Chinese students and even, if he did not qualify, the very fact of his being enquired about might draw him to the attention of the local authorities and make something happen.

That night there was a storm with heavy rain and the plain was flooded with shallow lagoons. We wondered how the fish guardian stopped his charges simply swimming away. The horses enjoyed splashing through the water, which was warm from the hot sand. In the mountains snow had fallen and lay halfway down the slopes, quite beautiful in the fresh morning sunshine.

In one of the ponds, concealed from the village by a dune, we came across eight of the children from the school frolicking naked in the shallow water. The scene was one of perfect innocence and they were happy to be photographed. They splashed each other and our horses, then lay in the sun to dry. They were neither overcome by our unexpected arrival, nor embarrassed by being watched

at play. In a country where the normal overcrowding, as well as political and social controls, tends to make everyone self-conscious and conformist, it was wonderfully reassuring to stumble on children behaving as they do anywhere in the world. It remains one of our happiest images of China.

One day we were caught in a dust storm far out in the desert. The wind blew huge quantities of sand horizontally across the ridge along which we were riding. It stung our faces like needles. The force of the storm increased until we were barely able to move. There was no danger of our being lost as we knew we had only to follow the compass, but it was frightening and uncomfortable, the sand hurting relentlessly and penetrating our clothes, mouths, eyes and noses. Staying close together we battled on for a couple of hours. At times the wind was so strong that we had to lie down, while the horses turned their backs to the storm and we held them by their head ropes.

With the combined effort of wind and sand, rain and man's depredations, it is extraordinary that any of the Wall has survived in these regions, and yet we found some quite well-preserved sections. At one of these there was even a large stone with Chinese characters carved on it. They read: 'Watchtower of the Great Wall. Important Cultural Relic. Anyone damaging or removing it will be liable to prosecution.'

On our last night in Gu Cheng we and our crew all went up into the dunes and had a picnic around a camp fire. We had brought a bucket of dried camel dung with us to make a fire. Over it we suspended our kettle on a couple of forked sticks. We made ourselves some coffee, lay back against our saddles wrapped in our sleeping-bags and talked about the two months of riding that lay behind us. Louella mused on all the nice, kind people we had met and how lucky we were to have seen so much of the Wall, something most people only read about. The restored sections in the east were magnificent and everyone who saw them was impressed. But now, as we approached the western end, we had a sense of the incredible scale of the building operation it represented.

It is often said that the Wall is the only man-made object visible from space. In fact, this is said so glibly that I strongly suspected it to be a myth. I therefore wrote to NASA to ask if any astronaut had ever reported seeing the Great Wall of China from space.

Disappointingly, the Chief of the Special Events Branch wrote to me to say that, 'recurrent reports that astronauts have seen the Great Wall of China from space cannot be substantiated. In fact, it would be difficult, if not impossible, to see the Great Wall from space because over the centuries the Wall has become overgrown with vegetation which causes it to blend in with surrounding terrain.'

As we lay in the still desert night, drinking our coffee out of tin mugs beside our camel-dung fire, we could see a short section of the Wall outlined against the sky. A Bactrian camel with a rider safely slumped between its two humps padded past, turning its head to look down superciliously and snort at the strange sight. The night was still and we heard a desert fox as the full moon rose unexpectedly behind the Wall. We were content to be there.

The Last Lap

The next day we set out for Jiayuguan and the great fort there which marks the westernmost end of the Ming Wall. That day was among the hardest and most exhausting of all. We had groomed the horses and saddled up by 7am. We were determined to try and follow the Wall as far as possible and this meant heading out into the desert to the north of Gu Cheng.

Through Mr Li we received conflicting advice which delayed us and was frustrating as we were anxious to be off while it was still cool. He had trouble understanding the local dialect and, like all our relatively cosmopolitan team from Beijing, found the peasantry intellectually inferior. 'I am dull from dealing with these sort of persons,' he said. When we tried to pin down specific information on directions, he would say, 'Nobody can tell,' which made us grind our teeth as our lives might well depend on not getting lost.

◀ Bactrian camels
silhouetted on a desert
horizon against a
spectacular setting sun.

After bidding farewell to the Han family, we set out through familiar country, across the plain and out to the dunes. It was a lovely morning, with a red dawn sky, fresh with a light breeze and even some dew glistening on the coarse grass. We turned west, following a piece of Wall we knew already, then left it to head by compass further out than we had been before and so, we hoped, cut a wide corner. There were several dry riverbeds to cross, the final fingers of flash floods from the mountains, which sometimes poured down into the desert to vanish under the sand. One of these looked suspiciously damp, and luckily I slowed Marco up as we cantered across it. In a moment he was sucked into a quicksand. As he floundered back towards the bank, I was just able to leap ashore holding on to his reins. I pulled and shouted, urging him as he struggled. For a moment I thought of plunging in to help, but then his feet came in contact with firm ground and he managed to drag himself out. His flanks were heaving but he was unhurt.

We found a safe way across by following some camel tracks and continued on our westerly bearing. This took us back to human habitation, a series of pleasant villages isolated on the edge of the desert and irrigated by canals. Through these ran a cart track, dead straight for several miles and in exactly the direction we wished to go. To our right we could see signs of the Wall from time to time, out in the dunes, and far ahead we began to make out the Black Mountains which guard one side of the pass at Jiayuguan.

Things were looking pretty good at eleven o'clock, when we stopped to give the horses a brief rest under some trees where the cart track ended. Ahead lay an open stony waste, with a curl of smoke beyond it which indicated Jiayuguan, our destination. A friendly local assured us we could ride straight there, and we set off optimistically. Four hours later we felt as if we had made no progress at all.

The plain was far more uneven than it appeared, and a great deal bigger. Out in the middle, all the horizons vanished and we were surrounded by mirages. For some time a surrealist factory had been visible dead ahead, smoke belching from its tall chimney. Then this was reflected upside-down in what appeared to be lakes of water and for hour after hour it seemed to get no bigger or closer. I felt an unfamiliar touch of agoraphobia, panic that we would never reach sanctuary again.

The horses found the going on the hot sharp stones painful and they were tired; so for much of the time we walked. Both of our pairs of boots were by now wearing out and in need of repair. Polo was quite stout-

▲ After hanging upside-down as a mirage for several hours, this factory finally appeared the right way up in all its grim reality.

hearted and plodded gamely on, but Marco seemed about to give up. Now it was my turn to lag behind and to have to urge my mount every yard of the way.

Another couple of hours of hard slog and at last the factory began to loom large ahead, two black slag heaps bracketing it, so that we did not have the energy to try to ride around. It was hardly the ending we had expected for our romantic ride along the Great Wall, but at least there would be water there for the horses, and we would be able to get directions for the fort. Some of the chimneys were pouring out black smoke, others pungent yellow and a rather sinister off-white, which smelt deadly. After total solitude for six hours, we were plunged into a bizarre world where gigantic gantries towered overhead, grotesque pipes carrying hot liquids between huge tanks and boilers bulged and leaked, sudden bursts of steam were released, and deafening bangs, shrieks and whistles rent the air. Fortunately, the horses were too exhausted to react but we found it hard to stay calm and confident.

Some friendly labourers gave us directions, pointing out a route through the heart of the industrial complex, which we deduced was an iron and steel works. We crossed a network of railway lines, dodging between a couple of noisy steam shunting engines, and came to an even worse man-made desert of slag and rubbish. Beyond this we found gates, through which we rode, to be stopped firmly but politely by an official. In spite of our urgent protestations that we were in a hurry, he insisted that we dismount while he telephoned for instructions.

There had been talk of a possible official welcome, with the governor of Jiayuguan and the local press turning out to greet us and we did not want to keep them waiting, but explaining this was beyond our ability in Chinese. Instead, we could only be patient as our guardian put a kettle on and told us to sit down and wait while it boiled. He read our handout through, then read it aloud slowly over the telephone. We found a tap and watered the horses, as a dreadful sense of anticlimax began to overcome us. Then we looked at each other and began to laugh. Here we were, buoyed up by the prospect of reaching the end of the Wall, expecting the plaudits of the local population and perhaps the world's press as we rode in triumph through the final gateway, only to find ourselves stuck in a dingy office, held prisoner by a kind man who was only doing his job. We dared not argue too vehemently as we strongly suspected that such an important factory would be closed to foreigners and that we should not be there.

He gave us glasses of boiling water which took an age to drink and at last he let us go, even sending a lad on a bicycle to guide us through the maze of roads between the factory buildings. Suddenly there was a roar of engines and a convoy of twenty police motorcycles overtook us. Each one had an armed man on the pillion and a sidecar in which sat another holding an automatic rifle. I looked down the barrel of each one as they passed. It seemed like a judgment. Tired after a day in the saddle and dazed by the din and smoke around us, I felt sure we were going to be arrested.

▲ The implacable face of officialdom—made all the worse by sunglasses, which lend these stern army personnel an added aura of menace.

Soon afterwards, however, we passed out through the main gate without being challenged by the battery of armed guards there, who just stared at us in amazement. Riding out of that inferno of blast furnaces and smokestacks we must have been a most unexpected sight.

The Strongest Pass Under Heaven

We were now, we discovered, in one of the main streets of the new city of Jiayuguan. At the central roundabout, a gratifyingly large crowd gathered round us and we were able to start a small riot by giving away handfuls of our handouts, which we were not going to need again. The people went mad for these, snatching them from our hands and fighting for them. It was an extraordinary example of mass hysteria, which we were able to watch in safety from our horses.

It took us an hour to ride out of town and up to the fort, known as 'The Strongest Pass Under Heaven', now clearly visible ahead, rising out of the plain between the mountains. This has always been a place of great strategic importance to China, lying in a narrow pass between the Qilian Shan mountains to

the south and the Black Mountains to the north, and guarding the entrance of the Silk Road into China proper. Through this fortress almost every foreigner entering China overland had to pass. Beyond it were the badlands to which Chinese citizens were exiled if they offended their emperor. Travel documents were needed to pass through and a garrison of 1,000 men was retained there to ensure that the law was upheld.

The fort and its surrounding defences were built in several stages by the Ming emperors between 1368 and 1574. It looked more magnificent than The First Pass Under Heaven at Shanhaiguan and we found it to be largely restored. At each of the four corners of the fort there is a turret and the thirty-foot-high walls are crowned by regular crenellations. The two great gates at the eastern and western entrances are fifty-six feet high and beautifully decorated, with painted pillars and carved beams below their curled eaves. Below these run brick-lined archways, like dark tunnels, sixty-six feet long, guarded by great wooden doors wrapped in iron sheets and painted black. The parapets, gates and towers are built of mud bricks, but the walls are simply rammed earth, made by a special process which gave them the immense strength needed to survive until the present day. The yellow earth was carefully sifted and cleaned of all weeds and seeds. Then hemp,

◀ **The great fort at Jiayuguan, aptly named The Strongest Pass Under Heaven, seems to have been built in a style inspired by its severe, imposing surroundings.**

lime and glutinous rice were mixed with it to create a strong cement. Each stretch of wall was tested by having an arrow fired at it: if the arrow bounced off, the wall was passed; if it stuck in then the job had to be done again.

Right under the shadow of the fort itself lay a small farm. One side of its courtyard was the Wall we had been following on and off for nearly 4,000 miles and against it there was a stable. Here, good old Mr Li had arranged that we could leave the horses; the perfect place. We fed and watered them there and quietly congratulated each other on having made it from Shanhaiguan at sea level to Jiayuguan, lying at 5,817 feet.

An Unexpected Mercy Mission

Next morning we decided to take things easy by going to the local market and strolling through the astonishingly varied stalls. Ducklings and chicks were crowded in high-sided trays like clockwork toys; goats, sheep and cows were tethered along a wall. Raw meat attracted swarms of flies; all sorts of exotic spices added their peculiar perfumes to the air. There were vegetables in profusion, sacks of animal feed, seeds and nuts, clothing stalls, trinkets and plastic sandals; it was a thriving, busy place.

As we were leaving I suddenly saw a young badger tied by its hind leg with wire to a bicycle. There was a crowd round it and it was trying desperately to escape, scrabbling to dig a hole in the hard, dusty ground. I tried to walk on and not interfere, but it was impossible. Badgers are rather special to me, as there are a lot on our farm in Cornwall. Moreover, we had undertaken our ride partly to raise funds for the World Wildlife Fund. How could I ignore a captive badger?

I quickly explained the situation to Mr Li and asked him to help me. He at once responded with more enthusiasm and understanding than I could have dared hope for.

'Why are you selling that animal?' he asked its owner.

'It will make good eating and its skin is valuable,' he replied. 'I caught it yesterday and I'm only asking 40 yuan for it.'

'Do you realise that it is a protected species in China and you are likely to go to prison if we send for the police?'

We were neither of us sure if this was the case, but it worked and he hurriedly dropped the price to 10 yuan, which Louella handed him. I ran back to our bus and fetched the empty sack in which the horses' corn had been kept. When I returned, I managed to guide the badger into the sack without getting bitten. Supporting the animal's weight from below, I carried it back to the bus and told our rather surprised driver to drive out along the road to the northeast towards the desert. After a time we came to a wild spot, where there was a grove of poplars at the junction of two streams and a patch of rough uncultivated scrub.

The release went unexpectedly easily. We laid Louella's thick saddle cloth over the sack to hold the badger down gently and eased its hind leg out. Fortunately, the skin below was unbroken and the bone of its leg felt straight and undamaged. We opened the sack's mouth and the badger shuffled out. Its face and eyes were still dusty from the market and for a moment it paused, disorientated, to look up at us. Then it moved off in a hurry through some thick grass and into a gully.

Badgers are needlessly persecuted the world over. With luck, the animal rescued by the author will have lived out its days in freedom, such as that enjoyed by the healthy specimen in this photograph. ▼

What impressed me about all the Chinese who assisted in this little exercise was not that they let me do something which must have seemed pretty silly to them, but that they understood exactly why I was doing it. Although conservation is not practised yet to any great extent in China, it is, thanks to television and a certain amount of propaganda, beginning to be a recognisable concept. Perhaps this is one area where, along with the tree-planting programme and the fight against the encroaching desert, there is hope for the future, even the near future.

Now we mounted our horses for the last time and rode out along the last stretch of the Wall beyond the fort. This runs across a flat gravelled plain towards the Qilian Shan mountains to complete the defence of the pass. Here we found the Wall to be very well preserved, as much as thirteen feet high in places and running straight as a die for five miles. At the very end there was a watchtower, and as we rode up to it we came to what was without doubt the most spectacular place we had seen since leaving the sea. A gigantic canyon lay between the desert and the mountains, its sides dropping 300 feet sheer to the Taolai River below. It was the most impregnable end to the Wall imaginable and completely unexpected. We had known the Wall must end somewhere there, as its final role was to bar the valley, but we had vaguely assumed that it would meander off up into the mountains, much as it did at Shanhaiguan where it began. Instead, here was vivid proof of how effective the Wall must have been at keeping everyone out of China. Although its sides were crumbling, the last watchtower, perched on the very edge of the canyon, demonstrated more clearly than all the books we had read about it that the Great Wall meant business and there was no way round.

Directly across the valley from us, the mountains rose steeply up from the riverbed. In one gulley opposite a shepherd stood guard over his flock of sheep, but otherwise it looked harsh, impenetrable country. A cormorant, white feathers showing below its steadily beating black wings, flew past us at eye level. The only thing spoiling the moment for me was that I was overcome by an acute attack of vertigo and could barely move. I became convinced that Marco was going to step off the edge and had to avert my eyes from the space below us.

It was almost over now. All that was left was to return the horses to Jiuquan— a couple of days' ride along the road. We had done what we had set out to do, and we had had a rare chance to see something of a maddening, confusing—yes, inscrutable—country, from a perspective which no one else has been granted since Liberation. Mounted on our horses, we had had time to think and to observe the country with a much greater freedom than those hemmed in by the claustrophobia all tourists feel in China.

One day, I hope, the Chinese authorities will feel able to allow foreign travellers to see the whole of the Great Wall, all the way from Shanhaiguan to Jiayuguan without a break. If they are lucky, they should be able to do it comfortably in the eighty days we originally allowed ourselves. If, by then, the security neurosis has been calmed sufficiently to let them camp *en route*, they should have a wonderful time. The people they will meet along the way are among the kindest and the most hospitable to be found anywhere, and the scenery, enhanced by the thread of Wall running through it, is unrivalled. Whoever they are and wherever they go, I beg them to do it on horses. Then they will, I believe, experience China at its best and from the finest vantage point, as we did.

▲ After weaving its way some 4,000 miles from Shanhaiguan, the Great Wall runs straight across the desert plain towards the snowcapped Qilian Shan mountains. It ends on the edge of a river canyon somewhere in the middle distance.

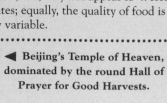

Preparing to Go

Options China has a great deal to offer its visitors in terms of history, culture and scenery. Its landscapes range from tropical rain forest, to mountains, to desert, and many of its towns and cities have strong identities of their own. The country is so large and so varied, however, that most trips can do no more than touch on a few highlights and give tantalising glimpses of an exotic civilisation.

Travel in China used to be virtually impossible for foreigners, and even today certain areas may be closed to them. However, the country is now far more open than before and is even (relatively) accessible to the independent traveller keen to get around on a tight budget. For those who are daunted by an entirely foreign language and culture, numerous organised tours are available. Some companies also offer adventure trips to remote areas, treks, special-interest holidays and cycling tours.

Travel Most major airlines fly to Beijing, some also to Shanghai. Alternatives include flying to Hong Kong and then crossing to the mainland by hydrofoil, ferry or train; or taking the Trans-Siberian railway from Moscow to Beijing, a fascinating journey of about a week.

Within China itself, the domestic air network connects most major cities, but rail travel provides a more memorable, if hectic, experience. The views are excellent and trains are a good way of meeting the people of China. Tickets can be bought (at a premium) from travel agents more easily than from railway stations, which are often very crowded. For anything but the shortest journeys, book well in advance and take a soft- or hard-class sleeper. Hard-class seat-only carriages, the cheapest option, can get extremely crowded, not to mention uncomfortable.

Tour buses are useful for seeing the sights; and bicycles, which can be hired from hotels and rental shops, provide an enjoyable means of exploring the cities.

Practicalities All foreigners need visas. Tourist visas have to be used within three months of being purchased, and are valid for a maximum of two months from the date of arrival.

Within China, some places off the beaten track are closed to foreigners. Check with the Public Security Bureaux, found in all provincial capitals, as to whether you need Alien Travel Permits for any of the areas you intend visiting. Independent travellers to Tibet need special permission to make their journey.

Language Mandarin, or *Putonghua*, is the official language of China, but Cantonese is common in the far south, including the colonies of Hong Kong and Macau; there are also dozens of other minority dialects. None of these languages is easy to learn, so it is worth taking a phrasebook with useful questions and statements written in Chinese script: in spite of the variety of spoken languages, they are all written virtually identically. In large cities, however, many Chinese people do speak English.

Health Travel insurance is essential. Check with your travel agent and GP concerning any current health requirements and precautions, particularly against hepatitis, Japanese encephalitis, tetanus, typhoid and malaria. Note that if you are travelling through Asia and arrive from an area recently affected by yellow fever or cholera, you will need vaccination certificates.

When to go China encompasses a great range of climates, with long, hot summers accompanied by typhoons in the south, and harsh, icy winters in the north. Spring and autumn are therefore generally the best times to travel.

A word of warning Tourism is not evenly developed in China, so be prepared for many hotels to fall substantially below Western standards. Away from the main tourist areas, foreigners can find themselves being stared at almost constantly, and will often attract instant crowds. Some people may find the lack of hygiene and the Chinese propensity for spitting off-putting. Certain types of cuisine, too, may not appeal to Western palates; equally, the quality of food is very variable.

◀ **Beijing's Temple of Heaven, dominated by the round Hall of Prayer for Good Harvests.**

▲ A fairytale ice palace, built as part of the Ice Lantern Festival at Harbin.

◄ Tourists explore a well-preserved section of the Great Wall of China.

Where to Go

Beijing The Chinese capital sprawls across an area the size of Belgium. Much of it was rebuilt after the 1949 Revolution, but numerous back streets recall an earlier era. In the heart of Beijing lies the Forbidden City, a palace complex covering 180 acres, and one of the great sights of Asia. To the northeast lies the Summer Palace, with an impressive collection of buildings and landscaped parklands. Other attractive sites are the Temple of Heaven and the Pavilion of Perpetual Spring, which offers fine views over the city.

China's most famous edifice, the **Great Wall**, is also accessible from Beijing—specifically at Badaling, 46 miles to the northwest. This trip is usually combined with a visit to the tombs of the Ming emperors, approached by a 'spirit way' or avenue of carved stone figures.

Canton (Guangzhou) The southern gateway to China is a large, prosperous city with imposing monuments and attractive parks. Excursions include boat trips along the Pearl River (Zhu Jiang) and luxurious rides on the Tourist Hotel Train to visit rock formations and caves.

Guilin The southern town of Guilin, with its open markets and floating restaurants, is the starting point for a memorable trip along the Li River. This leads into a surreal landscape of karst

Rice being harvested along the Li River, near Guilin, with the area's distinctive limestone hills in the background. ▶

limestone hills and crags that have inspired poets, painters and photographers through the ages.

Harbin The city of Harbin, in the far northeast of China, is strongly influenced by Russian architecture and culture. In January and February the Ice Lantern Festival transforms Harbin into a fairytale city as artists create ice carvings of fabulous buildings, beasts and flowers.

Kashi Formerly known as Kashgar, this distant western city was once a vital haven on the Silk Road, the ancient trade route between East and West. Kashi offers an experience of China unlike any other. Its culture is strongly Islamic, and its population an exciting mixture of peoples, among them Uigurs, Kirghiz, Kazaks and other minorities of Xinjiang. Kashi offers access to the

spectacular Karakoram mountains and, via the Friendship Highway that runs through these mountains, to Pakistan.

Leshan Situated at the confluence of three rivers, Leshan provides access to some of China's most dramatic scenery. Ferries take visitors to see the Great Buddha—at 233 feet, the largest Buddha statue in the world. To the west of Leshan is the holy Mount Emei (Emeishan), rising to 10,170 feet; numerous ancient monasteries cover its slopes, many offering accommodation.

Lhasa Because of its extremely high elevation (12,000 feet), the Tibetan capital of Lhasa can cause some travellers to feel unwell. Careful acclimatisation is the best remedy. The city is dominated by the 1,000-room Potala Palace, formerly the winter residence of Tibet's exiled religious leader, the Dalai Lama. Other spectacular sights are the Jo-Kang temple and nearby Drepung monastery.

Shanghai This vast city is often called the Paris of the East. There is a riverfront area known as the Bund, characterised by European colonial architecture, which contrasts strongly with the old Chinese city, itself vibrantly oriental in flavour. The Shanghai Museum has an excellent collection of Chinese art.

Xi'an The walled city of Xi'an stands beside the remains of China's ancient capital, Chang'an, and in close proximity to numerous magnificent historical sites. These include a Neolithic settlement in the village of Banpo, several tombs and temples of the Tang emperors and, perhaps most famous of all, the vast terracotta army guarding the tomb of Emperor Qin Shi Huangdi.

Index
and Acknowledgments

Note: page numbers in **bold** refer to captions for illustrations. Robin and Louella Hanbury-Tenison are referred to as RHT and LHT respectively, and the Great Wall is referred to as GW throughout the index.

Acknowledgments

The editors gratefully acknowledge the use of information taken from the following books during the preparation of this publication:

Architectural Guides for Travellers: Imperial China by Charis Chan, Viking 1991
China: The Economist Guide, Hutchinson 1990
China: A Concise Cultural History by Arthur Cotterell, John Murray 1988
China: Tradition and Transformation by John K. Fairbank and Edwin O. Reischauer, Allen and Unwin 1989
Collins Illustrated Guide to All China by Charis Chan, Collins 1988
A Companion to China by Frances Wood, Weidenfeld and Nicolson 1988
Cultural Atlas of China by Caroline Blunden and Mark Elvin, Phaidon Press Ltd 1983
Discovery and Exploration: Beyond the Horizon by Malcolm Ross Macdonald, The Reader's Digest Association Limited 1978
The Encyclopaedia Britannica
Encyclopedia of China Today by Fredric M. Kaplan and Julian M. Sobin, Macmillan 1982

The Forbidden City by Roderick MacFarquhar and the editors of the Newsweek Book Division, The Reader's Digest Association Limited in association with Newsweek 1972
The Genius of China by Robert Temple, Prion 1991
The Great Wall by Luo Zewen, Dick Wilson, Jean-Pierre Drège and Hubert Delahaye, Michael Joseph Ltd 1982
The Insider's Guide to China by Derek Maitland, Moorland Publishing Co Ltd 1994
Insight Cityguides: Beijing, APA Publications 1989
Insight Guides: China edited by Manfred Morgenstern, APA Publications 1994
Journey into China, National Geographic Society 1982
Library of Nations: China by the editors of Time-Life Books, Time-Life 1984
The Macmillan Family Encyclopaedia
Nelles Guides: China, Nelles Verlag 1995
The Pride that was China by Michael Loewe, Sidgwick & Jackson and St Martin's Press 1990
Whitaker's Almanack, J. Whitaker & Sons Ltd 1995

Picture Acknowledgments

T=top; *C*=centre; *B*=bottom; *L*=left; *R*=right; *I*=Inset

Cover *Spine* Windrush Photos/David Tipling *L(T—B)* Robin Hanbury-Tenison Keith & Liz Laidler Eye Ubiquitous/L. Fordyce China Photo Library Robert Harding Picture Library/Explorer *R* ChinaStock/Dennis Cox 2 Keith & Liz Laidler 3 Ffotograff/Patricia Aithie 5 Papilio/Robert Pickett 6 Caroline Blunden 7 Robin Hanbury-Tenison 8–9 Britstock-IFA/Tetsuo Sayama 12 *B* Lowell Georgia 12–13 Eye Ubiquitous/Chris Gibb 13 *TR* Eye Ubiquitous/Julia Waterlow *B* Robert Harding Picture Library/G. & P. Corrigan 14 *TL* Keith & Liz Laidler *BL* Windrush Photos/Les Borg *BR* Minden Pictures/Jim Brandenburg 15 *T* Oxford Scientific Films/Chris Caxton *B* Oxford Scientific Films/David Tipling 16 *T* Robert Harding Picture Library/Peter Ibbotson 16–17 Robert Harding Picture Library/Simon Westcott 17 *T* Lowell Georgia *BC* ChinaStock/Dennis Cox *BR* ChinaStock/John Eastcott/Yva Momatiuk 18 *T* Robert Harding Picture Library/G. & P. Corrigan 18–19 Impact Photos/Alain Le Garsmeur 19 *T* Tibet Image Bank/Norma Joseph *BR* Impact Photos/Matthew Kneale 20–21 Spectrum Colour Library/D. & J. Heaton 22 *TL* Robert Harding Picture Library/Jon Gardey *BL* Ontario Science Centre, Toronto, Canada *BR* Ontario Science Centre, Toronto, Canada 22–23 Magnum Photos/Hiroji Kubota 23 *B* The Science Museum/Science & Society Picture Library 24 *B* ChinaStock/Dennis Cox 24–25 The Bridgeman Art Library/Freer Gallery, Smithsonian Institution, Washington DC 25 *B* ChinaStock/Dennis Cox 26 *T* ChinaStock/Dennis Cox *B* Lowell Georgia 26–27 Ann & Bury Peerless—Slide Resources & Picture Library 27 *B* The Bridgeman Art Library/Christie's, London 28 *TL* Biofotos/Heather Angel *TR* Wellcome Institute Library, London *B* Minden Pictures/Jim Brandenburg 29 *T* Minden Pictures/Jim Brandenburg *B* Michael Holford/Wellcome Institute Library, London 30 *T* The Bridgeman Art Library/Zhang Shui Cheng *B* The Bridgeman Art Library/Percival David Foundation, London 31 *T* Werner Forman Archive/Sotheby's, London *C* ET Archive/Bibliothèque Nationale, Paris *B* Comstock/Georg Gerster 32–33 Robert Harding Picture Library/Peter Scholey 34 *C* The Bridgeman Art Library/Museo Correr, Venice *BL* ET Archive/Bibliothèque Nationale, Paris *BR* Collection of the National Palace Museum, Taiwan, Republic of China 34–35 Robert Harding Picture Library/G. & P. Corrigan 35 *B* Kadokawa Shoten Publishing Co Ltd/Akira Soda 36 *B* Zefa Pictures/Sunak 36–37 The Bridgeman Art Library/Cecil Higgins Art Gallery, Bedford 37 *C* The Bridgeman Art Library/Christie's, London *BL* The Fotomas Index *BR* Werner Forman Archive/Christie's, London 38–39 *T* The Bridgeman Art Library/Taylor Gallery, London *B* Peter Newark's Pictures 39 *TR* AKG London *C* The Bridgeman Art Library/National Maritime Museum, London 40 *T* AKG London *BL* Ann & Bury Peerless—Slide Resources & Picture Library *BR* Zefa Pictures/Dr H. Kramarz 41 *T* AKG London *B* Windrush Photos/David Tipling 42 *T* Minden Pictures/Jim Brandenburg 42–43 ChinaStock/Dennis Cox 43 *T* Eye Ubiquitous/Julia Waterlow 44–45 Zefa Pictures/Kurt Scholz 47 Perren Tracey 48 Telegraph Colour Library/Colorific!/Jerry Young 49 Tony Stone Images/Ed Pritchard 50 The Hutchison Picture Library/Melanie Friend 51 ChinaStock/Dennis Cox 52 The Hutchison Picture Library/Melanie Friend 53 Rex Features Ltd/Wang Zhiping 54 Sygma/Gianni Giansanti 55 Robert Harding Picture Library/Rainbird 56 Panos Pictures/Tim Chevassut 58 Kai Ulrich Müller 59 Robin Hanbury-Tenison 60 Robert Harding Picture Library/G. & P. Corrigan 61 NHPA/Roger Tidman 62 *BL* Biofotos/Heather Angel *BR* Ffotograff/Patricia Aithie 62–63 Impact Photos/Matthew Kneale 63 *TR* ChinaStock/Dennis Cox *CR* Aspect Picture Library/Michael Ma *BL* Mountain Camera/John Cleare *BR* The Image Bank/Harald Sund 65 Robert Harding Picture Library/Robin Hanbury-Tenison 66 Aspect Picture Library/Ma Po Shum 67 Aspect Picture Library/Peter Carmichael 68 Aspect Picture Library/Peter Carmichael 71 Aspect Picture Library/Peter Carmichael 73 Robert Harding Picture Library/Maurice Joseph 75

Windrush Photos/David Tipling 76 Lowell Georgia 77 ChinaStock/Dennis Cox 78 Eye Ubiquitous/Julia Waterlow 79 Robin Hanbury-Tenison 81 The Hutchison Picture Library/J. G. Fuller 82 *TL* Telegraph Colour Library/Colorific!/Patrick Morrow/Black Star *TR* Retna Pictures/Chris Beall *CR* Michael Holford *BL* The Hutchison Picture Library/Sarah Errington 82–83 Trip/Gill Suttle 83 *T* AKG London/Erich Lessing/National Museum, Beijing *BR* NHPA/Gerard Lacz 85 Windrush Photos/David Tipling 86 Robin Hanbury-Tenison 87 Windrush Photos 88 Impact Photos/Alain Le Garsmeur 90–91 Biofotos/G. & P. Corrigan 92 Aspect Picture Library/Tom Nebbia 93 Ffotograff/Patricia Aithie 94 Magnum Photos/Thomas Hoepker 95 Eye Ubiquitous/Julia Waterlow 96 Eye Ubiquitous/Frank Leather 97 Robin Hanbury-Tenison 98 Impact Photos/Alain Le Garsmeur 99 Spectrum Colour Library/I. Meredith 100 *T* ChinaStock/Dennis Cox *B* ET Archive/The British Library 101 *TL* Ffotograff/Patricia Aithie *TR* Biofotos/G. & P. Corrigan *BL* ChinaStock/Dennis Cox *BR* Eye Ubiquitous/Julia Waterlow 102 Robin Hanbury-Tenison 103 Retna Pictures/Paul Slattery 104 Lowell Georgia 105 China Photo Library 106 The Hutchison Picture Library/Felix Greene 107 Camera Press/Roger Whittaker 108 Sally & Richard Greenhill 109 NHPA/Morten Strange 112 *TL* Sally & Richard Greenhill *TC* NHPA/Anthony Bannister *BL* China Photo Library/Jacky Yip 112–113 *T* Biofotos/Heather Angel *B* Impact Photos/Alain Le Garsmeur 113 *TR* Impact Photos/Alain Le Garsmeur 114–115 Camera Press/Imapress/Chamberland 116 Aspect Picture Library/Peter Carmichael 117 Robert Harding Picture Library/Vision Poster Co 118 China Photo Library 119 The Ancient Art & Architecture Collection 121 Ffotograff/Patricia Aithie 122 Aspect Picture Library/Peter Carmichael 123 ChinaStock/Dennis Cox 124 Zefa Pictures/Kurt Scholz 126 Eye Ubiquitous/Julia Waterlow 127 Rex Features Ltd/Kazuyoshi Nomachi 130 *T* Lowell Georgia *BL* Lowell Georgia 130–131 Lowell Georgia 131 *TL* AKG London/Erich Lessing/National Museum, Beijing *TR* The Bridgeman Art Library/Zhang Shui Cheng 132 Biofotos/Heather Angel 133 Robin Hanbury-Tenison 135 The Hutchison Picture Library/Titus Moser 136 Robin Hanbury-Tenison 137 Robin Hanbury-Tenison 138–139 Panos Pictures/Alain Le Garsmeur 140 Mary Evans Picture Library 141 Zefa Pictures/Fritz Rauschenbach 142 The Image Bank/Guido Alberto Rossi 143 Robert Harding Picture Library/Simon Westcott 145 Eye Ubiquitous/Julia Waterlow 146 *CL* Magnum Photos/Hiroji Kubota *BL* Eye Ubiquitous/C. Portway *BR* Magnum Photos/Hiroji Kubota 146–147 Robert Harding Picture Library/Peter Ibbotson 147 *TR* Kadokawa Shoten Publishing Co Ltd/Akira Soda *B* Magnum Photos/Hiroji Kubota 148 The Bridgeman Art Library/Private Collection 149 ChinaStock/Dennis Cox 150 Telegraph Colour Library/Colorific!/M. Clark 151 Ffotograff/Patricia Aithie 152 ChinaStock/Dennis Cox 153 Biofotos/G. & P. Corrigan 156 Biofotos/G. & P. Corrigan 157 The Hutchison Picture Library/Trevor Page 158 Windrush Photos/Tim Loseby 159 Robert Harding Picture Library/Robin Hanbury-Tenison 160 ChinaStock/Dennis Cox 161 Biofotos/G. & P. Corrigan 162 Robin Hanbury-Tenison 164 *T* Ann & Bury Peerless—Slide Resources & Picture Library *BL* Robert Harding Picture Library/G. & P. Corrigan 164–165 Caroline Blunden 165 *TR* AKG London *CL* Robert Harding Picture Library/Ken Gillham *BR* ChinaStock/Dennis Cox 167 Robert Harding Picture Library/Robin Hanbury-Tenison 168 Robin Hanbury-Tenison 169 The Image Bank/Guido Alberto Rossi 171 Biofotos/G. & P. Corrigan 172 Robin Hanbury-Tenison 174 Keith & Liz Laidler 177 The Image Bank/Guido Alberto Rossi 178 Robin Hanbury-Tenison 179 Nik Wheeler 180–181 Aspect Picture Library/Tom Nebbia 182 Windrush Photos/George McCarthy 183 Robert Harding Picture Library/Tom Ang 184 *B* Aspect Picture Library/Gavin Hellier 184–185 Retna Pictures/David Corio 185 *TC* Kai Ulrich Müller *B* Britstock-IFA/Bernd Ducke

SEPARATIONS David Bruce Graphics, London
PAPER Townsend Hook Limited, Snodland, Kent
PRINTING AND BINDING Mohndruck, Gütersloh, Germany